Zen
and the Art of
Recording

Zen
and the Art of
Recording

Mixerman

Hal Leonard Books
An Imprint of Hal Leonard Corporation

Published in 2014 by Hal Leonard Books
An Imprint of Hal Leonard Corporation
7777 West Bluemound Road
Milwaukee, WI 53213

Trade Book Division Editorial Offices
33 Plymouth St., Montclair, NJ 07042

Printed in the United States of America

Cover design by Jeff Mutschler
Book design by UB Communications

Library of Congress Cataloging-in-Publication Data

Mixerman.
  Zen and the art of recording / Mixerman.
      pages cm
  ISBN 978-1-4803-8743-0
1. Sound recordings—Production and direction—Vocational guidance. 2.
Popular music—Production and direction. 3. Sound recording industry—
Vocational guidance. I. Title.
  ML3795.M58 2014
  621.389'3—dc23

                              2014035146

www.halleonardbooks.com

Acknowledgments

Special thanks to:

John Dooher
Scott Paterson
The Saint
David Wozmak
Bob Olhsson
Jeff Lorber
Patrick Moraz
Adam Topol
Bill Gibson
Bernadette Malavarca
Tanya Rodriguez
Brandon Gresham
Wyn Davis and Total Access
    Studios
Adam Arnold (or Double A)
Tim Gilles
Jennene Mildenhall-Gilles
The Entire Big Blue Meanie
    Studios Staff
Jessica Tomasin
Steve Wilmans
Julian Dreyer

The Entire Echo Mountain
    Recording Staff
Joe McGrath
Steve Jackson
Pulse Techniques
Lewitt Microphones
Randy Fuchs
Antelope Audio
Dusty Wakeman and
    Mojave Audio
Royer Labs
Tascam
Jason Fee and Empress FX
Peter Montessi and A-designs
EveAnna Manley
Millennia Media
Steven Slate
Clayton Joseph Scott and all
    the boys in Brightside
The Broadcast
Max Sarafin

ℤ Contents

Chapter Two
The Recordist's Tools   65

Chapter Three
The Source and Capture

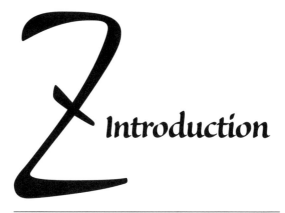

Introduction

Anyone who is familiar with my writings knows that I do all that I can to avoid discussing technical information beyond the very basics. There's a very good reason for this—musical decisions are of far more consequence than technical ones. However, in preparing to write this book, I realized there's just no way around it. Recording is an art that requires some measure of technical understanding.

This was especially evident on the Internet, where I found literally hundreds of posts asking how to set the attack and release times on a compressor. Many posters just wanted to know a preset that they could use for a particular source, which ignores a fundamental principle of what we do—listen.

As humans we are exceptionally good at recognizing patterns. Only an idiot savant could pick up a Rubik's Cube and solve it within the first few minutes. For the rest of us, we must learn how to solve the puzzle, and if you experiment with the toy long enough, you will eventually pick up the patterns that will help you solve it.

Music also has patterns, as does recording music, and you will come across recognizable patterns over time that will help you to streamline the decision process. But before we're able to recognize patterns we have to see them in the first place, and in the case of recording, we have to hear. This requires you to develop and fine-tune your hearing to the point that you trust it above all other senses.

The good news is that you're already familiar with musical patterns, you just don't necessarily know it. I could play three notes in such a way that most all of you will sing the next note in the series without prompting. If you play the notes C, up a fifth to G, and down a minor third to an E, most all of you will sing an F. That's because the resolution of those notes forms a recognizable pattern. Scales are patterns. Chord progressions are patterns.

There is no doubt that we are far more comfortable with our sight than we are with our hearing when it comes to evaluating information. I've brought up this example before, but the original *Star Trek* theme sounds completely different when you're not viewing the main titles along with it. The whooshing of the Enterprise flying past is far more obvious sans the picture, mostly because it seems almost random in nature.

When we discuss sound we often use terms that relate to our other senses, such as *warm, dark, brittle, bright, like ass, transparent,* etc. These are all feeling terms, which makes sense since the whole point of music is to evoke an emotional response. We tend to use feeling terms to describe sound because music and sound are inextricably attached.

Frequency information is often viewed more within the purview of the recordist than the producer, but this would ignore the fact that frequency relates directly to musical notes. Therefore, arrangement decisions can be made based not only on a part, but how all the parts work together within the frequency spectrum. Beethoven didn't have EQ—he had to create frequency balance and contrast through his instrumentation and arrangement choices alone.

Tone is also often viewed within the purview of the recordist, but good tone requires good performance. As a producer, I listen to tone as an indicator of performance. As a recordist, I first need to pull a tone that inspires a performance. The musician is therefore an integral part of the tone. Which would explain why some people can make an instrument sing, and others can only make it sound. A musician who makes her instrument sing feels the sound as music, and that in turn will often evoke a reaction from the listener.

There was a time when a recording session required a designated engineer—one whose only job was the capture. These lines have been blurred significantly over the years, and more often than not, the recordist is operating in some other capacity, either as a musician, artist, or producer. And if you're the chief engineer at your own studio, then you are likely a Default Producer—a role we will discuss in more detail later.

These days I operate as a Producer Recordist, which means I'm performing two operations that require my full attention. That's impossible. Fortunately, many processes that I must perform as a recordist are nearly automatic, which allows me to prioritize the musical decisions.

Given the realities of recording today, it is often best to simplify the capture process, so as to allow you to concentrate on what's most important—the music itself. That said, I can only simplify things for you so much, as there are still technical considerations that can't be ignored. Stereo miking alone, done improperly, can cause auditory anomalies that will weaken the overall impact of a recording. The good news is, once you learn the sound of negatively interacting microphones, you will become virtually allergic to it such that it becomes difficult to make that kind of mistake in the first place.

There's a reason why recording is so difficult. The thousands of tiny decisions that you make all day long are subjective in nature. This requires some modicum of self-confidence. If you don't believe that you're an adequate arbiter of what's good, or more accurately, what's effective, then your first reflex will be to leave yourself as many options as possible. Taken to its extreme, tonal decisions are often left in flux with the idea that you can make it all work somehow come mix time. Or worse yet, you'll leave all those decisions to a third-party mixer such as myself.

I'm more than happy to make those decisions for you as your mixer, but this will likely lead to some surprising results, as you will have provided me with no clear indicators of intent. If all that you supply me are the DI'ed electrics on a guitar-driven track, you leave me with nearly infinite possibilities. When it comes to a successful recording, it's far more effective to limit me as a mixer than to leave me so many options that I have no idea what you were trying to achieve. And if you're mixing it yourself, I'm not sure why you would want to go out of your way to make the job more difficult.

There have been several scientific studies over the years revealing just how difficult a time we have when we are presented with too many options. Our brains are built to choose between A and B. Given the choice between chocolate and vanilla ice cream, a selection is relatively easy to make. Given the choice between 30 flavors, you will likely find yourself nothing short of overwhelmed.

This is no different in recording. If you leave yourself every option imaginable, you will only manage to paralyze everyone on the session. I personally find an overabundance of options so overwhelming that I often ask someone from the team to "produce" my dinner for me. Perusing a menu full of options as my brain is subconsciously sorting through dozens of recording decisions can make a simple dinner selection tantamount to making a choice with potential global repercussions.

Since every decision in recording affects the next, everyone on the session can quickly find themselves confused, as there is nothing concrete to work on. You can't know where your recording is at if you're not willing to commit to both musical and sonic decisions along the way.

Those times in my career that I was working purely as a recordist, I was able to focus my creativity on recording techniques alone. This allowed me to geek out on sound rather than performance, as I had a producer who was in charge of that. I sought to apply my daily observations of how sound travels—*especially* how it reflects, as parabolas and long corrugated drain pipes can be used to harness and direct sound.

I've also spent an enormous part of my career ignoring creativity where recording technique is concerned. Whatev. I'm trying to make a record, I'm quite possibly behind, and I don't have time to be creative in how I capture until there's an obvious problem. That doesn't mean I sloughed off the recording. It means my creative energy was best served elsewhere. Such are the pitfalls of working as both producer and recordist simultaneously—at all times one is suffering.

The good news is great performances usually result in great sonics, so long as you put the effort in to pull the appropriate tone in the first place. In fact, I can always tell when I'm in the wrong mindset as a producer, because I desperately want to touch shit. Balances and tones often fall apart as a result of performance issues. Good performances tend to manifest as good tone. And bad tone is inconsequential in the context of a poor performance. In the recordist's mindset, I will first notice the bad tone, and in the producer's mindset, I hear the bad performance. Make no mistake, if you pulled good tones before making your take, you would do well to keep your hands away from all knobs—virtual or otherwise.

It's natural to reach for knobs when you're just starting out, especially today, because the tools available for mangling tracks are far more powerful and plentiful than ever. And while that may seem like an advantage, in many ways, you'd be far better off learning how to record with a limited supply of recording gear rather than an overabundant one. Limitations force creative adaptation, which is an exceptionally good skill set to have in this business.

Meanwhile, as the price of entry into the digital world of DAWs and plug-ins has come down considerably, analog compressors and microphones still require significant capital investment over time. Which means your initial investment into recording will provide you enormous power to mangle, and limited power for accurate capture. That's a bad combination, as it promotes all the worst habits when it comes to the art of recording.

This book is about recording music, so just about everything I present to you will be from that perspective. And when you're recording music, your first allegiance must be to the music, performance, and production. Not the recording. Even as a designated for-hire recordist, you must often put the needs of the music first and foremost. Recording technique is nothing more than a means to an end—to capture a performance.

I'm certainly not suggesting that you abandon creative recording techniques. Quite the contrary. I encourage it. Especially if it's on your time. The more skills you develop, the more effective you are in the studio, and experimentation is a great way to learn new things. As a producer, I give my recordist the latitude to get creative with technique. Believe me, I've gone down a great many four-hour (and longer) rabbit holes in search of a tone that lasts all of five seconds in the context of the production. And even when this sort of Science Experiment ends up unfruitful, it's rarely a waste of time. Unfruitful ideas often lead to useful ones, and there is almost always something to be gleaned from your failures—even the little ones.

Anyone who has acted in some capacity as my recordist knows that as the producer, I will often grab the closest mic, even if it's not the best mic for the job. That may seem strange. I mean, I'm a seasoned recordist, yet as the producer, all of that falls to the wayside? That's right. Because as a producer-for-hire, I have to constantly consider time, and the closer the mic is to my performer, the sooner I can start recording her. The best recordists will protest my choice, and I will often acquiesce, so long as I can record my performer in relatively short order.

There's a natural push and pull between time and creativity. Time restraints push us forward, as creative forces pull us back. A balance must be achieved between the two, regardless of whether you have stupid amounts of time, or far too little. Frankly, given the choice, I'd choose the latter. An unlimited budget removes time pressure as a tool for pushing the session forward.

Recording an album without time constraints requires the kind of discipline that would prevent most of us from attempting it in the first place. I'm not talking about the discipline to work. I'm talking about the discipline to *finish*. I know several musicians who have been remaking the same album for over a decade. Needless to say, you've never heard of them. What's worse, the more time it takes, the more pressure there is to deliver something worthy of the time. We've all heard about great albums that took a week to make. But how many great albums took 10 years to make? I can't think of one. Nothing can live up to the inherent hype of that. Great art is made with intent to its completion. No album requires years to make.

Art only exists if it's been completed. A finished work is a clear expression of an artist's intent. Conversely, a work in progress has no intent whatsoever. How could it? How can we determine the artist's intent from an unfinished work? The *prima facie* evidence of intent can only be found in a completed work, one in which no excuses can, nor should, ever be made.

If you're the kind of person that has trouble finishing things, then you would do best to curb this tendency if not eradicate it completely from your recording personality. One album does not a career make, especially if it's never done in the first place.

I'm a big proponent of aggressive recording techniques. I advise that one records with intent towards a finished product, even when you're just learning, partly because it promotes good recording habits, and partly because it's the most effective path to quality results. One of your more important duties is to keep your artists and musicians in the right mindset—inspired.

Given the opportunity, I want to make my decisions along the way, and record towards a vision. If I want the cymbals distorted, I record them that way. If I want the guitar to swim in a spring reverb, I choose an amp with a good spring and record the tone that way.

Of course, this methodology has its pitfalls. Sometimes you fuck up, and bad. When that happens, you'll surely curse me. To which I say, I can't save you from your bad decisions, nor can I prevent you from making them in the first place. That's also kind of the point. Working aggressively creates good decision-making habits that will benefit you in the long run, no matter how badly you might fuck up in the short run. When you record aggressively, you will make mistakes. That's okay. That just means you're doing things right.

Working aggressively will force you to think about the end game. Believe me, you can record with intent, and still leave yourself some wiggle room, and we'll talk about how throughout the book. But there's really no better way to overcome the debilitating effects of fear than by operating in a fearless manner. A phobia of flying I can understand—irrational as it may be, death is a possible consequence. To date, and as far as I know, there have been no documented reports of death by bad recording and I don't expect that to change anytime soon. So what are you worried about? Your reputation?

Well, you should be worried about that! But not at the expense of learning how to record well in the first place. If you approach recording with trepidation, if you worry about doing things the wrong way, you're going to retard your improvement. I assume you're reading this book in order to advance your skills. Recording aggressively with intent is the best way to accelerate the learning curve.

As a pure recordist, your job is to capture sound. If you record music, your job is to capture sound as it relates directly to *music*. If you're both musician and recordist, then your job is the same, it's just that your musicianship is considerably more critical than your recording skills. As a performer, you'll have far more to do with the quality of a track than you ever will as a recordist, that is, unless you're getting in the way.

You really have to work in an assiduous manner in order to fuck up a recording from a technical standpoint. Oh, it can be done, and likely occurs on a daily basis, but that's often a result of trying too hard. You want to simplify the recording process, not make it a chore. Once you get your instrument to sound exactly the way you want it in the room, recording becomes a straightforword process of placing a mic where it most accurately represents the tone.

The tone of an instrument in isolation is almost irrelevant. Your tones must work together to form one coherent recording, and I can provide you with the key to success in this regard. Think musically! Don't think sonically. Don't think technically. The moment you start to think in musical terms, your recordings will improve a hundredfold.

I'm not a technician, not even close. So if you're looking for a book about recording that focuses purely on the technical aspects of electronics, then this is not the book for you. In fact, none of my books are. I record music, and therefore, I'm a student of music first and foremost.

While we must discuss a number of technical realities where recording is concerned, I can assure you, there will be nothing in this book that can't be conceptually understood by anyone with an interest in recording. For the most part, we will discuss the art of recording in terms of both musicality and practicality.

Perception

I don't think I'll ever forget the first time I recorded myself. It was sometime in the 70s when I was just a lad. My best friend had moved to Chicago, and long distance telephone calls were expensive (according to my mother). Rather than writing a letter, I decided to record one on a compact cassette recorder instead. Imagine my surprise when I played it back.

That's not what I sound like!

Yes and no. It was me, obviously. But it wasn't a perfect replication of my voice, certainly not as I heard it.

Much of that perception has to do with the fact that our ear canals are nestled within a resonant chamber—our skull, which is, of course, attached to our beautifully absorptive body. This greatly influences how we hear ourselves, which is somewhat warped in comparison to the way others perceive us. In an age where a microphone and a camera are never more than meters away, most of us have experienced playback of our own voice and the usual discomfort that follows.

Oh, I did everything I could to alter the way my voice sounded on playback. I tried speaking in a softer tone closer to the mic. I tried speaking louder from a distance. I tried altering the pitch of my voice by accentuating certain words, much like a television announcer. After a number of hours of experimentation, dejected, I gave up. And while I'd managed to improve my results through trial and error, I was far too uncomfortable with the tone of my voice to continue.

Just about all of you have likely experienced this. Disdain for one's own voice is common, especially when we're first exposed to it. Eventually, most of us get over it. These days, I don't even notice my own voice. Recording countless radio shows, interviews, an audiobook tends to do that.

Then there was the time I recorded my high school rock/ska band with a single microphone in the guitar player's basement.

That's not what we sound like!

Again, yes and no. The recording was certainly skewed, as a single mic placed randomly in an acoustically flawed room is not an ideal way to record a band. Upon playback, the drums were overbearing, and the singer completely garbled. Clearly the mic was too close to the drummer. Move the mic, try again.

That's not what we sound like!

Too much guitar, not enough vocal. Move the mic closer to the PA speaker.

That's not what we sound like!

Too much vocal, and you know something? This mic sucks.

The balance of the instruments captured by a single mic clearly had everything to do with the placement of the mic. Of course, it was a $35 dynamic mic at a time when a Shure SM57 was just under $100. In other words, it was a piece of shit. It was also all we had. Besides, we weren't looking to record a track for purposes of release. We just wanted to hear for ourselves what we sounded like, and if memory serves, it was somewhere in the range of atrocious and horrendous.

Recording is like a mirror. Unfortunately, it can sometimes feel as though we're looking in an airplane mirror—which is typically magnified, warped, and lit in the most unflattering manner possible. I imagine this is done purposely to prevent people from spending countless hours admiring themselves. A recording is similar, in that it will reveal your flaws with brutal accuracy.

Our basement recording was a mess. The snares rattled from the bass. The low end was uneven, at times blossoming and resonating uncontrollably and thereby consuming the recording. And that stupid mic picked all of it up!

At the time, we chalked up the poor recordings to our subpar equipment. And while that surely didn't help, the bottom line is, it *did* reasonably pick up what was happening in the room, at least how it sounded from that location. Frankly, a high quality mic and pre would have only managed to illuminate the truth of the matter. The problem was us. Put in recording terms—the problem was the source.

The room sounded like shit. Our instruments sounded like shit. And we performed like shit. The recording, while somewhat obfuscatory in nature overall, revealed these particular maladies with absolute fidelity. I mean, how could we listen back to a recording of our lousy playing, on our crappy instruments, in an awful acoustic space, and still manage to blame the gear?

Human nature, I suppose.

Had we recorded the identical poor performance in a stellar recording space with the same crappy mic and receiver, we would have significantly improved the recording, as many of the room maladies would be eradicated. A larger space would give the low end more room to blossom, thus preventing a frequency buildup that consumes the recording and rattles everything in the room.

Had we hired well-seasoned studio performers the results surely would have improved significantly, even on our crappy instruments. And were you to give these great performers instruments worthy of their talents, the difference would be staggering, even using a single crappy $35 mic to capture the performance.

Most of you reading this (certainly anyone born after 1985) likely had childhood access to far more sophisticated recording gear than I did. As much as I'm a proponent of analog gear, a cassette deck captures with considerably less sonic fidelity than even the crappiest computer soundcard. That said, were you able to supply me today's prosumer technology to record my childhood band, that recording would still be horrendous. The problem wasn't the gear. It was the source.

Source, Source, Source

I'll warn you now. I'm going to hammer this to death throughout this book, and for good reason. There is nothing more important to a recording than the Source itself. When you place a great player with a great instrument in a great room, you actually have to go out of your way to fuck up the recording. I could record an amazing band with a wire recorder (that's way before my time too), and it would still be clear upon playback that you're listening to something special, despite the limited bandwidth of the recording.

Conversely, if we put a terrible player, with a decrepit instrument, in a problematic space, the best recording equipment will capture the awfulness before us with absolute clarity. Therefore, the Source is of paramount importance.

The moment the Source is compromised, you are merely engaged in damage control. A lousy room will have obvious artifacts. A lousy player is incapable of exciting even a good room in a manner beneficial to the recording. A subpar instrument can even cause a virtuoso player fits, as the brainpower required to deal with the inadequacies of an instrument will certainly affect his ability to perform. An instrument that has intonation issues, dead notes, live notes, generally anemic tone, or any other malady, will greatly limit even the most talented performer.

The Source is the totality of the tone, and can be broken down into three components. The player generating the source. The source instrument itself. And the room in which the source is performed. I will refer to these from this point forward as Source Player, Source Instrument, and Source Room. Make no mistake, all three of these Source Components determine the overall quality of the source itself. At that point, it's all about the capture.

I'm not suggesting for a moment that you should, or even could, always record the most professional player, with the best instrument, in the best sounding room available. That's not really how this business works from a creative standpoint nor a practical one. Besides, raw everyman performances, even reckless ones, can be exceptionally effective. Desired, even. So I'm not here to cast judgment in some abstract manner as to the definition of good. *You* are the arbiter of that.

There will be times when you will find yourself unable to verbalize the sound you seek, no matter how well formed the tone might be in your imagination. Such is the nature of creating art that must be performed. On those occasions you'll be faced with a choice. Record the part and deal with the problematic tone later (which promotes uncertainty), or spend the time during the recording process to find the right tone. Even on those occasions when you choose post-processing to manipulate a source into compliance, you would be far better served to mangle the part the moment that decision is made. This way, both you and your musicians are monitoring the production with intent in place.

Surely, microphone selection, mic pre selection, and microphone placement will all have a great influence on the tone. On those occasions when you are stuck with a particular source instrument or player, how you capture becomes one of your more important weapons. Once that happens, you're in some measure of damage control.

Frankly, I can teach you about mic placement in relatively short order, and while you'll improve and refine this skill over the course of a career, what takes decades to learn is how to manipulate the tone at the Source to match a sonic vision. I can reduce that learning curve significantly. But even if you memorized everything in this book regarding Source Instruments and how to manipulate them to your recording needs, we won't even scratch the surface of what you'll encounter over the course of a career recording music.

I certainly won't be able to remember every situation that I've ever come across, and even if I could, you will discover all sorts of things that I may not have experienced myself. Until you sit down to write a book on recording, I'm not sure you can really fathom just how much there is to learn. There are no shortcuts to experience. However, once you understand all the basic concepts and realize just how much control you have over the Source, you will have the tools necessary to record well.

Source Player

The player has the greatest impact on how the source sounds in the room. An act as simple as striking a drum is directly affected by the person hitting it. A great player will make that drum sing.

It's almost as if they pull the tone from the instrument itself, such that it excites the room in an optimal manner. A masterful musician is capable of making quick adjustments to a Source Instrument in order to achieve the desired sound within the context of the space surrounding her.

It literally takes me 10 minutes to get tones with amazing drummers like Jim Keltner, Matt Chamberlain, or John Robinson (just to name a few). Yet your average band drummer, even a relatively good one, can require a full day for tones, regardless of the quality of instrument or room. Were I to put an average drummer on Matt Chamberlain's kit, I would likely have to engage in numerous processing and placement calisthenics in order to shape the tones and overall internal balances of the drums.

That said, this does not automatically make the player and the room more important than the Source Instrument itself. If I seek a kik drum tone with the identifiable thud of two closed heads, I'm going to have difficulty capturing that sound on a kik drum sporting a hole in the resonant head, regardless of who's playing the instrument. And if the feeling I seek from the drums is one of almost infantile abilities, then I'll probably need to fire Matt and hire someone capable of playing in such a childlike manner. Sorry Matt!

Further complicating matters is the fact that no professional musician, no matter how good, is the perfect player for any given situation. Matt is one of my favorite drummers around, but if I want just stupid aggressive, in-your-face rock drums, I'm more likely to seek out someone like Chad from The Red Hot Chili Peppers. If I want beautifully detailed jazz drums, I'm more likely to reach out to Steve Gadd. Does this mean that Matt couldn't do a convincing job in both situations? Certainly not. He's amazingly versatile. But if I want to make my life easier, and I do, then I'm going to attempt to hire the player that I feel best fits the requirements for a particular production.

As a recordist, one who is being hired by an artist or producer, you don't always have a say in the hiring of players. This is especially true with bands, in which the unique lineup of personnel dictates the overall sound of the band. Replacing band players is fraught with problems politically, but musically too, as changing out a band player can have a significant impact on the musical dynamic. You don't always get to choose your Source Players. Fortunately, there are two other Source components that you can control, starting with the room.

Source Room

Wouldn't it be great if we could just play an instrument, and then have it magically *reproduce* for us *exactly* as it sounded in the room?

The problem is that defining "exactly as it sounded in the room" gets a bit sketchy. Sounded to whom? You, as the player, who is being influenced by the physical vibrations of the instrument at the time of recording? The person on the far side of the room? The person sitting three feet away?

Sound does not live in a vacuum. Sound moves through, reacts with, and dissipates within a space. Therefore, the source of a sound is wholly dependent upon the space in which it occurs. How you perceive that sound has everything to do with your proximity to the Source Instrument as it relates to the space. You can't separate the source sound from its space. You can ostensibly reduce the size and reflectivity of a space in order to alter how the sound travels and dissipates, but in practical terms there are limitations that you can't overcome. At the end of the day, you need a space that is appropriate for the recording itself.

Were you to cover all of your walls and ceiling with heavy moving blankets, the cloth would absorb many of the higher frequencies, thereby preventing them from bouncing throughout the room. This will have the effect of attenuating (reducing) how the high frequencies are heard in relative balance to the low frequencies within the space. In other words, you'll suck up all the high end, but the low end will continue to resonate unabated throughout the room.

The cloth from moving blankets don't absorb the lower frequencies, and if your space is inadequate in size for the large waveforms of the low end, knocking down the high end will negatively impact the tone of the room. If you were to place a singer in a small closet-sized room covered with an absorptive material like carpet, "boxy" would be the most likely adjective for the tone. The only reasonable way to extract that boxiness from your recording is to remove the singer from that atrocious room before you record her. Should you choose to deal with that boxiness after the fact, I predict a very long and tiring day as you learn a valuable lesson in the limitations of removing resonant frequencies from a source through processing.

Next time you're in your shower (or my favorite, a large concrete parking garage), belt out a low note and sweep up the scale as you evaluate the reaction of the sound within that space. At some point in your sweep, you'll notice one or more frequencies that resonate considerably louder than the others within the room.

This sort of resonance is perfectly acceptable for showering or parking your car. It's not so great for recording. Resonant frequencies will be picked up by the mic no matter how closely you place it to the source. And while some mics are better at rejecting ambient room information than others, a resonant frequency that causes you to feel as if your entire head has been engulfed will most assuredly be captured. This is true regardless of the mic and its placement.

Suppose you determine your bathroom has an obvious resonance at 98 Hz. What do you think is going to happen when you try to record a bass cabinet in your shower stall? Every time the bass player hits a G (which just so happens to sound at a fundamental of 98 Hz, go figure), that frequency is going to increase greatly in amplitude (volume), causing a swell every time a low G sounds. Your microphone will pick this up perfectly. Clearly, this is not optimal.

Amplitude has a great deal to do with how sound reacts within its environment. If you and I were to stand in the middle of a large field and have a normal conversation, there would be very little reflectivity perceived from our position. Were I to increase the amplitude of my voice by yelling, I could very well excite the sound sufficiently to reach a building 100 yards away. This would result in an audible slap-back of my voice to our position in the field. Amplitude affects just how far the sound travels before complete dissipation occurs.

Amplitude is what excites a room. Drums, being generally loud in nature, tend to reveal the sonic maladies of a room. A kalimba, on the other hand, doesn't have enough amplitude to adequately excite a room, which greatly reduces the room's influence on the capture. As a result, you can record a kalimba just about anywhere.

Directionality of sound also comes into play. If you've ever watched a marching band perform towards the opposite side of the stadium just before they turn around to blast you with everything they've got, then you have experienced the directional properties of sound firsthand. You will lose an exceptional amount of high end brilliance as the horns face the opposition direction. If the sound isn't traveling towards us, then we're not perceiving the direct waveform of the sound, but rather the return of that sound, which will generally return with an attenuated high end.

High frequencies are extremely directional and a trumpet facing us, even from many yards away, will send the waveform directly to our ear, thereby reducing the relative level of the ambience in relation to the direct signal. Low frequencies, on the other hand, are long, slow-developing, and insidious in nature, as they do not travel directionally. This is why you can place a subwoofer anywhere in a room.

High frequencies are also more readily absorbed and reflected than low end. All objects have absorptive and reflective properties at different frequencies. Thunder can sound like nothing more than a low end rumble from a position five miles away. The high end from the initial crack was likely absorbed by several miles of foliage. Yet if lightning strikes just 100 yards away, the high end of the crack will be nothing short of earsplitting.

Low end tends to travel along walls and floors, and is absorbed by solid objects. With the kinds of distances we deal with in the studio, bass frequencies tend to be trapped rather than absorbed. If you sit on the couch in the back of the room of most studios, you will be enveloped with all the low end that's getting trapped against the wall and the couch. The couch and the back wall are acting as a bass trap.

Position, distance, amplitude, directionality, and frequency, along with the exact properties of the environment, cause an acoustic reaction within a space, all of which affects the sound as it reaches your position. The good news is, no matter how large the space, and regardless of the makeup, sound will react according to known laws of physics. Theoretically, we could predict with absolute accuracy how a sound will react in a room based on the laws of physics. Practically speaking, there are far too many variables to forecast beyond an educated guess. Even a slight change in environment and our position can significantly affect how the sound travels and what we hear from our location.

The room, and how you adjust it by placing absorptive and reflective objects within it, is critical to how the microphones pick up the tone. If you place a drum kit in the middle of a rather sizable concrete room, you will collect an enormous, perhaps overbearing, amount of room information. The drum sound will slap off any solid material, excite the room, and return to the microphones. Even your close mics (that is, microphones placed in close proximity to the sound source) will pick up that returning ambience. Without some treatment, your drum recording could offer you nothing short of an undefined mess.

Surrounding a source with absorptive baffles can help tremendously towards cutting off the returning room information. Even if you seek a rather bombastic tone, you'll still likely want some control over the balance between the direct attack of the drums and the ambient tone of the room. Those close mics are there so that you can control just how immediate your drums sound.

Surrounding the drums with too many baffles can be equally undesirable, as you can effectively choke their tone. You've gone too far. At least you've determined where the line is. Once you have the close mics performing their intended duty, you will have some control over your ambient information through balance.

Room reflection folding into the microphones, no matter how short in absolute time, can't be removed electronically—certainly not without significantly degrading the audio with obvious artifacts. This is no great revelation, and it's why so many green recordists often capture tones as dry as possible (a dry sound being defined as a sound with minimal reflectivity). The thinking is that space can be added later through digital reverbs and delay tails. And while certain genres call for this treatment almost as a matter of course, an organic room tone is difficult to mimic convincingly through digital reverbs. When you're looking for an organic room tone, the only effective means is through the capture. This requires choosing a room that fits the needs of the recording.

What matters here is intent. If your *intent* is that of a natural space, it's far more effective to actually record in the appropriate space than it is to mimic a space after the fact. If your intent is that of unnatural space or a space much larger than you can reasonably achieve, then you will likely want to reduce the apparent ambience in the room. Thus, called neutralizing the room.

This is not to suggest that digital reverbs are a sum negative where drum tones are concerned. It's just that the ambience of a natural room manifests a more honest feeling than the illusion of space does. And that statement has nothing to do with personal preference. This is about how a recording makes you feel within the production itself. I'm far more likely to use a digital reverb on a pop recording than on a straight rock production.

Ultimately, it's the music itself that evokes a reaction from the listener. But how that music is recorded and presented will influence how a song makes us feel. If the recording and all the decisions that go into that recording don't fully serve the song in how it affects us emotionally, you will only mange to dilute the overall impact of the track.

Microphone placement will directly affect the nature and level of the room information. A room mic placed 10 feet into the air will collect far more high-end room excitement than a mic just a foot off the floor, where the low end information travels. Over time you begin to figure these things out, particularly if you get into the habit of placing your microphones purely by ear.

I frequently witness recordists and producers placing microphones by eye. I've even had producers ask me to move microphones that didn't look right despite how they sounded. Moronic, I know. It's also stupidly common. The listener never sees how you record.

All the listener can react to is what they hear. Given this, I fail to see the logic in worrying about what a mic placement looks like. If it sounds right, it is right.

That said, if you pull your tones out of context by getting a snare drum tone, and then a kik drum tone in isolation, without ever considering how the mics work on the kit in context, you could have a big surprise later when you realize there's more hi-hat coming through your snare mic than the snare drum itself. Having a drummer whack a snare in isolation is useful. Isolating a snare in the context of a beat is far more informative, particularly as it relates to discovering potential problems.

Using the room to your advantage requires forethought, and it can be treacherous to record a part with too much ambience. You'll be stuck with it. Your best option is to record the part again. Unfortunately, if it's a great performance, that quickly becomes the worst option. So, if you're going to err, it's often best to provide yourself some latitude to increase room information later.

A relatively small room with significant absorption will give you less latitude for acoustic adjustments than a larger room. It's easy to add absorptive baffles to knock down a live room. It's not so easy to start tearing the carpeting off the wall, and such a solution could cause the studio owner some marked consternation.

There are ways of extending the apparent size of a room without using reverb. Compressors are quite handy for increasing your space. A compressor, especially one set with a fast attack and a fast release, will effectively bring up the ambient information relative to the direct signal. This, of course, can also work against you, as compression used for dynamic purposes can increase the apparent ambience. Yet another reason to record with intent.

Many of you reading this book will have general access to one particular recording space, whether that's your own studio, a studio you work for, or your home. Let's face it, any space can be used for recording. Really, the most critical difference between a designated studio space and one in your home is isolation. It doesn't do you much good to record a beautiful violin part if you can hear ambulances driving by, children screaming, or the low-end rumble of an air conditioner that hasn't been decoupled from the room. So, as much as any space can be used for recording, there are a number of factors that must be considered beyond the sound of the space itself.

I can promise you, I'm not, by any stretch of the imagination, a snob when it comes to this. I like any room that's a perfect fit for the production, regardless of its usual purpose. Interesting spaces can offer unique results, which is why we often prefer to record in the controlled environment of an acoustically purposed recording room—it removes surprises from the equation. When I operate as a freelance recordist, I'm almost always involved with room selection.

A multiroom facility, one in which you have a variety of spaces with which to work, is often ideal. Those of you with but one recording space available will be restricted by what that space has to offer. Musicians are often far too willing to spend copious amounts of their time dealing with a fucked-up room with poor results. And while I understand you'd rather not ask your client to pony up anywhere between $500 and $2000 a day for your tracking session, the time savings alone could make it worthwhile. When it comes to recording, there is little to no difference between time and money. In life too, really.

The sooner you accept the room is just as critical to the recording as the Source Instrument and player, the sooner you'll find yourself recording with a plan. If you want to be successful at recording, recognize the space as an extension of the player and instrument itself.

Source Instrument

Recording a fucked-up instrument, particularly one outside the intent of the production, can be exceptionally frustrating for both the player and recordist alike.

Setting aside instruments that should be taken behind the studio and shot, the overall tone of an instrument will greatly affect how it works within the production. In simple terms, a relatively clean guitar tone will create an entirely different feeling in a production than a distorted one. There are literally hundreds of guitar and amplifier models, each with their own unique sound.

If you're looking for the distorted tremolo twang of a James Bond-style lead guitar line, you're going to have a difficult time getting the tone with a Gibson Les Paul through a Marshall cab. A Telecaster through a Supro will get you much closer, and a baritone guitar might bring you closer still. Of course, if you don't have a Supro, a Tele, or a baritone guitar available, and most of you don't, your choices are limited. Either you spend your time trying to locate the right guitar and amp combo for the job, or you get as close as you can through copious amounts of processing and mangling. The latter is an exercise in futility. Even if you come close, you will have invested a great deal of energy to achieve a tone that is nothing more than a pale imitation.

When it comes to a tone as iconic as a James Bond-style guitar (and nearly all of you will have a sonic picture in your brain as to what that sounds like), you can't get there using the inappropriate instrument and amplifier. The part has to correlate to some degree as well. The feeling that a James Bond-style monophonic electric guitar lead line provides will never sound similar to a part that's chordal in nature. If you find my use of the words "feeling" and "sound" incongruous, I can assure you, they're not. When it comes to music, they are one and the same.

Too often, instruments are recorded almost haphazardly, and then mangled to somehow fit the track. For starters, this rarely works for anything aside from electronically driven tones found in EDM tracks, which are often characterized by their uniquely uber-processed sound. As a fan of electronic music (which might have something to do with the fact that I don't produce the genre for a living), I totally appreciate the nature of electronic musical tones, which is more about production and mixing than actual recording.

There is generally no skill involved in *recording* electronic music. The skill is in the manipulation of the tones to create constant sonic motion in conjunction with its definitive pulse. Anytime you're looking to create a sound that doesn't exist in nature, the organic quality of a tone is rendered nearly irrelevant. If you make electronic music exclusively, much of the information contained in these pages won't necessarily correlate, and you'd be well served by *Zen and the Art of Mixing*.

There are so many variables that affect how a source sounds that we are often dealing with a slightly hit-or-miss process. While it's true that I can make an educated guess as to my desired guitar-amp combinations, I must actually hear the tone in context of the production in order to cast judgment. Even string gauge will make a significant difference in the tone of a guitar, although string choice often has much to do with the comfort and performance needs of the guitar player. Putting 14-gauge strings on a guitar for a player who routinely performs with 10s will likely prove problematic, as they could be far too heavy for her to perform well. The comfort of your musicians as it relates to their performance shouldn't be ignored.

There is no substitute for experience where Source Instrument selection and alteration is concerned, particularly when you start to get into tones as varied as electric guitar. You can't really comprehend what a Marshall amp sounds like until you've experienced one, and even then you'll only understand its tone in relation to the guitars you have available. And no, the plug-ins aren't going to help you much to understand the overall tone of the real thing. You never have any guarantee that a plug-in sounds like its graphic suggests, and the illusion is rarely all that convincing when you're familiar with the analog model it's meant to emulate.

That said, if all you have available are amp simulator plug-ins, then eventually you will learn how to get the best out of them. You'll recognize patterns, which will speed up the selection process as you pull tones with less guesswork. And that certainly has some value. Unfortunately, those patterns won't correlate to analog amplifiers, which push both electronics and air.

The bottom line is this: You can mangle parts, you can manipulate them, change their timing, alter their tuning, distort, modulate, EQ, compress, limit, expand, etc. You can certainly alter how a particular source sounds through all sorts of processing. Everyone does this, and I don't begrudge anyone the technique, as it certainly has its place and time. But anyone who records with some regularity will soon realize that no matter how aggressively you manipulate a part, you will never eradicate its overall sonic fingerprint. Therefore, it's far more effective to capture the right tone than to alter a generic tone later through electronic mangling—sometimes called "fixing it in the mix" (a phrase that I would ask you never to utter). And since time is money, and budgets limited, it behooves us to record in a manner that's both effective *and* efficient. Unfortunately, recording a sound with the intention of manipulating it later is neither of those. Once you have this particular "aha" moment, recording will come much more naturally.

The closer you can get your recordings to the desired end game throughout the process, the more successful you'll be at accomplishing the goal for your clients, yourself, and hopefully millions of fans.

Two Schools of Thought

There are two basic schools of thought when it comes to recording. While any given recordist may lean towards one approach over the other, the realities of a specific recording scenario will often dictate the best approach.

The first school of thought is to record your tones as close to your desired outcome as possible, using compression and EQ as needed to achieve the goal. Brought to its extreme, this recording method leaves little room to maneuver later as you work aggressively towards the end game. By the time you're done your last overdub, the mix is nearly there.

The second school of thought is to record with little to no processing, and in a manner that leaves you the flexibility to change your mind later. We'll call this passive recording.

At first blush, leaving yourself room to maneuver will likely seem the more appealing option, particularly if you're light on experience. Your experience or lack thereof, while certainly a factor, shouldn't be the main impetus for choosing one school of thought over the other. More than any other factor, the situation should dictate this.

My good friend Slipperman leans towards passive recording, and for a number of reasons. For starters, he has a multiroom shop, with an entire production team, and he will often take on more than one project at a time. He doesn't carefully select his projects like I do as a freelance producer and mixer. He has an enormous overhead and must keep the studio time booked in order to cover expenses. Given the reality of multiple staff engineers capturing the tracks on any given project, he prefers to retain control by recording in a manner that leaves him room to manipulate the tracks later. Speed in conjunction with an adequate capture is the goal.

Slipperman also has loads of analog gear, all of which can be available come mix time. This is an important consideration. It's not uncommon for a recordist to have access to analog gear during the tracking phase and none during the mixing phase, and you would be wise to take advantage of the analog gear when you have the opportunity. If for no other reason, so you can have the experience. There are an overwhelming number of tools at our disposal, and you only learn what they sound like by using them.

That said, if you want to keep your clients comfortable with the direction of the recording, you're far better off aggressively recording towards the final product. For starters, compressing a signal at the tracking phase will affect how much ambient information you're introducing. If you wait until you've already recorded a part that is in desperate need of compression, you could find yourself with more apparent space than you desire once applied.

I advise neophyte recordists to learn how to record aggressively towards the end game. It's important that you make decisions as you record. If you end up overcompressing the snare drum because the drummer played 10 dB louder on the take, you'll learn a valuable lesson. Don't make your final compressor settings until you're making a take.

Of course, you could take away a different lesson. You could decide to never compress the snare during the recording phase. That would be the wrong lesson. The jump in volume by the drummer was predictable. Players tend to dig in more during a take.

Let's face it, you're going to make plenty of mistakes as a recordist. I make mistakes and learn new lessons (or relearn forgotten ones) on every session. So, if you're going to make mistakes anyway, why not make them in a manner that will tend to improve your skill set? Anyone can record a drum set badly and try to make it work later. Very few can record a drum set well in the first place. The former method leaves the product wholly to chance (especially when your experience is limited), and the latter gives you something concrete to build upon. Personally, I don't like leaving things to chance, and I don't enjoy telling uncomfortable clients that I can fix it in the mix. I can't. I can improve it in the mix. I can possibly make it work within the context of the mix. I can surely mute it. But as your mixer, I can't always fix problems that were ignored at the time of recording.

The argument, of course, is that you can spend as much time as you like on the mixing phase, but you may only have a player for a few hours. This is a valid argument, and on those occasions that your recording time is limited, from a practical standpoint, speed is more important than exactitude. Practicality wins the day.

When I was a recordist for hire, I leaned toward working in an exceptionally aggressive manner. I frequently went out of my way to tie the hands of the mixer. I started doing this purely to protect the producer from a Super Mixer granted power of veto by the label—a common occurrence at the height of the major label insanity. I wasn't going to spend hours getting tones that fit within the context of a producer's vision, only to give a mixer an opportunity to destroy it, all because I left them too many options. I'd much rather force the mixer down a particular path, thereby affording the producer some measure of predictability.

Even if you should choose to lean towards passive recording techniques in general, you still want to come as close as possible to your tone. You can just as easily compress the snot out of a room mic after it's been recorded as you can while you're recording. As the recordist, when you feel you're lacking the information necessary to make a proper decision, then the best option could very well be to leave yourself some room to maneuver later. You can add compression. You can't really take it away.

Now, as much as I *prefer* to aggressively pull tones that are designed to work cohesively toward the end game of the mix, this can't be done at the expense of the talent. If you take too long to pull a tone, you could completely wipe out your performer before he's even begun. This is especially so with singers, who are best captured when they are most inspired to perform. If you're not prepared to record a vocal the moment your singer is inspired, or worse yet, if you spend hours trying to achieve the perfect vocal sound, you could very well kill your vocal session before it even began. Thwarting inspiration is a cardinal sin in recording. No tone can survive a lackluster performance.

In general, I'm going to push you towards aggressive recording techniques throughout this book. Just how aggressive you choose to be in this regard is up to you. As I've already pointed out, the situation will often dictate your procedures, as will the music. But if you want to improve your recording skill set, source-centric aggressive recording will be the most accelerated path to good results.

The Overdub Method

In a world of DAWs with unlimited track counts, the process of building a track one part at a time through the overdub process is certainly the most common method of recording. Overdubbing requires some forethought and imagination on your part, since you're never hearing all the parts at once, but rather building them one on top of the next. The problem is, if you've never spent any time trying to mix, predicting how it's all going to go together in the abstract can be difficult at best.

Those of you who generally construct your tracks with loops and MIDI are already accustomed to building a track from the ground up. You've probably sat in front of your computer for hours searching for just the right combination of loops. From an arrangement and production standpoint, there's not much difference. You're still building your track from the ground up. Surely constructing a track with loops allows you to swap samples in and out at will. That's the advantage. But at some point you begin to lock in decisions, one after another, until eventually you have a track.

Unfortunately, swapping tones during the overdub process isn't nearly as instantaneous. Once you commit to a tone, it must then be performed. It's prohibitive and destructive to the process to recut performances purely for tone. This should be treated as an option of last resort.

Therefore, for all intents and purposes, once you record a part, you're pretty much stuck with it. So you need to build your track with intent and forethought. Even using more passive recording techniques, you should only defer processing and shaping decisions. You still have to capture the right performance with a tone designed to work within the context of the track. This too takes practice.

In some ways, it's actually far easier to record an entire band at once, because you can judge how it all goes together. If you attempt to capture drums alone, both you and the drummer are going to have a difficult time judging without any other context. Certainly, you can make a good drum recording without any other instrumentation, but without that information, you could find yourself more than a little lost.

The more sonic information you have at your disposal, the better your recording decisions will be. While one can become quite adept at pulling tones in isolation, until you have some experience, context is somewhat crucial. Even if your only goal is to capture the drums, you would be best to include the rest of the band. Not only will this supply you with the context that you need, it gives the band an opportunity to perform.

The advantage to recording in the overdub mode is your ability to focus on parts individually for both part and tone. The advantage to recording an entire group during the tracking phase is it provides you full sonic context. A band of high-caliber musicians who listen to each other as a unit don't necessarily need the focused individual attention that you might supply a band of average musicians. The fact that they're average musicians doesn't limit your ability to record an amazing product, it merely affects your strategy.

Much of how I will discuss technique in this chapter will be based on the overdub process, mostly because it's such a common way to record. Partly because it allows me to explain the considerations necessary for various source instruments.

Distortion

Much like room tone, the level of distortion you record with should be considered. And while you can certainly add distortion after the fact, analog front end distortion done right is generally much more pleasing than digital distortion applied upon playback.

I absolutely love when gear manufacturers tout their low distortion specs on gear. Not only is it usually a lie, or at the very least presented in a somewhat deceptive manner, it's just plain stupid. Frankly, I'm more interested with *how* a piece of gear distorts, not *whether* it distorts. Distortion is a critical component to good recording, and the day you figure out how to record without any distortion whatsoever is the day you'll have discovered precisely how to make the most uninviting recording of all time. A recording without any distortion will offer the most lifeless, uninspiring tones ever. The good news is, it's difficult, if not impossible, to record without some level of distortion.

Further complicating matters, there are many different kinds of distortion, all of them useful given the right circumstances. Even outright digital clipping, which is likely the harshest distortion there is, can be used to positive effect in the right production and recording.

All analog gear distorts; it's more a matter of how much audible distortion you seek on a given part (if any), and how that distortion sounds, especially within the context of the track itself. Just to be clear, I'm not suggesting you should go out of your way to distort everything—that can be equally as detrimental.

This is one of the reasons why I suggest you should take advantage of analog gear when you're recording. It distorts well. We'll talk more about distortion as it relates to specific instruments.

Capturing Performances

I'm going to speak to you more as a producer for a moment because there are philosophies that you should be aware of when it comes to process. And while I discuss these concepts in *Zen and the Art of Producing,* I must touch on some things with you here in this volume—in particular, how we use the technology to affect performances.

There are two basic approaches to recording. The first is somewhat organic in nature, in which the player is more responsible for his performance than the technician. The second is somewhat inorganic, in which the technician is more responsible for the performance than the player.

You should use all tools available to you when you find them appropriate. I have no issue with using the power of a DAW to fix minor performance problems. Unfortunately, it's often abused, not necessarily out of intent (which I also have no problem with), but rather out of some misplaced belief that this is how records are made today. It's certainly how *some* records are made. Is this the right way to make every record? Definitely not.

If you insist a player fully perform his part, you will achieve a wholly more musical result than if you use your DAW to edit, cut, paste, tune, and time a less-than-stellar run-through. I'm not here to lecture you on how aggressively you choose to use your DAW. I admit, when you find yourself tediously punching-in on every measure under the guise of capturing a performance, you will question my sanity in this regard. And in those cases, it may be worth using the power of your DAW to help out a struggling player. But insisting that a player perform is not always a tedious process, and there are a number of benefits to compiling a performance, over constructing a collection of notes.

The 13-year-old kid next door can play notes. The main distinction between greatness and mediocrity in music is the difference between musical performances that affect the listener's emotions, and notes that serve only to fill space. If you're recording music, then you are in the business of manipulating emotions, and you best accomplish this through the capture of musical performances.

There will be times when a player must develop and learn the part as she records it. By the time you finish your punch-fest designed to develop the part, she'll likely be able to perform it in convincing fashion with little more than a few touchups. It's never a bad idea to try and beat what you've got, particularly if it was labor-intensive to get there in the first place. Take a break first. Both you and your artist need to clear your heads.

A musician can't bring a part to performance standards as it's being developed. All you'll have upon completing the part are a collection of notes that you can now put in time and in tune. And while this can seem efficient, you have to ask yourself what are you trying to achieve? Notes or music?

It's the nuance that makes music interesting, and when you use technology to copy and paste, or when you align a part perfectly to grid, you lose all that is human from the performance. If your goal is to create a track in perfect time, and there are certainly situations and genres that call for this, then the grid is perfectly acceptable. That doesn't mean you're not greatly diminishing the human element. That's exactly what you're doing. It's just that there are genres in which this is common, if not desired.

You should be mindful of what you're trying to achieve with the music. Is your goal to provide a hypnotic beat for purposes of a trance-like feel, or is your goal to convey an emotional message? If it's the latter, you would be ill-advised to remove all human feel from your music.

When you insist that your player perform his parts, regardless of how many punch-ins are required, you provide him with a feeling of self-satisfaction and worth. As much as some performers might bitch at you for making them record every note (and some will), most musicians will appreciate your conviction upon hearing the results. More often than not, they will thank you for the experience.

Your performers will have an immense feeling of accomplishment when they are responsible for their performances. Further, if you give up on your performer too quickly, you could very well destroy his confidence. This will result in nothing more than a self-fulfilling prophecy.

Young musicians are all too familiar with the editing power of a DAW, and some even expect you to use it. That's just lazy, as far as I'm concerned. I'm not going to have a performer play down the song twice, and then create something from that unless I'm doing so specifically for production purposes. This is why I always fully investigate a band well in advance. I don't like these kinds of surprises.

By guiding your player to perform, you allow yourself the opportunity to evaluate the performance rather than tone, timing, and tuning. There could very well be times when a well-played part is detrimental to the production. If you want the sound of reckless, then there is nothing better than a ratty, slightly detuned guitar played on top of the beat. I mean, what are you going to do? Ask the performer to play it well, and then use your DAW to put your performer out of tune and time?

Surely, you scoffed at that suggestion (at least I hope you did). The point is, very few recordists and producers would even consider using a DAW for purposes of making a part more raw. So why then would you automatically use the DAW to polish it up? Give your performer an opportunity to deliver the goods. Besides, raw might just be the best way to go, and if you don't evaluate the music and the performance based on how it makes you feel, you're not basing your decisions on what causes a listener to react.

Not to put too fine a point on it, but if your only goal is to get down the part, and get it in time, then you're completely missing the point of music in general. Even as the recordist, and especially if there is not a designated producer, it's important that you constantly evaluate the overall feel of the track. The time to experiment with that is before you spend two hours editing a part you really didn't pay attention to in the first place. You can't manipulate and mangle your way into a high rate of success.

Some, if not many of you, likely recoiled at that last statement.

"What are you talking about? I manipulate and mangle my way to success each and every day!"

Perhaps you do, but let's examine the meaning of the word "success."

Where do you see yourself in five years? How about 10? Do you want to be recording shitty bands with little to no musicality in 20 years?

Your DAW is a powerful tool. And you can indeed manipulate and mangle your way into the illusion of a performance. Perhaps even convincingly so. And who is that going to attract?

More shitty bands, of course. And why not? You've developed your skills to manipulate and mangle one band, and then another, and the next thing you know, you have the reputation as the expert in manipulating shitty bands.

And if you think you're going to break out of that cycle, I have to wonder, how? You will only have managed to become a master at the least important skill set there is, unless your goal is to be the king (or queen) of recording shitty bands.

A hit would help. But what happens when that hit manifests into a gig with a seasoned producer and a really good band? All of a sudden, those editing chops of yours aren't worth dick, as those skills are neither required nor welcome on the session. How are you going to manipulate and mangle your way out of that predicament? You've developed all the wrong skill sets by becoming a whiz at editing bottom-of-the-barrel talent.

We all had to learn how to deal with relatively poor source material from the start. That's how it works. It's called paying your dues, although I fucking hate that phrase, and the only reason I just used it was to express my disdain for it. Call it what you like, but you would be wise to consider what skill sets you're developing, and how they will affect your career.

There are, of course, certain genres that nearly require being placed to grid, but most of those tracks have a dual purpose as dance songs. Not that you have to work to a grid in order to make a smoking dance beat—quite the opposite, really. Still, one must consider how one's art fits within the grand scheme of pop culture and fashion, and while it can be quite lucrative to establish the next big trend, it's also a long shot that requires impeccable timing.

Some rock music is highly edited to grid, although I'm hopeful this trend is finally winding down. I personally find rock bands cut to grid exceptionally boring, as it's the antithesis of rock. Rebels don't care whether they're in perfect tune or time. They just want to rock.

If you're using loops and samples, obviously you're going to be to grid. That doesn't mean you have to put every part you record to grid. Allowing the performed instruments to breath can help tremendously with the feel.

I dissuade you from recording to grid when you can avoid it, not because I don't like it. I wouldn't ever do it if I didn't understand its benefits. But too often, neophyte recordists default to technician-centric performances, with little to no consideration for experimenting outside of that realm. Not all records are cut to grid, nor should they be, and as the recordist, you should be interested in experimenting with all forms of record-making. This will only add to your arsenal, and make you better at recording in general.

Chapter One

The Recordist

The recordist is often viewed as the least important creative contributor. Mixers and mastering engineers have far more perceived importance and value than the recording engineer. In reality, the recordist (in conjunction with the producer) sets the plate for everyone else that follows. I can assure you, I can mix a well-thought out, quality recording much faster (and consequently much better), than a haphazardly poor one. And while I can certainly perform damage control—there are limits.

I suppose the thinking is that one should pay more for each engineer down the line so as to fix the fucked-up job of their predecessor. From that perspective, it kind of makes sense. I'm being facetious, although only partly. I'm sure that theory has some merit to it. Still, it's the short supply of exceptional mixers and mastering engineers that puts them in high demand. Further problematic: a really good recordist is almost invisible to the process.

The recordist doesn't get the same benefit of comparison as those down the line. The final mix is compared to a one-hour rough mix, the master is compared to the unprocessed raw mix. What's the recording compared to? The demo? Sorry, you get no credit for beating the demo. That's expected, and the producer and the artist will receive those dubious accolades.

No wonder the recordist is so underestimated in this business. Everyone else in the process improved upon the product in which your greatest contribution was to stay out of the way. Ultimately, you set your worth through your results. If you get consistent results, then you will eventually be recognized for your contributions—invisible or otherwise.

A strong producer with a clear vision could indeed render the recordist a relatively unimportant position, but only because she's picking up the slack. Only a small percentage of recording projects actually have a legitimate producer. This serves to elevate your importance as recordist, as you will likely have to help with some of the producing duties.

Recordist Roles

People seem to struggle with the definition of the roles when it comes to producers, recordists, artists, and mixers. There's a good reason for this. The lines are blurred—more so today than ever before.

This has made writing this book a bit challenging. It doesn't make sense for me to approach the subject of recording purely from the perspective of the recordist, since the large preponderance of us often serve more than one role. It's almost a requirement given the current state of the business.

You will automatically put less importance on the recording aspects in order to serve your primary role. This is not only natural, it's appropriate and necessary, which makes your quest to become a good recordist all the more important, as many of your recording duties must become second nature. This way you can focus on your more important job, without completely sacrificing your secondary role as recordist.

I understand the thinking that goes behind grabbing any mic that happens to be nearby when it comes time to record a quick tambourine. Guilty as charged. I mean, I'd rather spend 20 minutes trying to find the right tambourine than 10 minutes wanking off over microphone selection. It's a fucking tambourine. Even if the part is designed to be outrageously loud in the mix, it's not likely to be the main focus point of the track. At least it shouldn't be.

From a strictly purist viewpoint, choosing the closest mic to record my tambourine means I've sloughed off my job as recordist, at least to some extent. From a practical standpoint, I've put more importance on my role as the producer at that moment. And while I could certainly spend time auditioning mics and pres and carefully placing my microphones before I return to my producer's duties, I risk pulling myself from my preferred headspace.

As the producer, I'm thinking about the big picture, including running the session in a manner that gets the best performances possible. My focus as a recordist is purely on the capture. It can be challenging at times to switch between those two head spaces, even after doing it for years.

A great recordist can be a Buddha-send to a producer. Recording and producing are two distinct jobs, and while they work in concert (done successfully), a recordist allows the producer to concentrate on performances. The irony being that the less effective the producer is at pulling performances, the more you will struggle at your job as recordist. Where the performance crumbles, so goes the tone. Break out the compressors!

There are three types of recordists. The Designated Recordist, the Musician Recordist, and the Producer Recordist. There's also the Assistant Recordist, but the studio assistant should be able to fill that role regardless, and will often gladly take on the role of Designated Recordist.

The Designated Recordist

By definition (and yes, it's my definition), there must be a producer on the session in order to call yourself the Designated Recordist. If the band or artist are producing themselves, you become the producer by default, whether your client sees it that way or not. Should you find yourself encouraging performances, making arrangement suggestions, and monitoring the pace of the session, then you're operating as a Default Producer.

Don't get me wrong. That doesn't make you the producer. You're not in charge of the session, and you obviously don't have the artist's trust in that role, otherwise they would have hired you for it in the first place. If you don't have some minimal power of veto and total control over the budget, you're not the producer. But there is really no way around taking on some of the producer's roles. Essentially, you get much of the work without any of the responsibility. Oh, and without any of the credit either. That could be a good thing.

How involved you want to be as the Default Producer is up to you. If you're recording a band that is generally leaderless, you'll probably have to take on more responsibilities than you might with an artist who has a clear vision for her work. No matter the scenario, the talent can't do it all, and you should help them in any way that you can. Their success becomes your success, and that can be parlayed into more work in the future.

For those of you who operate as a Designated Recordist, I will warn you now, I'm going to be much harder on you in this section than I will on the Musician Recordist. Many of the responsibilities I'm about to explain to you here are not required of the Musician or Producer Recordists, mostly because they have a more critical job to do.

As a truly Designated Recordist, you have several responsibilities: capture the tones in the most appropriate manner possible, document how you got there (i.e. amp, guitar, settings for both, mic, pre, levels), watch the producer's back, and deliver a complete and fully organized recording session.

Capture Appropriate Tones

I'm sure you're wondering what the definition of "appropriate" is here. That adjective certainly leaves a ton of wiggle room.

I mean appropriate to the production, of course, but also appropriate to the song itself.

This brings us back to the concept of aggressive recording. Should a production call for trashy drums, it would be appropriate to record them that way. As far as I'm concerned, it's *inappropriate* to record them any other way. All you'll really manage to accomplish is more work for yourself, more work for the mixer (which just might be you), and more confusion for your artist and producer.

Get your hands on a crappy kit, and stick the drums in a place that maximizes the trash. Low ceilings and undersized live rooms work well towards the sound. Drums tuned poorly, broken cymbals, fucked-up rims, old heads, and obnoxiously raucous cymbals performed with excessive force are all good strategies for capturing a trashy drum tone. Notice that everything on that list has to do with the source and nothing to do with the microphones (although if you really want to accentuate the trash, try a Shure SM57 as a mono overhead).

Distortion is another great tool, and if the intent is for a part to be distorted, then distort it. For instance, if a production calls for ultra-distorted cymbals, it's appropriate to record them that way. Of course, many of you might be thinking, "but I can distort them later!"

Let's not get hysterical now. Yes, you can distort them later, and if there's some trepidation from your clients as to whether distorted cymbals are the right approach, then you should defer that decision. There's no reason to be dogmatic about this. Record the part clean if that will make the team more comfortable, but if the intention is indeed to distort, then either record both the distorted and clean signals simultaneously, or add the distortion on the return. This way you're monitoring with the intended tone. Believe it or not, that aggressive distorted cymbal tone will affect how your musicians perform.

Whatever you do, don't record the entire production monitoring clean drums, only to distort them come mix time. Work towards the mix as you go along, otherwise you leave everyone unsure of where the production is going. If you're not monitoring the cymbals distorted as intended, then you won't know how your overdubs fit within the big picture. And if your performers aren't monitoring that distortion in the headphones, then you are losing an opportunity to adequately agitate them, which is kind of the point of distorting cymbals in the first place—to agitate the listener. If you want to agitate the listener, there's no better way to accomplish this than to agitate your performers.

What your performers are monitoring will have a direct effect on how and what they play. As the Designated Recordist, you are responsible for the players' headphone mix (cue mix), and there are a number of strategies for this. Many studios have portable multi-input headphone mixers, which will allow your players some individual control on their cue mix. That may seem like a great time saver, that is, until you check out some of the atrocious cue mixes at the various stations. At times you will wonder how your musicians even managed a take. You would do well to go through and give your talent a good starting point on the cue mix.

It can be difficult to come up with a stereo cue mix that satisfies all the players as you're tracking, since each of your performers will want their part loudest in the balance. Typically far too loud. Given this, compact headphone mixers are often the better alternative.

During the overdub phase, you can send the control room monitor mix to one stereo input, and the part you're recording to a second input. This allows the performer to boost their part without affecting your own monitor balances. Be forewarned, any fader move that you make during the course of the performance will be heard by the performer in their cans. This can be distracting, and you should leave the balances static when possible.

There are certain performance maladies that can be a direct result of a poorly balanced cue mix. Players who are out of time may not have enough rhythm instruments in their cue mix. Out-of-tune horns can be a result of monitoring too little harmonic information. Surely, you will record players that are incapable of playing in time and tune regardless of their cue mix, but this is certainly a good place to investigate when you come across perplexing performance issues.

If you don't have multi-channel cue mixers available, you can always pick up a prosumer sub-mixer for the task. Without it, you could very well find yourself setting up multiple cue sends. Don't underestimate the importance of a good headphone mix. This is in your domain, and it's not a duty to be taken lightly.

Document

Documentation is critical for an efficient session. This falls under the purview of the recordist, although it's often delegated to a studio assistant. Regardless of who performs the documentation, it's your responsibility to make sure it's done properly.

Any information that you document could very well come in handy later. Taken to its extreme, you would document everything, including the particular instruments used, amps, mics, pres, compressors, EQs, and all of their individual settings. Admittedly, when I was working primarily as a recordist, I almost never documented all of that, but rather reserved certain signal chains for particular combos. When you're recording with a $500,000 budget, you have that latitude.

Documentation isn't nearly as necessary for acoustic instruments. You can certainly make drawings of where you had the mics, but you'll likely waste more time than you'll ever save. You should definitely document a change in snare and kik drum. You should document acoustic guitars used. The most important documentation has more to do with amplified electric guitars.

If you're going to spend valuable time trying out guitar and amplifier combinations in order to find the right tone, you might as well be able to get back to it later. There is nothing more deflating than attempting to match an electric guitar tone without any documentation. You may be able to pick out the guitar and amp by ear, and your mind might even be a steel trap for such details, but I wouldn't rely on either of those solutions.

The aggravation you'll feel by neglecting to document *what* guitar and amp were used, let alone how they were set, can be described as nothing short of all-consuming. When the eighth song of a session would benefit from a similar guitar tone from the first, good documentation will have you up and recording in short order. Without notes, not only will you attempt to backwards engineer that tone, you'll likely never feel like you quite got there. You'll probably feel that way even if the new tone is somehow better. Don't do that to yourself.

If you think that documenting your mic selections will help later, then by all means, write them down. Some people include the mic in the filename, which isn't a bad idea. Where you placed the instruments in the room can be valuable information later. Documenting who played is certainly useful, especially if you've recorded a variety of sidemen. The level of detail you apply in your documentation is up to you. Just keep in mind, when you save a producer time because of good documentation habits, she will likely hire you again.

Listen

If you're taking a gig with a producer who you've determined is a hack, don't take the gig in the first place. Your most important responsibility is to help the producer achieve success. George Drakoulias once told me that my job was to make him look good. Which was absolutely how he viewed it, and no matter what you or I think of that, this was the gig. If we asked five more producers the job of the recordist, we'd get five more answers, the theme of which would be the same. Watch my back.

What does that mean? It means you're always paying attention in order to prevent mistakes by the team. You're going into the room to make sure that mics are where they belong. You're making sure that parts aren't overlooked (like the guitar part on the entire second chorus). The producer will likely have a long queue on her mind throughout the course of a production. Consequently, it's easy to fuck up. You're her safety net.

As the Designated Recordist, you're also responsible for running the DAW, a task sometimes referred to as tape-op, which is a seemingly anachronistic term at this point. Tape-op can be a rather mundane part of your job, but it still requires your absolute concentration.

An inattentive recordist is a time and energy sap to the session. You need to listen to what your producer is relaying to the performer, as it will directly involve you as the tape-op. For instance, if the producer and player are discussing problems on the first chorus, you should immediately locate to that chorus, which you surely have markers for by now. The moment communication is complete, you should be in record, preferably with an appropriate amount of preroll. Some artists require more pre-roll than others. Pay attention to how tight your player likes her pre-roll, and adjust to her preferences.

As the recordist, you have the power to disrupt the pace of a session. Inattentiveness to your job will frustrate everyone on the team, regardless of how they feel about you as a person. Even sessions operating at a breakneck pace will have many periods of inactivity, so there is no reason for you to fade. Should you find yourself losing focus, you can always temporarily pass the tape-op duties to the producer, although admittedly, I know several producers who will look at you like you grew a second head when you attempt to hand over the Con. Proceed with caution.

Tape-op is the position where everything tends to break down on a session. Musicians often noodle between takes (and some recordists won't interrupt). Why? It may have something to do with the fact that you keep taking 30 seconds to hit record. Unless the performer requests a moment, interrupt the noodling. Set an efficient pace. Your performers will be thankful to be recording the moment they have their instructions.

This may all sound rather stressful, and outside of what you imagined recording to be like. Believe me, unless you're on a jingle session, or a union hit, the pace tends to be fairly relaxed, even with an aggressively fast producer.

Setup is critical to speed. Markers make it far easier to locate sections. Creating tracks in advance of an overdub, cleaning tracks, organizing your session, and naming your inputs by microphone will all serve to increase your efficiency. The more efficient you are, the more valuable you become.

Even when I'm in overdub mode, I tend to set up a large variety of mics in the room and assign them to certain inputs in the DAW. As my recordist, if you name your inputs based on the microphone, you will be able to access them quickly, without searching through a patch bay of spaghetti. This way, when I stick a tambourine player in front of the AKG C12, you can easily locate your "C12" input and be in record.

Your producer needs to concentrate on the parts and performance, and if you don't keep the session moving, you will distract her attention from her supremely important job. I'd sooner take over the tape-op duties myself than have to deal with a recordist who doesn't understand how to keep a session moving.

When you're working with a fast producer, you will likely use playlists for takes in your DAW. Whatever your DAW manufacturer calls it is of little consequence. Playlists allow you to record multiple takes on the same track, which you can then compile into one performance. How you use your playlists depends on the operation. If you're recording entire passes of a track, you should make a playlist for each take. If you're punching in on sections in order to nail a difficult part, there's no point in making a new playlist every time the player fucks up. Command-Zed will save you from having to go through useless takes later. It saves on disk space too.

That said, the moment you undo and then record again, the abandoned take is gone. Make sure that there is nothing useful in a take before using the undo command. In general, it's fairly obvious, and an efficient producer will tell you when to toss a take. If there's some question, keep the take and move on.

I can't possibly come up with every scenario that you might come across on a session, nor should I have to. This is about being attentive and thereby prepared. When you find yourself unable to keep up, it's incumbent upon you to devise an efficient system regardless of the methods. A producer might prefer to work in a manner in which you're unfamiliar. Your best defense is to figure out an efficient way to operate within the producer's workflow.

As the Designated Recordist, one of your primary jobs is the capture. Disk space is cheap. When your band is playing, even if they're just fucking around, you should be in record. When your musicians are running down the track, you should be in record. There is absolutely no good reason not to be in record if there's even the slightest chance of capturing something useful. A performer could play something brilliant purely by accident, and describing it back in words will only serve to baffle. It's far better if you can play it back to her. That would make you the hero.

While recording is certainly a creative job, it's also one that requires some modicum of efficiency given the time restraints of a budget. As a recordist, the moment the performer is ready to record, you should be rolling. Believe me, if the pace is overbearing, you will surely be informed of this. Don't be defensive. Just slow things down accordingly. Whatever you do, don't sit there like a bump on a log waiting for the producer to explicitly tell you to start recording, when she's already told the performer the plan. You're sitting in the same room as the producer. Listen!

Deliver

As a third-party mixer, I'm blown away by just how poorly organized many recordists keep their sessions. There is nothing worse than receiving a session with missing parts. This is almost guaranteed to happen if you don't keep your session clean. Not only will you piss off the mixer because he's trying to mix with incomplete information, you'll piss off your client too, as they will have already experienced the pleasure of your disastrous organizational habits.

An unorganized session is an inefficient one. It's also death to the session, as your clients become more frustrated every time you have to stop to search for missing parts. The moment you can't find a part because of your lack of organization is the moment you've failed to capture an appropriate tone, you've failed to watch the producer's back, and you've pretty much failed in documenting the session. After all, recording is the very definition of documenting.

Once you've finished recording a part, it's incumbent upon you to clean up any edits or audible punch points, to label the track in a manner that describes it ("Twang guitar" is far more useful than "Guitar 3,") and to delete (or at least hide) from the session those parts that have been rejected. You also need to make sure you're backed up, which should be performed at least once per day, if not more.

Impatient producers may insist that you move forward before you've had an opportunity to fully tidy up your takes. You can perform your janitorial duties during the next break, or at the end of the day, or the start of the next—whichever makes the most sense. Whatever you do, don't let your organization duties pile up for days.

Cleanup time is session time, and you're not required to do it for free. If you're charging a day rate, and the producer uses all the time for himself, then insist on the first hour of the session for organizational duties. Frankly, most sessions take a good hour to begin (mine do anyway), and you can use that time for yourself. This also allows you to get paid for the work.

By the time you're finished with a session it should be devoid of pops, obvious edits, punches, superfluous or unwanted noise, and all failed parts. Even if you're also the mixer for the project, this should be done in advance of your mix session. This way, you can concentrate fully on the job at hand.

It's always best to compile and clean up a track the moment you're done recording it. As the Designated Recordist you don't have full control over how the session is run, but you can do some of the more macro work by eye as the producer and performer listen to the final take. Your fine tuning can be done by ear later, but at least you've laid out the basic compilation decisions. This sort of work can accrue fast, so you may want to keep a ledger or whiteboard listing your unfinished tasks.

At the end of each day, you're responsible for keeping your session backed up two times: one local, and one offsite, like in the cloud. If there's a disaster that takes out your computer and hard drive at your recording location, you will still have a safety backup that you can access from elsewhere. While your recording project may be the least of your concerns after an incident described as a "disaster," you surely wouldn't want to compound your problems.

When delivering a session to a mixer, it's unlikely, although possible, that she will not want to use your DAW session for the mix. It's far easier to start from scratch on a mix than it is to work off someone else's session. Typically, you're going to consolidate the audio for the mixer, which means you will deliver nothing more than fully contiguous audio files, all of which will start at the same mark.

If you really want to be swell, make sure the new audio tracks have revealing names. "Marshall Overdrive Guitar" is far more telling than "Guitar 3_03," especially when there are a number of guitar parts in the session. You might choose to name your tracks "Rad Guitar," "Chime Guitar," "Arp Guitar," or even "Marshall-Les Paul," as these sorts of naming conventions make them much easier to find for everyone involved. This habit alone will make your session considerably more efficient because the moment someone starts referring to a part as "Rad Guitar" everyone on your session will tend to follow suit. Your talent will even start to come up with their own names for future parts.

Of course, when you're in the heat of battle, and you haven't heard a part to name it, your audio files will probably be referenced generically, i.e. "e gtr_08." You can, however, rename your track in the playlists, and this will be the term that your team tends to reference. Either that or "green guy," but if your track colors are dynamic, it could be "orange guy" later that day. That makes waveform color references nothing more than transitory in nature. "Rad Guitar" is far easier to deal with, and you'll make your guitar player really happy. I mean, who doesn't want to be responsible for a rad guitar?

If you've been listening to your session with a plug-in designed to mangle a part, you should include that processing as part of the audio file. In other words, if you've been monitoring a guitar part with some kind of whacky envelope filter, deliver it that way to the mixer. If you're using a simulated amp on the return of a DI'ed guitar, bounce the track with the amp before delivery. Don't send the mixer the DI guitar signal, other than as a safety, and I wouldn't even bother doing that. Trust yourself and the producer.

When you send me a production to mix, your tones and decisions should indicate your intent. If you send me a track with direct injection guitars, I'll have absolutely no idea what the intention was. I'm perfectly comfortable and capable of deciding the kinds of simulated guitar tones that I think work best for a production. But if you leave it to my imagination, both you and your producer could be in for a very big surprise. And if you call me to describe the tone, I'm going to tell you to send the part that way.

So when you wonder why I decided to overdrive the guitars when they were designed to be lightly distorted, it's because you gave me no indication whatsoever as to what the team was thinking as they were recording. The fact that you didn't commit to a guitar tone doesn't bode well for your commitments on the rest of the recording.

Before consolidating files for a third-party mixer, you should organize your tracks in a logical order by category, and start each audio filename with a number. Not only will this force you to clean up your session, it will prevent sending a folder with missing parts. Even if you're not happy that the mix is being sent out to a third party, it is incumbent upon you to deliver organized tracks.

Delivery Instructions for Mix

This section contains detailed instructions on how to deliver files for mix. If a mixer has her own specific set of instructions, follow those. Most don't, so I'm providing you with my own. You are free to use it as your own, and make changes to it based on your own personal preferences.

All files should be delivered tuned and timed appropriately. All tracks should be free of pops and obvious edits before consolidating.

All electric guitars with amp simulator on the return should be bounced that way for delivery. Send me the guitars as you've been monitoring them. Please do not send me DI guitar tracks.

Any part that you've altered significantly through plug-ins on the return should be bounced and delivered that way. Please do not have me recreate aggressive processing that's an integral part of the tone, especially if you've been monitoring it that way throughout your session.

Consolidate all other files as they were recorded without processing of any kind.

Stereo files should be delivered stereo. Mono files should be delivered mono. There is no need to indicate in the filename whether a track is mono or stereo. Don't indicate the sample rate in your filename. The DAW will tell me the sample rate of a file.

NAMING CONVENTIONS

Any parts that don't belong in the mix should be removed. Any part that's questionable in nature should include a "?" in the filename (if possible).

Please rename all of your files so that they start with a number, then the instrument. Include any information in the filename that will make it easy to distinguish. A part that is recorded as a double should have a "Dbl" indicator in the filename. Harmonies should include the name of the singer, and an indicator of its pitch relative to other harmonies, i.e. "Katy *Hi* Harm." If you've printed certain FX returns, like an analog plate or delay, include those in your session.

Organize the files in your session by category in the following order:

Bass	Percussion
Drums	Harms
Electric Guitars	Vocal
Acoustic Guitars	Horns and Strings
Keys	Miscellaneous and FX

Rename all of your files so that they start with a sequential number that keeps them in that category order. Here is an example of how the audio tracks should be named for delivery.

01 Bass DI	23 Intro Ac Gtr	45 Katy Ooh
02 Bass Amp	24 B3	46 Katy Ooh Dbl
03 Kik	25 B3 Lo	47 Katy Ooh Tpl
04 Sn Top	26 Piano	48 Katy Ooh Quad
05 Sn Bot	27 String Pad	49 Ld Vocal
06 Tom I	28 Lead Synth	50 Ld Vocal Dbl
07 Tom II	29 Wurli	51 Outro Ld
08 Tom III	30 Rhodes	52 Trumpet
09 Hat	31 Tamb	53 Alto Sax
10 OHs	32 Shaker	54 Tenor Sax
11 Room L	33 Djembe Top	55 Bone
12 Room R	34 Djembe Bottom	56 Clarinet
13 E Gtr	35 Cabasa	57 Hi Violin
14 E Gtr Dbl ?	36 Congas	58 Mid Violin
15 Arp. Gtr Stereo	37 Bongos	59 Cello
16 Crunch Gtr	38 Washboard	60 String Bass
17 Chime Gtr	39 Claps ?	61 Sound FX
18 Chime Gtr Dbl	40 Claps Dbl ?	62 Party Track
19 Tele-Supro Gtr	41 Tim Hi Harm	63 EMT 140 Vocal
20 Gibson-Twin Gtr	42 Tim Hi Harm Dbl	64 Echoplex Chime
21 Ac Gtr	43 Tim Lo Harm	Gtr
22 Ac Gtr Dbl	44 Tim Lo Harm Dbl	63 Rough Mix

Put all the audio files in a single folder. The folder name should include the following information: Project, Song Title, BPM, Recordist Initials. Abbreviate song titles when necessary. If the track was recorded without a click, indicate this.

Ben Harper.Steal My Kisses.112BPM.ES

Or

Ben Harper.Steal My Kisses.No Click.ES

Organizing your audio files sequentially like this prevents mistakes. I recently mixed a song only to discover upon delivering the first print that I was missing parts. A whole slew of parts, in fact, all of which made no sense within the context of my mix. This was a headfuck of epic proportions because not only did I like my mix better without those parts, I now had to reconsider a great many decisions down the line. This only serves to piss off the entire team, and you'll get the blame for it as the recordist.

Most mistakes can be avoided by good habits. Get into the habit of meticulously cleaning and organizing your sessions.

The Designated Recordist Rules of Conduct

As a recordist for hire, you're in a service business. That means you're there to serve your client, no matter how great you think you are at recording, and regardless of how clueless your client may be. Honestly, you shouldn't be recording if you're not having fun. Yes, it's work, but it's creative work, and you affect the personal dynamic in the room. The last thing you want to be is a hindrance to a session. If you're all pissed off because you're dead broke and feel you should be getting paid more, then either stop taking gigs that don't meet your financial needs, or do something else entirely.

One of the producer's most important jobs is to keep everyone on the session happy and relaxed. It's part of the recordist's job too, but only at the pleasure and lead of the producer. One malcontent on the session can destroy the vibe and bring a session to a grinding halt. This can't happen, certainly not from the position of the recordist.

It seems some recordists are nothing more than frustrated producers, and if that describes you, then you shouldn't accept the position of recordist in the first place. You will only make the producer miserable as you second-guess her decisions and undermine her authority, all because you know better. It's not unheard of for a good recordist to be miles ahead of a young producer. In fact, a young producer would be smart to hire a veteran recordist, just as she should hire top-notch musicians.

Should you find yourself resentful because someone who can't happens to be smart enough to hire someone who can, which in this case would be you, then you have only yourself to blame. That young producer convinced an artist or band to allow him to lead them. You didn't. When you accept the gig as a recordist for a producer whom you don't respect, you will only manage to provide a lousy experience for everyone involved. If a kid that has both the gumption to produce a record, and the wherewithal to seek out a professional such as yourself, then why would you not do all that you can to help? His success becomes your success.

This doesn't mean you shouldn't have an opinion nor express one. You're not proving anything by allowing a producer to struggle when you have suggestions for arriving at a solution. You're just being a selfish cunt.

If you find that statement offensive (and you should), then you have some idea of just how offensive I find a recordist who isn't a team player. It's a pet peeve of mine. Admittedly, I've been far from perfect in this regard. How do you think I learned this lesson in the first place? I'm being no harder on you than I am on myself.

No matter how skilled you are as a recordist, and no matter how overwhelmed the producer might be, you are in a subservient role. The producer is the boss, and you are her second in command. The client is also technically your boss, but you should generally limit your day-to-day negotiations to the producer. It's not for you to second-guess the producer, and if you're confused by conflicting instructions, allow the producer to deal with the issue.

Everyone on a production has a role. You're a team. If you do a great job and make yourself valuable to a producer, you also make yourself valuable to the client, the musicians, and the artist. This will only work in your favor in the long run, as the client could very well remember how helpful you were and recommend you as a producer in the future.

The Musician Recordist

As the Musician Recordist, you're a musician first, and a recordist by default. You're probably your own producer too. Given this, we have to simplify things a bit. I'm sorry, but it's impossible to perform all the roles of a Designated Recordist as I've laid out, and also carry out your duties as the musician and producer. Something has to give.

With all that you must think about as the Musician Recordist, you should concentrate on one thing where recording technique is concerned, and that's the capture. I'm also going to recommend that you simplify the way you record. You're a musician first, and as such, engineering duties need to be streamlined. There's no need to use two mics on a guitar when one will suffice, particularly if you have no assistance.

Surely, if you want to get creative with recording technique, you should, especially when you find yourself with some time to experiment. Unfortunately, you only have so much creative energy to put forth on any given day, and most of that creative energy is best spent on the music.

As far as documentation is concerned, I'd recommend keeping it down to the bare minimum. It makes sense to document amp and guitar combinations you might be interested in returning to later. Beyond that, it's not practical to keep extensive notes while performing multiple duties. You have too much on your plate.

A large percentage of you reading this likely have a camera in your phone, and there is no easier way to document than by taking pictures. This method requires that you organize your photos by track, that is if you want to actually find anything. So you'll still have to take time out for documentation purposes. If you're anything like me on an understaffed session, you'll likely fall off of that pretty quick. For the most part, documentation goes to the wayside.

As a Musician Recordist, you should go out of your way to make your sessions as clean as possible. Otherwise, you will bring your project to a grinding halt in order to take care of some basic janitorial work. You want to perform your cleanup work on your terms, preferably at the time of recording the part. It's a mistake to leave comping for another day. Comps are best done at the time of recording while the takes are relatively fresh in your mind. Besides, you don't have a take until it's been compiled and verified, so there's no point to moving on before you've gone through that process.

The Producer Recordist

The Producer Recordist takes care of both producing and recording duties. Given that the jobs of producing and recording each require your full attention, it can be difficult to perform both jobs well. As a Producer Recordist, you should get an assistant on your session who is also a relatively strong recordist in her own right. Even with an Assistant Recordist available, it's best to simplify recording technique whenever possible.

Don't confuse a Producer Recordist with a recordist who is also the producer by default. A Default Producer is merely a recordist who is consulting on the production, and if the job entails more than that, you should be getting credit for it.

You might think that operating as the Producer Recordist would simplify matters, as you wouldn't have to deal with trying to communicate a tone to a recordist—you could just pull it yourself. Of course, as producer, you're the boss, so if you want to pull a tone yourself you can. So I'm not sure where the advantage lies. This is why it's critical to at least have an assistant. You need someone there to help you place microphones, patch in processing, operate the deck, and attend to your clients as you concentrate on the task at hand.

Engineering duties tend to be left-brain functions, and if you keep yourself in that headspace for an extended period of time, it can be difficult to pull yourself back into the preferred right-heavy mindset necessary for producing. Bad performance will often result in poor tone, and this is best dealt with from the position of the producer. Keeping yourself in the right headspace requires constant vigilance.

The Recordist's Tools

If you read the Internet audio boards, you're probably familiar with the countless debates over our tools and their relative importance to the recording process. We've already established the gear is far less important than the performer, instrument, and room. But "less important" doesn't necessarily mean *un*important.

You can't record a sound being emitted in a room without a microphone of some sort. You can't record without some form of recording and storage medium, whether that's analog tape or a DAW. You can't run a DAW without a computer. You can't monitor what you're recording without speakers. And you can't do any of it without electricity.

Therefore, you can't record without technology, which means your tools have some bearing and importance to the process. Yet, despite this rather obvious flaw in the argument, the Internet abounds with neophyte recordists who are absolutely convinced that gear has no bearing whatsoever on the ultimate quality of a record.

As if.

Yes, a compelling performance will certainly transcend any recording technology. Does that mean we should all go back to ADATs?

It should come as no surprise to you that I have no shortage of confidence when it comes to my engineering capabilities. My multiple books on the recording arts shall serve as *prima facie* evidence of this. Yet, there have been times in my career that I have literally been rendered artistically impotent by subpar gear in a fucked-up critical listening space.

Is the cheapest mic pre available going to do your recording harm? According to some on the Internet, no. According to me, absolutely. That crappy mic pre that comes stock with your digital interface will compound your recording with unintended distortion that isn't all that musical in nature. There's no getting around the "tools" part of this. The large preponderance of this book will address source and capture techniques, but your tools can, and will, affect the overall quality of your recordings. That's not even debatable. Yet here we are.

Then there's the numbskulls who insist that gear means everything to their success as a recordist—a claim that often leaves one to ponder the definition of success, given that it's an argument typically raised by weekend warriors who have never made a record of note. This is an equally delusional position.

The truth is somewhere in the middle. We've already established that there's a bare minimum of gear required in order to record. Therefore the technology must have some bearing on the recording process. We can't perform our job without it. So just how vital is quality gear to a recording? It depends on the function of the gear.

While you can make a record without a single compressor or EQ, converters are a requirement for digital recording and reproduction. Your converters are directly responsible for the overall audio quality, making them one of your more important gear considerations.

You certainly can't record a voice without a microphone or a microphone preamp (although you can amplify the mic with an analog compressor if you really like stupid amounts of line noise on everything you record). And while it's true you can build an entire instrumental album using prepackaged loops and MIDI instruments, the moment you want to record an acoustic instrument, you'll need a mic and a preamp. We use these tools in order to convey our music and art to others; therefore, they have relevance to the process.

We have a wide array of choices where our tools are concerned, many of which perform the same basic functions in slightly unique ways. Our recording tools can run anywhere from ridiculously inexpensive to prohibitively expensive. Supply and demand principles are alive and well when it comes to recording gear.

There's no doubt that a well-maintained vintage Telefunken ELAM 251 is an amazing microphone. Is it $24,000 good? Probably not. If money was of no consequence, a 251 or two would surely be worth owning. Do my recordings suffer when I don't have that mic available? Of course not, and neither will yours. But I sure am happy when I see a 251 on the studio gear list. That said, just because I have a 251 available on my session doesn't mean it's the mic I'll use in any given application. Circumstance could make the $100 Shure SM57 the far superior choice.

There is no doubt the source has the most impact on the quality of your recordings. But our tools surely play a role. Once the source is right in the room, our job is to capture it in the best way possible. Mics, preamps, EQ, and compressors allow us to shape the tone in the most compelling and fitting manner possible.

Notice I used the word "fitting" in conjunction with "compelling." There's no such thing as good sound or bad sound. There is only sound as it works relative to music. So I'm not making an abstract subjective determination of what good sound is. If the overall sound is effective and fits the record, then that's good sound.

By the time you deliver the final product, the sound should be so interwoven with the production and the song that it's unnoticed. Much like dark matter, good sound should be invisible other than how it pulls on those within its sphere of influence. A sound itself is of little consequence. It's how the sound affects the musical presentation that should be of primary concern.

At any given time in your career, you will have access to a finite collection of gear. You can only use the tools available, or that you can creatively (and legally) acquire. From a creative and musical perspective, there is nothing limiting you from making a great record other than your skill. From a technical perspective, there are certain tools that can and will limit that skill set. Your abilities only serve to maximize your results relative to the gear available.

It can be a bit overwhelming to explore the sea of recording gear available, both vintage and new, especially when you consider the expense. So how the hell do you decide what to purchase when you don't really have the experience to choose wisely? You could go on the Internet and ask a bunch of strangers, most of whom are likely in a similar position to you. Or you can provide yourself some basis of comparison. I recommend the latter.

I realize this is a book on recording, but the best way for me to explain to you the power of direct comparison is to discuss my early experiences with some desks. When I started the LA portion of my career, I was absolutely convinced that the Neve V in Hollywood Sound was the mix console of choice over the API and 8068 in the other two rooms. The Neve V was newer! It had processing on every channel!

I had the opportunity to work in the Neve V room for half the day before moving the project over to the API room. Let me tell you, that was probably the most dramatic aha moment I've ever had in my career, and I've had a number of them over the years.

The API was far more open in tone. The music and recording were way more inviting. Here I was listening to a console that was decades old, and it blew away the Neve V!

Of course, if you listen to the expectation bias conspiracists out there, I should have preferred the Neve V regardless of what the API sounded like. I mean, that was my expectation, right? Apparently not.

Now, just because I prefer the API, doesn't mean I couldn't or wouldn't mix a record on a Neve V. Let's be real here. As much as I find the Neve V clearly inferior in sound to an API, it's still a useful piece of kit for mixing. For starters, any studio that spent hundreds of thousands for a Large Frame Analog Console invested in their buildout too. As a result, the Vs are typically placed in good critical listening spaces. But then so are APIs.

The Neve V consoles are worthless for recording other than as a monitoring desk, as are SSLs. Yet I've mixed countless albums that I'm proud of on those consoles—just as I have on various APIs. There have been instances where a Neve V made my life easier despite the inferior sound. Further, its deficiencies are not so great that they prevent me from accomplishing an effective mix. Essentially, a Neve V doesn't get in my way when mixing.

All of this might cause you to wonder why I wouldn't just work on my preferred desk as a matter of course. Simply put, there's far more to consider than the console. Here are just some of the things I take into account when I choose a room, in no particular order: accuracy of monitoring; size of the project (track counts); distance from home; artist and/or producer preferences; proximity to good food (gotta feed the brain); price as it relates to budget; availability, automation, quantity, and quality of outboard gear; studio staff; the general vibe of the place; and even the overall comfort of the room.

Suppose I spent a month recording in a good API room and then moved to a studio full of prosumer gear. Do you really think I'm going to be happy using prosumer mic pres and converters? Certainly not. But then I understand just how overtly that prosumer gear will get in my way, to the point that I won't even be able to adequately operate. And if you think that I (or anyone else) can get the same results from an inaccurate room littered with prosumer gear, think again. There are some things that skill cannot overcome. Experience, on the other hand, prevents me from accepting that fucked-up situation in the first place.

Where skill fails, experience prevails.

Then, of course, there's the subjectivity involved. I personally can't stand mixing on an SSL. I've mixed many albums on SSL desks (just about every model) and I detest how they sound in general. I feel as though I'm fighting those consoles tooth and nail every step of the way, and I often struggle to pull what I want from them. Is that a failure on my part? Probably not, since I've mixed countless records on SSL consoles that I'm proud of, but the experience would have been significantly improved had I mixed on a console that I can easily make sing. As much as the SSL gets in my way, it doesn't prevent me from an effective mix. It just makes my life considerably more difficult. Of course, I know many well-regarded engineers and mixers who have similarly negative feelings about the Neve 8068 desk, which is by far my favorite mixing desk. This is why it's so critical that you come to your own conclusions when it comes to selecting gear.

I don't share this with you to beat up SSL, but I haven't been shy over the years with sharing my disdain for these desks. I only state this opinion because of the weird perception by the Internet Chatter Class that SSL desks are somehow the panacea of sonic quality where recording consoles are concerned. Nothing could be further from the truth.

Clearly, there are a ton of records mixed on SSL consoles, which would explain the beneficial brand perception. Despite my preferences, or anyone else's for that matter, there really can be no debate over whether a Neve is better than an SSL or vice versa. That depends purely on your taste, and your taste alone. Your preferences will fit neatly within the confines of how you hear. It's really that simple.

My friend Dave Pensado likes to say, in his beautiful drawl, "People hire me for my taste." It also stands to reason that some people don't hire him because of his taste. The same goes for me or anyone else. There is no one so talented that they can satisfy all of human consciousness with their style. Everyone hears differently, and you will gravitate towards the gear that aligns with your own musicality, or lack thereof.

There's a scientific principle called *Nullius in Verba*, which is Latin for "see for yourself" or "question authority." And while I present my strong opinions from a position of authority, it's not for some misguided purpose of trying to convince you to do things my way. It's to provide you with a starting point for making your own decisions with confidence. It doesn't matter what anyone else claims. Ultimately, you need to "see for yourself."

You must develop your ears in order to adequately evaluate the gear, and you require experience in order to pass judgment. So when you read suggestions that the SSL is the best desk to mix on, not only should you question whether that person has an actual basis of comparison to make such an absurd claim, you should recognize that the only opinion that matters is your own. This is true regardless of how many top-flight engineers might agree with the statement. There will likely be just as many that disagree.

Further complicating matters is the purpose of your work. If you desire to learn how to record for your own personal hobby, then you can absolutely use the bare minimum requirements to record. There's nothing at stake other than your own enjoyment, and if it makes you happy then I'm all for it. Let happiness abound. The stakes, however, increase significantly when you're creating records for commerce. Competition alone will force you to regularly consider what gear is preventing you from doing your job at the highest level possible, whether you're a musician, a producer, or a recordist.

Business perception issues also come into play. How are you going to charge $800 a day for a mix room that has nothing but a DAW and a Sound Blaster card? Given the kind of room you can get these days for that price, you will have a difficult time selling that rate, no matter how skillful you are, and no matter how great your tracks sound.

Now, many of you don't have access to an API or a Neve 8068. Worry not. I've been mixing in a DAW in my own suite since 2008. After a long and sometimes frustrating process, I now actually prefer this method of working for a number of reasons—all of which ultimately make my life easier. For starters, I don't have to travel, I can have a life, and I can mix what I want when I want regardless of budget, which gives me more freedom to take low-budget jobs that I believe in. I also don't have to constantly reset for the idiosyncrasies of an unfamiliar room. Best of all, I can mix in my pajamas!

Notice: none of those reasons had to do with sound quality. That's because I personally put together a system that stays out of my way sonically. That's where the experience comes in. All the components are handpicked based on what I like, and how that gear influences my work. More importantly than the gear itself, my room is sonically accurate, which means I don't get whacky mix notes that have more to do with translation issues than mix decisions. This allows me to concentrate wholly on the music, rather than committing valuable brain resources towards compensating for the gear, or worse yet, the control room.

The more I get out of my way, the faster I can work, and the easier it is to deliver an effective and compelling mix. It's experience and time that have allowed me to put together a system that doesn't get in my way, and it's been a long and difficult road on the digital front, particularly given my many years of mixing in the analog domain.

Recording tools are no different in this regard, other than perhaps the stakes. A bad mix can be redone or adjusted until it meets your standards. Most clients don't have that luxury where the recording is concerned given the sheer time, money, and effort involved to record a production in the first place. Yet somehow, despite this logic, conventional thinking at all levels tends to put the emphasis on mixing. This is backwards, as a mix is wholly dependent on everything that came before it.

While it's true that *how* you use the tools available matters more than the tools themselves, this does not mean that you aren't facing limitations. As your skill improves, these limitations will reveal themselves, at which point you will be all but forced to remove subpar gear from your arsenal. This is a natural and organic process.

Digital Technology

When I see arguments from those in the Internet Chatter Class who insist digital technology is fully realized, I can only roll my eyes. People have been claiming that for 33 years!

Not only is digital technology not fully realized, it's still relatively young technology in which there's plenty of room for improvement.

Market forces have kept us perpetually stuck in a flawed digital format that was rushed to market in the late 70s. Improvements in digital have been slow, as we face some rather problematic technical limitations. That said, digital technology and sound are getting better all the time, and the demise of physical reproduction systems will serve to open new possibilities for improvement in digital. You can currently reproduce 24-bit, 96 KHz WAVE files in your iTunes app. Your CD can only play one barely acceptable format. Good riddance.

Where recording platform and storage is concerned, digital won the day. This was never a matter of if, but rather when, and although the large preponderance of records are now recorded in the digital medium, we still require analog gear in the form of microphones and preamps. While compressors and EQs are available in the digital realm, plug-ins don't react in quite the same manner as their analog counterparts.

I don't want to get on a soapbox regarding the merits of plug-ins. Many are generally usable. I do, however, want you to accept a few things before you start to read about recording tools and my thoughts pertaining to them.

From the purely practical standpoint of the here and now, your gear is merely a means to an end. Your tools make it possible to record and mix music, and that's all you need to start. You have plenty to learn before you're even in a position to fully comprehend just how your tools are getting in your way, and I can just about guarantee that you will outgrow your prosumer gear as you gain experience.

It doesn't much matter whether you realize that your gear is introducing difficult hurdles. That reality exists regardless. But if you're new to all of this, you're not in a position to make these sorts of determinations about your tools. That happens over time.

Your hearing and recordings will improve concurrently with your gear.

The good news is that price point of digital recording products continues to trend downward as the quality increases. The cost to produce and sell a plug-in is front-loaded in the development stage. The plug-in maker's labor pool is typically small, shipping costs minimal, and a middleman unnecessary, as the product can be sold directly to the consumer at 10 percent of the price of the hardware it emulates. Which brings up the obvious question: Does the price advantage of digital plug-ins outweigh the quality advantage of similar analog processing? Unfortunately, even at a 10:1 ratio, the answer to that question is: not yet.

Plug-ins are built to mimic the qualities of analog gear. In all instances they fall short in that regard, just as there is no such thing as a convincing piano sample. Plug-ins don't react the same as their analog counterparts. There is no way to properly mimic a non-linear electronic reaction at this time. Slate Digital is coming closer than anyone else, but it's still emulation. It doesn't really matter whether you prefer a plug-in to the original analog unit. That just proves my point. They're different.

Now, is an analog SSL G384 compressor worth 15 times the price of the digital plug-in? Only you can determine that. What's important for you to understand is that emulation plug-ins aren't interchangeable with their analog models.

You can debate until you're blue in the face that any given plug-in version is "close," and I will have the same response. Close is not the same as exact and is a subjective determination. Your "close," based on a 10-minute A/B comparison between the hardware SSL G384 and its plug-in equivalent, is not going to be the same as my "close," given that I've had that analog compressor strapped on my 2-bus for over 20 years. I will have far more sensitivity to any and all differences in reaction to program material because I'm so familiar with the unit. That said, in the case of the SSL compressor, there's really no comparison between the two.

Don't pay any attention to those who claim to offer a results-based A/B test that somehow "proves" the plug-in is the same in tone and reaction as its analog counterpart. These comparisons are performed in a manner that all but guarantees a flawed conclusion. A sonic comparison made outside of process is generally useless. Nullius in Verba.

Evaluating and Choosing Your Tools

A test is only as good as its design. An ill-conceived test will result in a flawed conclusion. You can't judge a piece of gear casually on program material in which you have no stake in the outcome. All of your decisions regarding your sonic evaluations of gear must be process-driven, and performed on a recording in which you are the arbiter of all that's good.

You'll learn nothing useful by merely strapping a stereo compressor on someone else's finished mix. All you'll manage to accomplish is a comparison between a mix as it was intended, and a mix in which the balances have changed due to the introduction of the compressor. Therefore, you should evaluate gear based on how it affects your decision-making process. You have to use the compressor in context of your own mix in order to make an appropriate evaluation.

When you test a microphone by inviting a friend to sing *a cappella* into it, you have no context with which to judge the tone, musically speaking. Such a test will tell you absolutely nothing in regards to the overall versatility of the mic. You have no idea how that microphone will react to any other source, nor do you have a specific production with which to judge the sound of the vocal. The best time to evaluate gear is when you're most susceptible to the overall emotional impact of the music.

Blind ABX comparisons are useful at times, but this whole Internet Chatter Class concept that you have to perform all comparisons blind for fear of expectation bias is ludicrous. Even the most subtle sonic difference can change how a track makes you feel. That is of far more consequence than the specific attributes of the tone being imparted. A subtle difference on completed program material has no consequence. A subtle difference on a work of personal or professional importance is the very definition of consequence.

We have all turned the knob on a disengaged EQ only to perceive a tonal change that doesn't exist anywhere but in our heads. Clearly, our brains are subject to some expectation bias, and I wouldn't argue otherwise. But to suggest that we are completely incapable of making judgments without the influence of expectation doesn't seem to correlate with reality. Were that the case, it would be nearly impossible to make the thousands of tiny judgments we make in just a single day of recording.

Expectation bias really only comes into play on those occasions when the difference between A and B is so remarkably subtle that you're not entirely sure whether it matters. And while adding a touch of high end on a disengaged EQ can dupe even the most talented engineer, cranking an engaged high-end boost knob by 12 dB will quickly reveal we're turning a dead knob.

Do you believe that a 12 dB difference of a relevant EQ frequency requires an ABX test as your client runs from the room in pain? No one would miss that. Clearly, there's a line.

Further complicating matters is the method in which the A/B is performed. Switching between the A and the B in quick succession completely removes emotional impact from the evaluation. You're recording music. All of your decisions regarding sound should relate directly to how it affects the music. Balance decisions are not made purely in the here and now, but also within the context of what comes next in a production.

Music won't properly evoke an emotional response unless there's context. A chorus that dynamically explodes can offer great excitement for the listener. But that dynamic exists only within the context of the previous section. When you perform an A/B in quick succession, you remove the effect of musical dynamic and contrast from the evaluation, and those are actually more important than the internal balances at any given moment. Sonic differences can appear subtle, or even irrelevant, when the music is removed from the equation. It is precisely this kind of inattentiveness to emotional impact that likely explains the development of the MP3.

Performed as an A/B in quick succession, most people would be unable to pick between a 192 KHz MP3 and a 16-bit, 44.1 kHz WAVE file. If, however, you play your test subject a full WAVE file of her favorite song in its entirety, followed by the MP3, she will be far more likely to notice the degradation of quality caused by the compressed format. Further, your test subject will not describe the difference in terms of sound, but rather how the track makes her feel. Why? Because that's how people listen to music. I encourage you to try this experiment for yourself.

Expectation bias is a two-way street. To suggest that my bias would coerce me into the more expensive tool in a shootout (as some in the Internet Chatter Class suggest) ignores the possibility that I might be looking for the cheap way out. And there *are* times that I'm looking for the cheap way out, yet somehow, that particular strain of expectation bias rarely saves me money.

To complicate matters, a subtle difference could very well blossom into a significant problem under the right circumstances.

The negative effects of 32 subpar converters will compound, and if you compare multitrack converters by running program through the first two channels only to declare the difference as "subtle," your conclusion will be just as flawed as the test itself. That evaluation of subtle can add up to not-so-subtle once multiplied by 16.

When evaluating gear, you have to use it in the heat of battle, and not just momentarily, but in a variety of circumstances. This is the only reasonable way to evaluate how a piece of gear reacts. If you were to strap an analog Teletronix LA2A onto the kik drum, you might not think much of the unit, as it's often a bit slow for the job. That doesn't mean it's a lousy limiter. It's a staple. It just happens to be an unusual choice for that particular application, on that particular recording, on that particular day. Nothing more, nothing less.

You'll notice I put in "on that particular day." There will be decisions that you make as you progress in recording that will offer pure magic on one day, only to be deemed pure shit the next. Welcome to the whacky world of recording. That never really changes. You're human, and therefore susceptible to making poor decisions due to any number of factors, including sleep deprivation and hunger.

There are good and bad specimens of all gear, but even the most atrocious gear can be useful. It's just a matter of how long you have to wait before you discover where it shines. Therefore, when you're evaluating your tools, make sure you do so over the course of time, as this will illuminate a unit's best and worst features through trial and error.

The Microphone

As much as I loathe to go into a whole slew of technical information, when it comes to microphones this really can't be avoided. Your mic choices and applications will be affected by their types and patterns, and while you can learn all of this by rote, I can help speed up the process a bit. I'm not going to discuss the technical aspects of microphones beyond basic practical information. The technical minutia is irrelevant to the art of recording, there are scores of good articles available on the Internet that can fill in the details that are well outside of my expertise. I will, however, discuss with you exactly why I might choose one variety of mic over another in relation to specific sound sources. I could offer you nothing more practical than that.

When it comes to discussing particular mics, I'll choose models that are commonly found in commercial recording studios. Given the sheer scope of available microphones, it's quite likely I'll mention models that are currently unavailable to you. I'm going to pretty much stick to the classics, and you can extrapolate from there. It's far more important that you understand the thinking that goes into mic selection than the specific mic chosen. What you need to understand is how the general microphone design will affect your practical recording decisions, so we're going to stick with the basic principles here. If you know why you're choosing your mic, then it's more likely to be the right choice—"more likely" being the operative term.

The Capsule

Microphones have a capsule or a membrane that is suspended in a housing. The sound waves cause the capsule to react, which is converted into an electrical signal. That signal is then boosted with a preamp, which is ultimately replicated by the monitors.

Every capsule has a front and a rear pick-up pattern. The front pattern, which generally faces the source, picks up the direct signal. The rear pattern picks up some measure of ambient information, the level of which is wholly dependent on the design of the microphone.

The nature of the rear pattern is one of the major considerations when choosing a mic.

Pick-Up Patterns

Every capsule has a pick-up pattern, which describes the overall manner in which a mic collects and rejects sonic information. There are four basic patterns: cardioid, hyper-cardioid (or super-cardioid), omnidirectional, and figure-8. Some mics have selectable patterns. An AKG C12, for instance, can be set to cardioid, omni, or figure-8.

CARDIOID

Cardioid patterns are relatively tight in nature, with a small rear pick-up pattern, which translates into good rejection properties. Cardioid microphones are subject to proximity effect, which causes an unnatural boost in low-end information and the introduction of distortion. Either of these microphone reactions may or may not be desirable, and your decision in this regard falls under the category of mic placement. Reducing proximity effect is as simple as backing the mic off the source, which will introduce more ambient information. This too must be considered.

SUPER-CARDIOID AND HYPER-CARDIOID

The super-cardioid pattern is a much tighter pattern than the cardioid, which makes them highly directional in how they capture sound. They do pick up some rear information, but provide far more isolation than a cardioid, and are not generally optimal in the studio. However, they can be quite useful under the right circumstances, given their directionality.

The hyper-cardioid pattern is even tighter than the super, and can be nearly unidirectional in nature, which means it generally rejects off-axis information. These mics can be tricky to work with in the studio, and are often best reserved for live situations given their rejection properties. It is rare to see a super- or hyper-cardioid mic in the studio as they are not favored for this application. In general, we want to capture some measure of room information in conjunction with the direct signal.

Omnidirectional

As the name indicates, a true omnidirectional microphone picks up information in all directions evenly around the microphone, and therefore is not subject to proximity effect. Given the 360-degree nature of the pick-up pattern, you will be collecting considerably more room information than with the more directional cardioid patterns.

Figure-8

A figure-8 pattern picks up information from the front and the rear of the capsule, and rejects the side information. This can be useful for recording two singers facing each other, or for mid-side techniques, which we'll be discussing shortly. A figure-8 pattern can also help to maximize the collected room information without totally sacrificing the direct signal. Most ribbon microphones are figure-8.

Powered Microphones

Some microphones are designed with transformers, which require a power source. Most powered mics accept 48 volts of phantom power, which you can typically send to the mic from the preamp. This function is often labeled on the preamp as "48V." The inclusion of a transformer in a microphone is a technical decision, and isn't really part of the calculus for the practical purposes of mic selection. A mic that requires power won't reproduce sound without it.

Plugging a mic hot into a 48-volt power supply is a great way to give yourself a nasty shock. Do yourself a favor and make sure the power supply is off for at least 30 seconds before connecting your mic. You have been warned.

Tube Microphones

Some condenser microphones incorporate a vacuum tube for purposes of amplification. In general, tubes are probably warmer than solid state microphones, but that's a gross oversimplification. A tube mic requires its own power supply, which will power the tube for purposes of amplification. Any mic that has its own power supply will not require phantom power. The Neumann M49, U67, U47, U48, and the AKG C12 are all examples of tube mics with their own designated power supplies.

Pads and Rolloffs

Some condenser microphones include a pad, which allows you to reduce the output between the capsule and the mic's internal amp. This is used when the SPLs from the source are too hot for the mic to handle without distorting. The rolloff is nothing more than a high-pass filter (HPF), which can be used to deal with proximity effect, or a source that's heavy in the bottom end.

Microphone Types

The capsule design of a mic is your main consideration when selecting a mic. There are five basic capsule designs. This is not a list of every kind of microphone technology there is, but rather a practical inventory of what you will most commonly come across in the studio: small diaphragm condenser, large diaphragm condenser, ribbon, dynamic, and piezoelectric. Speaker cones, although less commonly used, can also be used as microphone capsules.

Condenser Microphones

Condensers have a fast transient response, wide frequency response, and robust gain, and don't require excessive sound pressure levels (SPLs) for a quality capture. These microphones can be found everywhere in the course of your day-to-day life, as they are by far the most commonly used mic in consumer electronics.

For studio use, there are two basic kinds of condenser mics—small diaphragm and large.

Small Diaphragm Condenser (SDC)

Small diaphragm condensers excel at capturing off-axis information and can offer a detailed sonic image when used in pairs for stereo miking. Given the SDCs generally wide pick-up pattern, they're great on drum overheads, particularly if you're using them for the aggregate capture of the kit. They're often the first choice on acoustic guitars, percussion, and occasionally drum rooms. The Neumann KM84, AKG 451, Mojave MA-100, B&K 4003, and 4011 are all quality SDCs.

Large Diaphragm Condenser (LDC)

The large diaphragm condenser is probably the most widely used studio mic there is. The LDC's capsule is larger than that of a small condenser, which seems to make a whole lot of sense given the definitions of "large" and "small."

LDCs aren't as useful for picking up off-axis information as their smaller counterparts. The size of the capsule leads many to believe that LDCs have a more extended low end, which is a myth. LDCs are often the first choice for vocals, drum overheads, room mics, stringed instruments, etc.

Large condenser microphones have the capsule suspended in a protective grating. With rare exception, the front of the capsule on an LDC faces the logo side of the mic. This way, you can be sure your performer knows precisely which expensive German microphone you've selected. The AKG C12, 414; the Neumann M49, U47, U48, U87, U67; and the Telefunken Elam 251 are all highly sought-after LDC microphones.

Ribbon

There is nothing like a good ribbon for capturing your more strident instruments like brass or woodwinds. Due to a generally steep roll-off above 16 kHz, ribbons have a rather smooth top end, which can often be perceived as dark in nature. The generally slow response of a ribbon will result in a natural rounding of transients.

Older ribbon mic designs like the RCA77 have low output and are best served by a preamp with a transformer in order to boost the gain appropriately. Given their nature, ribbon mics can be used to great effect to capture drum overheads, guitars, and even vocals. In general, ribbons can't take excessive SPLs, and you must be mindful of where you place them. A Sony 44 in front of an aggressive drummer's kik is an exceptional way to disintegrate the ribbon. The more modern Royer line of microphones, however, can handle excessive SPLs. As a result, Royer mics are frequently found in front of blaring guitar amps—especially on my sessions.

There have been a number of ribbon microphones manufactured over the decades. The Sony 44, RCA 77, Beyer M160, Coles 4038, Royer 121, and the ShinyBox 46U are examples of quality ribbon microphones.

Most ribbons are bi-directional mics, which means they have a figure-8 pattern—the rear pattern brighter than the front. You should avoid sending phantom power to most ribbons, as they can disintegrate the membrane under the right circumstances. This is not an issue for mics like the Royer 122, which requires phantom power. The powered ribbon allows for a much lower noise floor, which is nearly a requirement when using them to record extremely dynamic material.

DYNAMIC

A dynamic microphone's diaphragm operates similarly to a speaker in that the diaphragm is connected to an induction coil and magnets. That's about as technical as we need to get. These are workhorse microphones that are less susceptible to damage from abuse and moisture, making them exceptional for live reinforcement. They're a staple in the studio as well, and they tend to be far less sensitive to sound pressure levels than the other mic designs. This attribute makes them a good choice for close placement to an especially loud sound source.

There are times that a dynamic is the optimal vocal mic, although they can be a major pain in the ass for this application. The slightest movement from your performer can cause an enormous tonal difference. Given this, dynamic mics are often preferable on stationary sound sources, as opposed to upwardly mobile ones, but this is by no means any kind of rule.

Dynamics are exceptional at rejecting ambient room information, particularly when placed in close proximity to robust sound pressure levels. Dynamic mics do not require a power source. The Electro-Voice RE20; the Sennheiser 609, 421, 441; and the Shure SM57 are all commonly found dynamic microphones.

PIEZOELECTRIC

These are basically contact microphones that pick up vibrations directly from the instrument, although you can certainly put a Crown PZM on the wall or the floor to collect room information. PZM stands for Pressure Zone Microphone, and for all intents and purposes is classified as a piezoelectric microphone. Small piezo-electric mics can be used for drum triggers, and as mounted pickups for acoustic guitar.

Speaker Mic

A speaker placed in front of a sound source will act like a dynamic microphone with a massive diaphragm. You need only connect the woofer's terminals to a male XLR in order to convert a speaker into a microphone.

Clearly, speakers are not efficient as microphones given the size of the diaphragm (which is referred to as a cone when used as a monitor). They are however, great to supplement the sub-frequency information in your capture. Speaker mics can also produce interesting results on their own. I frequently use speakers as microphones on guitar cabs, bass cabs, and kik drums, although I'm equally as likely to implement the speaker mic as I am to reject it.

An NS10 in front of an amplifier can produce some rather unique guitar tones, and a 15-inch woofer is great for extending the sub-frequency blossom of a kik drum or bass. Be careful. It's really easy to blow out your monitors if you're not prudent with how you introduce the speaker mic signal. A little goes a long way, and a lot might send your monitor woofers flying across the room. I'm being hyperbolic, of course, if for no other reason than to help you remember this.

Headphones, being speakers, can be used as a "stereo" microphone, although I can't say I've ever used headphones this way in the studio. Headphones are, however, a great way to record a rehearsal.

Stereo Mic

A stereo mic is defined by the total number of capsules rather than their capsule and electronic design characteristics. The two capsules are mounted one above the other, and on some stereo mics, you can rotate the top capsule 45 degrees for purposes of tightening the width of the image. There are a number of stereo mics available, including the Shure SM69, the AKG C24, the Royer SF12, and powered SF-24.

Stereo mics can be extremely handy as the capsules are phase-coherent within the housing. We'll discuss phase coherency in great length, so if that doesn't make any sense to you at the moment, just keep reading.

DIRECT BOX

A direct box, while certainly not a microphone, is used to plug an unbalanced line level signal into a balanced microphone input. A direct box is often referred to as a DI, which stands for "Direct Injection."

Guitars, basses, and keyboards—anything with a ¼-inch unbalanced jack to be recorded directly without an amplifier—require a DI. Some recordists capture the direct signal of their bass, electric pianos, and guitars (which we'll discuss later). A DI has a thru-port, which will allow you to daisy chain the signal to an amplifier. This way you can record both the direct and amplified signals.

Since long unbalanced cable runs are susceptible to high frequency loss and interference, a DI can help counter these maladies. Most DIs include a ground switch. This can be particularly handy when using ungrounded vintage amplifiers. Most mic pres include a DI input for those times you might be recording in the control room, or for you nutbars who keep the mic pres out in your live room. And I use the term "nutbar" endearingly. Mic pres sound better the closer they are to the source, but very few recordists bother with that. I digress!

There are passive and active DI boxes. Active DIs (powered) are superior at reducing ground hum, and will supply more gain. I prefer active DIs, but there are plenty of adequate passive DI boxes.

Some examples of good DIs would be the Countryman Type85 and the A-Designs REDDI, but to be perfectly honest, I rarely worry about the brand of a direct box until it proves a problem. The better DIs can get a bit pricey, and you can probably get away with one high-quality stereo DI.

There will be some purists that read that last bit in horror. Sorry, but a DI is the least of my concerns so long as it's doing its job in an adequate manner, and most of them do. There's not much to a DI, and you can build your own if you're into that sort of thing.

Microphone Selection

Microphones influence and color the capture of our source, and you will often choose a particular mic based on its type and pattern. When placing multiple microphones in close proximity, rejection characteristics often become the main consideration.

Every microphone is unique. Even among particular models the variation in sound can be considerable. A microphone is similar to a fine instrument in that each and every one will have its own individual tone. Further complicating matters, environment and care of a mic plays a significant role in its overall quality. A mic that has been subjected to years of smoke is likely to offer inferior tone to one that was kept in a cleanroom. Not that you'd ever keep a mic in a cleanroom, but you get the point.

I would imagine I've heard anywhere between 50 and 100 different Neumann U47s in my career, and they can sound wildly different from one another, although most will have a certain identifying signature characteristic. Many of the older U47s have been cleaned and modded by Stephen Paul (who is no longer with us); others have been subjected to years of abuse with no concern for tonal degradation. As much as I like U47s in general, a particular specimen can fall anywhere on the usability scale from preferred to worthless. Given this, you should never purchase a vintage microphone without having heard it for yourself first.

You will notice far less variance between brand new microphones of the same model, mostly because the influence of its environment hasn't yet manifested. Make no mistake, there will be slight differences in tone and reaction between various microphones of identical models. That is, unless they've been sold as a matched pair by the manufacturer.

A matched pair of microphones must be identical in model and within certain tolerances of capture specs. You pay considerably more for a matched pair as some recordists swear by them for stereo recording techniques. Given that our left and right ears don't process sound identically, I've never really bought into the concept. Besides, stereo pairs don't align with my asymmetrical tendencies. I've been known to mic overheads with two different LDCs like a U47 and a C12, so there you go.

The decisions that we make when it comes to recording are exceptionally personal. Whereas I don't gravitate to matched pairs, another professional of high repute might prefer them. In fact, it's been so long since I've tried a matched pair, I think I'll try it again.

Microphone selection is often made based on capsule attributes. Dynamic cardioid microphones, for instance, are commonly chosen over condensers for toms. Believe me, every recordist gets the brilliant fucking idea to use condensers on the toms at some point in their career. The problem is that condenser microphones don't sufficiently reject the rear pick-up of the capsule for this application. As a result, this is a fantastic way to capture excessive cymbal information. The rear of a condenser placed on toms tends to face directly towards the cymbals, at least on every kit I've ever managed to record. That said, don't be dissuaded from trying condensers on toms. With a balanced drummer, it could be a fantastic choice.

Beautiful individual tom tones in isolation are pretty useless if the cymbal balance is causing you fits come mix time (if not earlier). And while a condenser will give you the most natural capture of a tom, I'm not sure how that offers you much when you're just going to have to choke the tone by stripping the audio down to what amounts to samples anyway. Rejection characteristics are an important consideration when selecting microphones for recording. Sometimes, it's the primary consideration.

When dealing with many mics in close proximity, you need to pay more mind to how the mics work together than how any specific mic sounds in isolation. The Sennheiser MD421 sounds absolutely wretched on toms in isolation as it tends to accentuate the low end and muffle the attack—a highly unnatural tone for a tom. Yet, used in conjunction with a good aggregate overhead sonic picture, the 421 can add exactly what's missing—the meat of the drum.

Don't take this as some kind of suggestion to always use 421s on toms, or worse yet, to run out and buy three of them. If I choose to use 421s on toms, that decision will have much to do with the fact that there aren't three Sennheiser 441s available, which have similar rejection characteristics in conjunction with a significantly more pleasing tone. While 421s are useful mics for a variety of applications, they aren't always the best mic for recording toms, especially when we start to take genre into account. There is rarely more than one reasonable approach when it comes to miking. This is especially true with drums.

It's not unusual for me to audition 10 different microphones on any given singer. While the goal is to find the mic that best matches the singer's tone, the individual production will also influence that decision. A singer could sound fantastic on an LDC, but if I'm looking for a more aggressive tone for a particular track, then I could very well choose a dynamic. I don't want to get bogged down on the specifics just yet. The point is both the source and production should be taken into account when selecting a mic.

As important as microphones are, and as much as they do shape and color the sound their design, they're still going to pick up the source as it sounds in the room based on their specific placement. It's always a drag to realize your microphone choice was less than ideal, but it's certainly not a catastrophe. We have tools for manipulating tone, and there's nothing wrong with using them in order to preserve a stellar performance.

Personally, I'm just as likely to choose a mic for reasons outside of sonic considerations. To name a few: my mood, recording fashion trends, immediacy of availability, and even the good feelings of my artist and producer are all valid reasons for choosing a particular microphone. Granted, the moment I deem a mic choice inappropriate, that mic is swapped out for another. Whereas there can be any number of reasons for choosing a mic, there is really only one reason for keeping it, and that's based on how it reacts to your source, regardless of accuracy.

I recorded an exceptionally talented singer, Caitlin Krisko of the Broadcast, recently. We were working at Echo Mountain Studios, which has a great selection of high quality mics. After auditioning a number of them, it came down to a choice between the AKG C12 and the ELAM 251. I personally preferred the sound of the C12. Caitlin was gravitating towards the 251. It's not like she sounded bad on the 251—she sounded great on both. But she sang *better* in the 251 because she liked what she heard. Any slight advantage I may have gained from a purely sonic perspective was completely eradicated by her preference.

Whether producer, recordist, or both, your instinct should be to put the comfort of the performer ahead of dogma. It doesn't make a difference whether Caitlin sang in the C12 or the ELAM 251. They both captured the performance well. May we always be so fortunate as to debate the merits of microphones that cost as much as new cars.

Caitlin's motives were pure. She was evaluating how the microphone made her feel, and there is no better measure than that. Not that it matters. Had she preferred the ELAM251 purely because it was the more expensive microphone I would have been just as amenable. Even misplaced feelings are real, and since performance comes from an emotional place, we are far better off capturing the right emotion regardless of how perfect the tone. You can compensate for tone within reason. Not so with flat performances.

PHASE AND COHERENCY

This will likely be the most difficult section to get through, as phase relationship and coherency are complex concepts to explain. They also happen to be the most critical for you to understand. You would do well to sit in front of your DAW and perform these experiments as I explain them. This will make it far easier to follow.

As much as I insist you put the source and the performance first and foremost, some Source Instruments take up far too much real estate to capture appropriately with a single mic. The moment you begin to place multiple microphones in close proximity to one another, you're greatly complicating matters.

Every microphone's pick-up pattern relates to the physical space surrounding them. When two microphones are within inches of each other, their pick-up patterns will intersect and interact. We call that interaction a phase relationship. A poor relationship can cause all sorts of whacky and audible frequency cancellation, often in a non-linear manner, as the balance between the two signals will directly affect the nature and severity of the cancellation. Multiple microphones placed on a source that isn't fully stationary can intensify the problem.

Phase coherency issues manifest in a number of ways in a variety of situations, the most severe of which causes total cancellation. In order for full cancellation to occur, the signals must be identical but inverted. You will never achieve full cancellation with microphones, as they will not pick up identical signals no matter how well matched nor how closely placed. That said, it's good to understand absolute phase before we discuss the lesser degrees that we deal with when placing microphones.

If you'd like to experience total cancellation you can do this in your DAW. Load up a *mono* track of audio into a blank session of your DAW and copy the file to another track. Make sure the audio is perfectly aligned and the modules are at unity gain (the faders should be at zero, the pan knobs center, and there should be no plug-ins or sends inserted).

Listen to the first mono track alone, then unmute the copy track. The result will be a 6 dB jump in level. Now pan the signals hard left and right. Notice how that mono signal now appears in the middle of the sound field.

Two identical signals set at unity gain, panned hard left and right will result in a center image. This is important, so stick with me here.

Panning a mono source to the left side sends 100 percent of the signal to the left monitor. As you turn the pan knob towards the center, you are bringing down the volume in the left speaker as you bring up the volume in the right. This results in the sound moving across the stereo field. Once you hit the center position of your pan, you are sending the signal to both speakers at unity gain. So you can't make a "double" track by copying and panning the two hard. All that's going to do is put the image in the center.

In order to get those two identical signals to appear as if they are coming distinctly from the left and right monitors (rather than appearing in the center), a time differential of at least 20 ms is required. Delay one side by 20 ms and listen for yourself. That's a cool trick, right? Not really, and it's probably the most common mistake made by neophyte recordists.

Although the sound appears on the sides, there is not enough time differential to prevent cancellation due to waveform interaction. The difference between a player performing on the front or back of the beat can be as little as 3 ms (depending on the tempo). Therefore, a 20 ms time differential is enormous as it relates to music, and will cause obvious flamming. Further, the phase issues will cause that stereo image to appear disembodied from the track in context of a mix, and the cancellation that occurs will be more obvious outside of the stereo field.

I call this *faux* stereo, and it should be avoided. If you want your guitars to sound like they're coming out of the left and right speakers discretely, then you need to record two guitar tracks. Copying a guitar part to a different track and delaying one side by 20 ms (or more) will result in a phase-induced stereo image. This will manifest as timing issues, but more importantly, whenever someone walks by the stereo field they will notice a strange sonic shift in those guitars. When the listener plays your mix through daisy-chained computer speakers, the level of those guitars will attenuate, as summing the left and right this way will cause some center cancellation.

Now that you understand how time differentials affect identical signals, let's realign the two tracks so that they start at the identical time, and insert a plug-in with polarity reverse function to the first of the two tracks. Polarity reversal is indicated as "Ø." Every DAW has a plug-in for purposes of phase reversal, as does just about every desk. In Logic it's the "Gain" plug-in. In Pro Tools the stock EQ has a polarity reversal function.

Just to be clear, your two audio files should currently be fully aligned, at unity gain, and panned center. Now flip the polarity on one track by engaging the Ø button. The sound will completely disappear.

Where did it go?

When you look at your sound wave visually in your DAW, you'll notice a horizontal line that the wave passes. Above the line is the positive portion of the waveform, below the line is the negative, and the line represents the null point, which is neutral. For all intents and purposes, the positive portion of the waveform represents the push of your speaker, and the negative portion represents the pull. When you flip polarity of the identical signal, you are causing a simultaneous and equally opposite push and pull, which results in no sound whatsoever.

Reversing polarity on one of two identical signal puts them 180 degrees out of absolute phase relative to each other, resulting in total cancellation of the signal.

Now, let's bypass the polarity reversal and set the pans to center. Nudge one of the tracks by samples as you listen to the results. Every nudge will result in an audible shift in the sound which will manifest as a reduction in level due to frequency cancellation. Notice how the sound hollows. You're hearing frequency cancellation. Now nudge the track by milliseconds. What you're hearing is *sonically similar* to how microphones react to one another in close proximity.

Two microphones placed on a single sound source will be subject to slight timing differentials, much like the one you caused by nudging the audio file. These differentials will cause cancellation of frequencies, among other possible maladies, due to a slightly shifting source.

Two microphones in close proximity to one another can never reproduce perfectly in phase, as even the slightest differential in timing will cause some frequency cancellation between the waveforms. How much cancellation has to do with time differential due to physical placements in conjunction with the relative balance between the two mics. The more severe the phase issue, the more cancellation that occurs, and this will reveal itself most obviously in the low end.

When you face the capsules of two microphones directly towards one another, they will be 180 degrees out of phase. This is the most severe phase difference possible out of 360 degrees. The only difference between two mics that are 90 and 270 degrees is the relative direction of the waveforms as they relate to each other. Either way, you're 90 degrees from phase coherency between those mics.

Snare drums are often recorded with a top and bottom mic facing each other. This placement will result in an obvious loss in low end information producing a papery thin snare drum. As a matter of course, you must reverse the phase on that bottom mic in order to reproduce the low end information. Make no mistake, that upward facing capsule on the snare is also negatively interacting with the other mics on the kit. Therefore, you want to reverse the polarity on the bottom mic.

A phase coherency issue between two mics panned hard left and right (for purposes of stereophonic recording!) will cause what I can only describe as a disembodiment of sound from the stereo field. Two mics panned hard that are anywhere near 180 degrees will cause the audio to practically wrap around your head. If you'd like to hear the maximum effect of reversed polarity, load a stereo track into your DAW and flip the polarity on one of the sides. Notice the skewed center image, the sonic disembodiment from your monitors, and the significant loss of low end information.

This sonic reaction occurs because when you reverse polarity of one side of a mix, you are essentially canceling out much of the center information. Swapping the terminal wires on one of your monitors will cause the identical effect. You should become allergic to this sound.

Our main weapon against phase interaction between microphones is placement. The severity of a phase coherency issue has to do with the size and shape of the pick-up pattern, the specific direction that the capsules face, and the distance the mics are from each other and the source. In general, you can greatly reduce phase coherency issues with what is called the 3:1 rule.

Two microphones in close proximity on the same source should be three times the distance from each other as they are from the source. A mic on a guitar cab placed 3" from the speaker requires a distance of 9" between the capsules. While the 3:1 distance rule may be handy for your initial mic placement, ultimately, you have to use your ears to evaluate phase coherency.

Unfortunately, you can't always achieve a 3:1 distance ratio. Therefore, we must rely on our ears to limit and reduce phase coherency interactions between mics. Further, there are other tried and true miking techniques that will reduce phase interaction to acceptable levels.

It's not uncommon for a recordist to use 10 mics or more to capture a rock drum kit. Even given the real estate a drum kit commands, that's a lot of microphones in rather close proximity. This can, and will, result in phase coherency issues, which must be dealt with. Phase coherency issues between two mics is as easy to deal with as adjusting the physical placement of one mic as it relates to the other. Once we start adding more mics to the kit, we are complicating matters exponentially.

All those microphones can be exceptionally problematic in how they interact, which is why a drum kit is one of the more difficult sources to record well. The best way to reduce phase coherency is to use fewer microphones. This, however, must be weighed against the skill and overall balance of the drummer. The more balanced the drummer, the fewer microphones needed for the task. Your average band drummer with limited studio experience is far more likely to require some help where his internal balance is concerned. Many band drummers whack their cymbals with far too much aggression in relation to how they strike the skins. Consequently, two microphones will not suffice. Once you add close mics to deal with those internal balance issues, you are simultaneously introducing phase coherency issues.

We'll discuss this further in the drums section, but I'll be using the phrase "phase coherency" throughout this book, and it's essential that you understand what that sounds like. If you don't know that you're hearing a phase issue, you can't avoid it in the first place.

INVESTING IN MICROPHONES

"What mic should I get for my vocals?"

This is without a doubt the most common recording question found on the Internet today, and it's often followed immediately with budget specifications unsuitable for a medical marijuana dispensary run, let alone a microphone purchase. I can't even provide you with an appropriate budget because I produced and recorded Australian phenom Pete Murray using an SM57. This, after auditioning just about every mic in Sing Sing's locker over the course of tracking. It wasn't until Pete chose to grab the talkback mic (which I always record) for a take that we finally discovered our mic of choice. That example would bring the recommended vocal mic budget down to around $100. If only.

Most every singer sounds acceptable on a 57. Very few sound *best* on a 57. Dynamics are susceptible to wide tonal shifts caused by physical movement at the source. Consequently, they're not typically the first choice for vocals. More often than not, you're better off using a condenser. When it comes to purchasing a condenser microphone for one specific application, the only reasonable course is to audition the mics that fit within your budget. Why invest your hard-earned money into a mic that isn't clearly superior for the task?

Some of you may purchase a microphone primarily for your own vocal recordings. If you're looking for a purpose-bought microphone, you should call the nearest commercial studio facility, and schedule an hour or two to try out their microphones. Just make sure that your wish list corresponds with what they have in their locker. If they don't have a particular mic, ask if the studio can find one for you.

I promise, there are many other people recording in your area. You should get to know every one of them. Wyn Davis owns Total Access down the street from me, and we loan each other our gear on regular occasion. My SPL Transient Designer has been in his room for a year, and I've had Joe McGrath's Chandler TG2 mic pre for months now. Loaning out your gear to friends and clients is the Social Contract of recordists. It goes something like this. You loan out your shit, forget where it is some months later, and then you borrow someone else's, until you can finally remember who has yours. In fact, there's a term for this sort of exchange. It's called Permanent Loan. That all may seem quite humorous, and it is, but every high level recordist that I know operates this way.

Most people starting out don't have a robust mic locker (or any at all). It would be foolish to put together a full-blown commercial tracking room without any experience, and unless you're a trust fund baby (and there's nothing wrong with that), it's really not feasible. Most of us start out with one or two microphones, loops, and MIDI. I started with a four-track recorder, two dynamic mics, some synths, a PA, and an Apple II+ (complete with 64KB of RAM!) for MIDI programming. We all have to start somewhere.

When it comes to investing in microphones, the most important consideration is variety. You need all sorts of mics to record effectively.

The Microphone Preamplifier (Mic Pre)

A mic preamplifier is necessary in order to amplify the low output signal of a microphone. As much as the mic will color the sound, the mic pre too will affect the tone. If you get really deep into the engineering side of recording, you can seek out the best combination of mic and pre on each and every source. That can become a bit of a wank, and many of us prefer to use the desk pres. As far as I'm concerned, you can't go wrong recording an entire album with the pres on an API or any Neve 80 Series desk (not to be confused with the 81 series).

Not all pres are created equal, and even if you have a recording desk full of stellar mic pres, you might choose an external pre for a particular application or microphone. Make no mistake, a pre will influence and color the tone of the microphone, and if you know the kind of tone a particular pre tends to impart, you can use that knowledge to your advantage. Frankly, you're better off using an inexpensive microphone than a cheap mic pre. A great mic pre can cost in the thousands, although price is not a foolproof indicator of quality.

Your better mic pres generally distort less easily, but also distort well, particularly if you push the electronics with signal. Should you ever find yourself recording with a Neve 1073 preamp (which includes a highly sought after EQ section), try cranking up the input gain and check out that distortion. I use these pres (and others) to distort toms, vocals, cymbals, etc. It's beautiful distortion, and you can break up the signal just slightly, or you really crank it up and make a part literally resonate with distortion. Of course, if you're recording an organic straight-ahead jazz quartet, you might want to keep that trick in your back pocket, as this is a generally undesirable tone for that particular genre. If you don't have a 1073, worry not. All mic pres distort, given enough signal. Your job is to find out which ones distort how, and use that information to your advantage as you record.

Many of you could very well use mic pres that come packaged with your converter interface. These are useless mic pres, and I realize that's going to be a tough pill to swallow, given the overall generalized nature of the statement. This is typically where the argument comes in regarding skill. Sorry, there are some things that skill alone cannot overcome, and one of them is a prosumer pre.

I've been accused on the Internet of being an audiophile elitist because I insist that some gear will get in your way. An audiophile would never talk about the importance of emotional impact and music the way that I do. Audiophiles think you can separate the evaluation of sound from music, and that's just stupid.

I mean, why would I suggest that a $100 microphone can be the best choice in any given recording situation, only to turn into some sort of audiophile snob when it comes to the device that amplifies that mic? And if my positions had to do with snobbery based on price point, wouldn't I be touting the glorious sound of a $500,000 SSL? Save yourself $250,000 and pick up a brand new Rupert Neve Designs 5088 desk. The point is, I don't choose gear based on price. I choose it based on quality and overall usefulness, as should you.

Even when I suggest to you that most cheap mic pres are dismally inadequate for the job, it's for musical reasons. The compounding effect of distortion from prosumer mic pres is anything but musical. Further, if you're going to spend time getting your tone at the source, it doesn't make much sense to hinder yourself with a tool that only serves to cloud your capture.

A quality pre with the right mic in front of a great source will capture with clarity. A lousy pre on that same mic and source will pale in comparison, the sound of which is difficult to describe in sonic terms. In visual terms, it's like snapping a picture with your smartphone with low light. The picture will be grainy, and no amount of processing will provide the kind of brilliance you could expect had you used a faster lens and a wider aperture. A cheap mic pre will deliver a tone that is grainy and one-dimensional in nature, and no amount of processing can compensate for this.

The difference between the poor sonic capture and the poor visual one described above, is the compounding effect. We don't tend to record one source instrument, but many, and you will have a difficult time overcoming the negative effect of 20 or more piss-poor prosumer pres. How's that for a tongue twister?

Once you find yourself in a studio with a number of mic preamp choices, you can get quite deep into how and when you choose to use them. I've gone way down that rabbit hole. There's no doubt you can always improve your capture if you're willing to try just one more pre, but time practicalities can be prohibitive. While no model of mic pre is necessarily perfect for every situation, a great one will rarely get in your way. The benefit you might gain from spending the time to compare mic and pre pairing is often outweighed by the time requirements of a session.

There are tons of great mic pres available, and they generally fall within the $700 to $2000 range. I'm not saying definitively that there aren't worthwhile mic pres for under $700. But I can assure you the quality drops off precipitously at that price point. Vintage pres are subject to the market forces of supply and demand. There's a reason why 1073s are so expensive, and it has nothing to do with hype, and everything to do with supply and demand.

There are also a whole host of companies rebuilding and repackaging vintage mic pres like the Neve 1073. Be sure that any repackaged mic pre (or reissued) hasn't somehow been "improved" in electronic design. "Improvements" should be viewed with suspicion, as it's difficult to imagine how one improves the most versatile and useful mic pre ever designed.

As a third-party mixer, even being somewhat selective, I occasionally get tracks that are obviously recorded through prosumer pres. A track captured in this manner will add hours to a mix and will limit my ability to make the track sing. A well captured track allows me to focus on what's really important—the music itself.

Just so we're clear, if a client sends me a track to mix that's produced and recorded lo-fi by design, in which distortion and filters are seemingly a staple, I'm not going to somehow try to turn the track into something big, broad and beautiful, nor could I. That's not possible. I'll be hammering this throughout, but good sound can only be evaluated within the context of the music. If a lo-fi treatment is appropriate for the music, then that would be considered "good sound."

Here's a list of some mic pres that will be more than adequate for the job: the Neve 1073, 1066, Brent Averill Neve 1272, Neve 1081, API 512, Chandler TG2, Calrec 1161, Great River ME-1NV, Tonelux MP5a, A Designs P-1, the Millenia HV-3D, and the RND Portico series.

The Recording Console

Most commercial tracking facilities will have a recording console in the control room. A recording console, or desk, will allow you to record many mics simultaneously, as each channel will have a mic preamplifier. This is by far the easiest way to record, as it keeps everything within your reach, and allows you to bus two micro-phones to a single channel.

A bus is nothing more than an audio path. In order to combine the output signals of two preamps, you must use a bus, and consoles have this feature built in. Depending on the size and the makeup of the console, you can simultaneously use it to monitor your returns. This may require splitting the console so that you're using the mic pres on one side, and the line level returns on the other. When summing two external mic pres to one channel, you either need to send the return to a console for purposes of bussing, or you need a two-channel mic combiner/splitter.

Rooms that are dual-purposed for recording and mixing will typically have a Large Frame Analog Console (LFAC). There are quite a few LFACs designed and sold over the last few decades, including half an alphabet's worth of SSL consoles (E, G, J, and K); Neve V, VR, VRP, 88R; API; Trident A-Range (which are quite rare); and Amek 9098s. The definition of "large frame" is a console that is contained in a stationary frame with a sizable footprint. Since all of those consoles listed above can be configured as small-scale production desks, we should probably also define an LFAC as having over 48 inputs, although that's certainly a debat-able line.

There's a whole slew of vintage consoles out there that have been converted to LFAC status by combining two consoles into one. This includes vintage APIs and the Neve 8028s, 8038s, 8048s, 8068s, 8078s, etc. While these double-wide vintage desks fit within the size parameters of an LFAC, they don't carry many of the bells and whistles of models built post-1980. Each and every console listed above is a superior recording desk, loaded with some of the most useful mic pres ever made. They do not, however include any dynamic processing found in the modern LFAC.

Most LFACs built after 1980 include the following on every module: A 48-channel bussing matrix, trim, polarity reversal, mic pre, dynamics section including a compressor and gate, multiband parametric EQ, high- and low-pass filters, eight stereo aux sends, a monitor fader, and a large-throw channel fader with automation.

The thinking at the time LFACs were first released was that studios could avoid filling their room with expensive analog outboard gear. All processing could be done on your very expensive desk. It's all you need!

That concept didn't quite pan out.

Unfortunately, the mic pres on SSL G series consoles were of such low quality that they were quickly rejected by the recording community in general. The same can be said for the mic pres on any of the AMS Neve desks—that is, until the 88R, which includes a package with 1081 reissues located in the recording room.

The closer you can get the mic pre to the source, thereby reducing the length of cabling necessary, the better the capture. That said, it's usually not worth the disadvantage of having to take a trip to the room every time you want to adjust the pre. The beauty of the 88R is it allows you to control the 1081 mic pres remotely from the console, giving you the best of both worlds.

Further problematic are the dynamic processors found on LFACs, which while effective for some program, tend to be one-trick ponies. They're fine in a jam, but they're not by any means versatile. I mean, I wouldn't want 60 of them! Which is exactly what you'll get on a 60-input SSL or Neve VR. Further, as much as diversity in preamps is unnecessary, the same can't be said about compressors.

The idea that an engineer would need nothing but an LFAC itself—the main sales pitch at the time of their introduction—was a naive claim at best. This illuminates an inherent and time-honored disconnect between manufacturers and music makers. Frankly, the mic pres on SSL and AMS Neve consoles predating the 88R aren't much more useful than today's prosumer pres. Which is why so few recordists ever use them. Most seasoned recordists will use these LFACs as nothing more than an oversized monitor desk when recording, preferring to use high-quality external pres, compressors, and EQ over the inboard selections. Given the automation packages and sheer size, fully loaded LFACs are often far more useful as mixing desks than tracking.

LFACs aren't generally known for their superior sound, but rather the convenience of their size and recall abilities. When it comes to quality of capture, the simpler the design and the fewer electronics in your way the better. Although, a simple design is certainly no guarantee of quality. The Rupert Neve Designs 5088 desk, which is modular in design, is a throwback to the early Neve desks. Their overall simplicity means you have very little coming between you and the capture of your microphone. This would be an example of a superior recording desk.

There are a number of other desks that are more than adequate for recording, including the Trident 80B, 80C, and the Neotek Elite. I've made records on all of these consoles, and I would describe them as nothing short of usable. You can find these desks for relatively short coin. Just be sure you take into account maintenance, wiring, and recapping when you're considering a purchase. And if you're on a budget, you might want to learn how to use a soldering iron. The labor costs for wiring and recapping a console can be substantial.

Recording consoles utilize capacitors, and over time they must be replaced. Failing capacitors manifest as an insidious fuzzy distortion. It's important a desk is recapped at the recommended intervals. How long you can go between capacitor replacements depends on your sensitivity to failing caps, and the desk itself. Desks that run exceptionally hot, like the Neve V series, will burn through capacitors in just a few years. Other desks could last considerably longer. So if you find yourself on a desk that sounds nothing short of fuzzy, you may want to inquire as to the last time it was recapped.

I would be remiss were I not to also mention the Toft ATB24, modeled off the Malcolm Toft-designed Trident 80B console. This is a relatively inexpensive desktop console, and could be an excellent choice as an entry-level recording desk. You will likely outgrow it in the future, but it's way better than many of the similarly priced alternatives out there.

A room with a good desk will make life considerably easier for your larger tracking sessions. For starters, you'll spend considerably less time dicking around with external pres, and bussing two mics to a single track from a desk is as easy as pushing two buttons.

Now, some of you might be wondering why I'd ever want to combine mics rather than record them separately on their own discrete tracks. Admittedly, it's partly out of habit. Analog tape required some measure of conservation, given the limited real estate of 24 tracks per reel. I certainly didn't want to burn two tracks for the snare drum if I could avoid it. And yes, I could and would regularly lock multiple analog 2″ machines together, but for various reasons, track counts were still a valid concern.

The DAW has mostly rendered track counts of little consequence. Yet I still frequently combine the top and bottom snare mics, and not purely out of habit. Why? Because any decision that I make early on is one I don't have to make later. Further, bussing the top and bottom snare mics to a track allows me to strap single analog compressor on the tone as a whole. While it's slightly risky to combine two mics to one track, I can assure you, it's nowhere near as treacherous as bussing the toms and overheads together on a single stereo track—a technique I've employed on many occasions.

Of course, when you manage to fuck up the balance between your top and bottom snare mics, or worse yet, fail to flip polarity between them (which can't be reversed once combined), you'll likely curse my persuasiveness in this regard. Curse away. I can take it.

Cursing Mixerman Intermission

Look, if you want to improve your skills as a recordist, then you should consider working aggressively toward the end game. While you may fuck up a recording or two in your early attempts, in the long run, you'll be a better off for it. You can always trigger a sample if you somehow pooch the blend between your bussed snare mics. And while samples certainly aren't ideal, you do have an out.

Your DAW is an exceptionally powerful tool for fixing mistakes. You can either exercise its power as a crutch, or reserve it as a safety net. I can assure you, there is no better way to learn recording than by having to spend hours dealing with your own poor judgments. Your path is clear. Don't operate from fear. Say, that rhymes!

Monitoring

A relatively accurate critical listening space is paramount to good recording. Otherwise all of your decisions will be based on a lie. I used to change studios on a weekly basis, and I became quite adept at adjusting to the idiosyncrasies of critical listening spaces. Minor issues that can be heard and identified are easy to overcome. It's the problems that you can't hear due to frequency cancellation that will make the job all but impossible.

There are some critical listening spaces that can't be compensated for, no matter how great your skill, no matter how incredible your hearing, and no matter how vast your experience. Room maladies that cause frequencies to completely disappear are all but impossible to overcome. How your mix works outside of your room is called *translation*, and if you can't hear everything across the frequency spectrum, your recordings won't translate.

There's just no way around this. Your recordings will suffer from a fucked-up monitoring environment. The monitors themselves, while an important consideration, will be wholly affected by the space that houses them. If you're attempting to perform critical monitoring in an inadequately treated environment, you really will have no idea what you're actually capturing. If the source is amazing, you might very well get away with a compromised listening environment. In general, however, inaccurate monitoring will not only limit your successes, it will retard your improvement.

Monitors

Some of the following information regarding monitor types and varieties I've pulled from *Zen and the Art of Mixing* and altered slightly for purposes of brevity. I can't explain it any better than this, and since all three of these books are designed to work together, I'd rather not force the issue. Thank you for your understanding in this matter.

There are three basic styles of studio monitor: bigs, midfields, and near-fields.

The bigs are typically soffit-mounted and require a rather large build-out in order to accommodate them. As far as I'm concerned, they're generally useless for anything other than making clients happy at the end of a long day.

Near-fields are small speakers with six- to eight-inch woofers. They typically sit on the bridge of your console or production desk, and are slightly less prone to the maladies of your critical listening space, but only slightly, and that also depends on monitoring levels.

Midfields are bigger than near-fields, and carry a woofer from 10 to 15 inches in size. Midfields are designed to be placed six to eight feet from the mix position. This provides the low end some room to develop before it reaches your position. That said, many recordists and mixers use midfield monitors placed in the near-field position. Space considerations can force such a decision.

It's not a bad idea to have more than one set of monitors, ideally near-fields in conjunction with midfield monitors, even if both are placed in the near-field position. The extended low end of your midfields can be far less tiring over the course of a day. Pay special mind to how your near-fields and midfields pair up. A radical switch in tone between monitors can send you into a state of shock, and some monitors pair better than others.

Seemingly every studio monitor manufacturer will tell you that their monitor is "flat." In theory, a flat monitor responds evenly across the frequency spectrum. In practicality, there's no such thing as a flat studio monitor. All you need to understand is how your monitors respond in the control room and how that response affects your decisions based on translation.

Monitor Varieties

There are two kinds of professional monitors—passive and active. Passive monitors require an external amplifier, one that should be carefully paired with the speaker. This too is a matter of personal taste, and in general the better the amplifier, the better the pairing. The power of your amplifier is also an important consideration, as improper power to your monitors will cause them to operate inefficiently.

Active monitors, which are not to be confused with active cross-overs, have the amplifiers built into them. This design offers a number of advantages, as the amplifier is matched specifically to the speakers. This allows you to take your monitors with you to external rooms, without having to worry about the amplifier. If you don't like the amplifier-speaker pairing of an active monitor, you don't like the monitor. That makes life simple.

Concentric monitors have the tweeter or horn placed in the middle of the woofer cone. The design keeps the high and low end in time alignment, which results in better imaging in the sweet spot (that is the center mixer's position), but attenuated high end outside of the stereo field. While I prefer concentric monitors, it's certainly not critical to results.

Whatever you do, don't purchase monitors without hearing them in your room first. This is the only reasonable way to tell if the monitors will work within the context of your room.

Choosing Your Monitors

There are countless models of studio monitors that are more than adequate for the job, and the price point of your monitors will have no correlation to your results. This, as evidenced by the 20-year reign of NS10M studio monitors, which only cost about $300 per pair when they were still in production.

In general, you want to choose a monitor that forces you to work in a certain manner. The overall frequency response of your monitors as they work within the control room will translate as a wholly opposite issue outside of that space. Put in simpler terms, a monitoring situation that reproduces an attenuated low end will translate outside your room as robust low end, that is, should you fail to compensate for the issue. You want your monitors to sound balanced within the room so that you can work aggressively towards your tones without constantly having to consider translation issues.

You're far better off spending a few thousand dollars on the accuracy and translation of your critical listening space, and a few hundred on monitors, than the other way around. A $7000 pair of midfield monitors are useless in a space that has major acoustic anomalies. You're also better off with a small pair of near-field monitors in a room with translation issues, although this certainly won't eradicate your issues. Commercial facilities of any worth will have purpose-built control rooms, most of which should offer reasonably accurate listening environments.

Some studios are built without a control room. These are typically privately owned studios, as most people can't fathom recording without an isolated monitoring space. I personally love single-room recording, but admittedly, it's a pain in the ass. It's also not particularly fun when your source isn't stellar to begin with. The procedure for pulling tones is a bit more random, as you must record, listen, adjust, and repeat until you're fully satisfied. This can greatly slow down the process of tracking.

Converters

There are some whacky motherfuckers on the Internet (one in particular) that suggest there is no audible difference between a Sound Blaster and a high-quality converter and clock. And people actually buy that crap! This is a myth.

I can assure you, unless you're nearly deaf, once I put you in a good critical listening environment, you'll be able to audibly pick out the quality converter over the prosumer card with ease, repeatedly, and blind. It would be the visual equivalent of asking you to choose between red and green.

Do not believe the nonsense. Your converters are critical to a good recording. They are the front line to your audio, and they affect the very core of your capture. Seeing as converters directly affect what you hear, they should be viewed as an extension of monitoring.

The AD (analog to digital) converter turns an analog signal into digital for purposes of capture. The DA (digital to analog) converter reproduces the digital signal as analog. Converter units that include both are called ADDAs. This is what you will require for both capture and reproduction of your audio.

There are plenty of acceptable converters for a reasonable price. Antelope Audio's Orion 32 is $3000 for 32 ADDA converters, and you will put yourself miles ahead of any other multi-converter unit I've used—especially when clocked with Antelope Audio's Isochrone 10M. In fact, I liked the combination so much, I recently agreed to endorse the products. That said, I'm not here to sell you on these particular converters and clock, but rather to point out the price point for a good capture has come down significantly in the past 15 years. The Orion32 is evidence of this, given that you're paying less than $100 per ADDA for professional-grade conversion.

You will damage your recordings severely with prosumer converters, and the sooner you can get away from them, the better. This is not about sound quality. It's about removing barriers, and when you use subpar converters, you're placing self-inflicted impediments between yourself and the music.

Orion, Lynx, Aurora, and Iz Technologies all make converters that I consider professional in quality. While I could certainly put that list in an order that would indicate my preferences, that's somewhat irrelevant. All that matters are your preferences.

There is a matter of subjectivity involved in conversion, as accuracy is in the ear of the beholder. In other words, my preferences in converters may not align perfectly with yours. To give you some measure of the bar, the HD192s made by Avid are what I would consider "barely acceptable" converters that are significantly overpriced for their level of quality. "Barely acceptable" won't prevent anyone from doing a good job, but they certainly won't make your life easier.

If you're a studio owner, or a recordist, you should get the best converters you can afford, as it's a smart business expense that will save you time. Even as a hobbyist, the buy-in for decent conversion is far from prohibitive. Given the compounding effects of poor conversion, an investment in good converters should be one of your early gear considerations.

The less you have to fight with your tools, particularly where capture and reproduction are concerned, the more time you'll save. Just keep in mind that like wine, price does not always directly correlate with quality. Given this, you would be well advised to audition a converter unit by recording and mixing through it before making a purchase decision.

The DAW

There are a number of DAWs on the market, and the manufacturers all realize that you are far more likely to stick with the DAW you learn to use first. I would imagine this is the main reason Avid also caters to the prosumer market. It can be exceptionally painful and time-consuming to learn how to use another DAW program. While all DAWs perform the same basic functions, they tend to excel in their own unique ways.

The most common DAW on the market is Pro Tools, and I can assure you, that has nothing to do with quality. The dominant argument for investing in Pro Tools is compatibility. That was a far more viable argument in 2004 than it is in 2014. Pro Tools may be dominant in the professional arena, but an entire generation of kids are using Reaper, Ableton, Cubase, Logic, and Digital Performer. I can't advise you as to what DAW to get, as it really depends on the nature of your music-making. Songwriters tend to prefer Logic for its massive sound library. DJs and live reinforcement engineers often find Acid or Ableton the best choices. Where the art of recording is concerned, the DAW that you use isn't all that relevant. Your converters are responsible for your capture and reproduction. Your DAW is responsible for manipulating your capture.

I will say this, however. Bang for your buck, Logic is a way better buy than Pro Tools. The stock plug-ins in Logic are exceptionally useful, and I can mix an entire record without using a single third-party plug-in. I can't say the same about Pro Tools. And no, I'm not a Logic endorser. Apple doesn't really have any, which might explain why they can't seem to overcome the market image that their DAW product isn't for professionals.

Lastly, the idea that your DAW can be used to completely replace external analog processing is as ridiculous as the notion was back in 1980 when SSL first unveiled their LFAC. Let history be your guide.

Processing Gear

If you're going to record, you're going to use a number of tools to process tone—our most commonly used being compressors and equalizers.

Compressors and Limiters

Compressors are used to reduce dynamic range, shape tone, boost output, and control low end. They are useful and effective tools, especially the analog variety.

The better the source, the more balanced the player and the instrument are in the room, the less compression you'll need. I can record a great drummer without any compression whatsoever. On the other hand, an average drummer could require copious amounts compression, particularly if he doesn't have full control over his balance. That said, I have no problem with crushing a phenomenal player with compression if the production calls for it. At that point, I'm making an artistic decision.

The more aggressive you think you need to be with your compressor, the better off you'll be using an analog one. And not just any analog compressor, but rather the best one for the task. If you're undersupplied with analog compressors, then use plug-ins. There is no getting around practicality. Use the best available compressor for the job.

There are several classifications of analog compressors and limiters including VCA, optical (opto), FET, tube, and vari-mu. These classifications describe how they work electronically, which translates to sonic characteristics, and it can get pretty deep from a technical perspective. I know—I've just been reading about them all, and I've learned all sorts of interesting things that are relatively useless where the art of recording is concerned. That said, we should go over the basics.

STEREO COMPRESSORS

Some analog compressors are stereo, which greatly simplifies compressing a stereo signal. Oftentimes, mono compressors (of the same model) can be linked together to operate as a stereo unit. The link will typically allow the first compressor to control the second in all aspects other than the output. Linking can be useful for preventing the center of the image from shifting in the sound field. The SSL G384, Neve 33609, A-Designs Nail, and Crane Song STC-8 are all high-quality stereo compressors, each with their own unique and identifiable tone.

LIMITERS

Limiters are basically high-ratio compressors, which prevent the audio from passing a certain threshold. Limiters should not be confused with brick wall limiters, which literally prevent a signal from passing a certain output level, regardless of the sonic consequences. When it comes to recording, there is really no reason to ever use one, and I would advise against it. A brick wall limiter leaves little room for error and can have the effect of placing a part into a steady state. Audio in which there is absolutely no dynamic variation whatsoever can be exhausting to the listener, even within the context of a mix. That said, there are situations in which a part put into steady state can be a desirable effect; it can also be performed on playback, as it should likely be considered mangling.

When it comes to technical descriptions of compressors, or any gear for that matter, one must be wary of terms being used for purposes of hype. Some manufacturers choose to use highly subjective and somewhat undefined buzz words in order to sell their wares. Further complicating matters, some compressors fall into more than one technical class, making even broad descriptions of how they sound suspect at best.

VCA COMPRESSOR (VOLTAGE CONTROLLED AMPLIFIER)

Solid-state VCA compressors are the most widely available, tend to have responsive attack and release curves, and impart minimal color in comparison to the other compressor types. A lack of color is often described as transparent, although a cheap VCA compressor is anything but. Their generally quick reaction times are handy for dealing with transients or peaks, and when set to the fastest attack will often impart audible distortion, which can be used to your advantage. VCAs used aggressively will tend to darken the signal, and may require brightening post-compressor.

Some examples of commonly used VCA compressors: the dbx 160 (the entire line all the way back to the original 160VU), the API 527, and the stereo SSL G384. The EL8 Distressor is also a VCA-based compressor, although it has emulation properties of optical and FET-based compression.

FET Compressor (Field Effect Transistor)

FET compressors and limiters are quite colored in nature, and are useful for both dynamic control and the shaping of tone. The most famous and widely used FET compressor is the Urei 1176LN originally manufactured by Universal Audio many decades ago. There are currently a whole slew of clones of the 1176, and even among the original 1176 line there are a number of versions. That said, regardless of version, 1176s have an identifiable and often aggressive sound, as they do tend to impart obvious distortion artifacts and tonal qualities that act much like an EQ. The 1176 is without a doubt the most useful limiter on the market.

Valve or Tube Compressor

Valve compressors are technically VCAs, and impart obvious color and pleasant distortion qualities to your tone. They are generally much slower than solid-state VCAs, and aren't particularly effective for the quick transients produced by drums unless you're looking for a very mushy effect. I cast no judgment in regards to "mushy" sounding drums. This could very well be a desirable tone for a particular production.

Opto Compressor (Optical)

Optical compressors use a light source and sensor to compress. In general, optos offer slower attack and release curves than VCA compressors, and often faster reaction times than tube compressors, although this should be viewed as nothing more than a rule of thumb. The overall attack and release characteristics should be evaluated based on the specific compressor. Optical compressors in general are more susceptible to distortion, although this isn't necessarily a bad thing.

The Teletronix LA2a and the Manley ELOP are examples of optical compressors, although they are technically leveling amplifiers, which employ higher compression ratios (which we'll discuss shortly). They still reduce dynamic range, they just happen to react slower than other compressor varieties. The reaction speed of a compressor is only relevant within the context of your source material and production.

THRESHOLD

The threshold on a compressor sets the level at which compression begins to be applied. It's essentially an input control. The lower the threshold, the more compression you're engaging. The threshold is directly affected by your attack and release settings.

ATTACK AND RELEASE TIMES

All compressors, limiters, and leveling amplifiers reduce dynamic range, regardless of the electronics. That's their main function. They also shape tone, and that's where the electronics come into play. The overall reaction speed, in combination with the electronic makeup of the compressor, will affect the shape of your tone, the quality of which requires subjective evaluation on your part.

Many compressors have selectable attack and release time settings. It's the overall reaction speed of a compressor that will dictate the fastest attack and release times available, and that's based on the electronic design. The attack and release times of a compressor are how you dictate the resulting tone, as they will affect how the compressor reacts to the program material.

The attack time of a compressor has to do with how quickly it can reduce the level of the source sound feeding it. The faster the attack-time setting, the more likely you are to lop off the initial transient. A slow attack allows more transient to pass unabated before compression takes hold.

The release time has to do with how long compression takes place. A fast release time allows the signal to pass almost immediately after the initial compression takes place. A slow release time can be used to clamp down on a signal for its duration.

You can use attack and release settings to great effect, particularly when it comes to shaping tone. For instance, if you wish to extend the apparent size of a drum room, you can do so with super-fast attack and release settings. This will attenuate the initial attack of the direct signal, while allowing the ambient information to pass unabated. It can also introduce copious amounts of distortion (which isn't necessarily a problem), depending on your threshold.

A kik drum with an overbearing ring can be dealt with through attack and release settings as well. A slow release setting in conjunction with a relatively fast attack setting will attentuate the amount of audible ring coming through on your kik drum capture. To accentuate the ring you would use a fast release setting.

Fast attack settings, depending on how fast, will tend to square and/or lop off the initial transient. A snare drum with an aggressive attack setting will sound as if the attack has been lopped off. This has a sound to it that may or may not be appropriate for a production.

The super-long attack and release times of valve compressors can be used to great effect, as they will bring up all of the harmonic artifacts of a source evenly throughout the sound. Used aggressively on a piano, you can bring the overtones to the level of the fundamental frequencies, creating an exceptionally rich steady-state tone.

Altering attack and release times will often require a threshold adjustment. Switching from a slow attack to a fast one, for instance, will increase the compression, and could require a lower threshold setting.

Used to the extreme, compressors can create fantastic effects. Used more judiciously, they can reduce your workload by allowing a part to sit within context of the track without losing important musical information. Passing notes can get swallowed up in the course of a production, and compressors are often the best remedy for this particular malady.

RATIO

Most compressors have selectable ratio settings. The higher the ratio, the more aggressive the compression as it relates specifically to the threshold. A ratio of 4:1 will attenuate the level of the signal to 1 dB of output for every 4 dB of signal above the threshold. Therefore a signal that goes 8 dB above the threshold setting will be reduced to just 2 dB of output.

A ratio of 1:1 offers no compression whatsoever, and will merely amplify your signal, which will impart some of the tonal characteristics of the compressor. A ratio of 2:1 is considered mild compression, 4:1 medium, 8:1 heavy, and a ratio of 10:1 or above means your compressor is technically functioning as a limiter.

There are certain effects that you can get from analog compressors, which you will be hard-pressed to achieve with the large majority of plug-ins available. As processing speeds continue to increase, the algorithms used to mimic the non-linear nature of analog compressors will improve. At the moment, plug-ins and their analog counterparts are not interchangeable. Given the complexity of how electronics react with program, analog compressors are often more effective, and take far less time to set. The time consideration alone is a good enough argument to stick with analog compression as much as you can during the recording process.

No matter how well you think you know your compressors, there is still some measure of randomness involved in the selection process. An 1176 on a kik drum will produce considerably different tone than that of a dbx 160. No matter how firm a sonic picture you have as to how these compressors will react to a given source, the production needs will dictate the best choice. If a compressor is imparting a tone that is counter to your goals, switch it out for something more appropriate.

If you find yourself recording in a setting with compressors that you're unfamiliar with or have never used, then you should have a discussion with the studio engineer. You don't usually have time to experiment in the heat of battle, and it's a good idea to get some general information on compressor's overall electronic makeup and reaction speed. Should you determine that everything the studio engineer told you is completely off base, at least you know not to seek his opinions in the future.

Regardless of your best guess or the counsel of others, compressors should ultimately be set by ear. The Internet Chatter Class can insist all they like on general rules and presets; that won't change the fact that *there are none.* You should, and will, use every combination of attack, release, and ratio settings available over time, and there is no ideal setting. It's all program-dependent.

A vocalist singing a long drawn-out melody, in which the tails of her notes all but disappear, will likely require a far longer release time than an MC performing a more percussive rap. That said, you could find yourself using more than one compressor on any given signal, particularly plug-in compressors, and you may choose to use different attack and release settings at different stages of your processing. I can't direct you on this as it's wholly program-dependent. That's pretty much my point.

Whether you choose to use a compressor in an aggressive and obvious manner, or in a subtle and transparent way, this is an artistic decision, not a technical one. Aggressive use of compression can cause blatantly heavy breathing and distortion artifacts—a tone that has artistic merits as a production technique. However, artistic decisions should be made with purpose and intent, even if the only explanation is that you like how it makes you feel.

There are all sorts of reasons to use compressors in an obvious and apparent manner, but those reasons should make sense within the overall vision and context of the production and recording. For instance, if I'm recording music that I want to present more aggressively and to appear slightly more rebellious in nature, I might want to push my compressors and limiters to the point of audible artifacts, such as pumping and distortion.

You can impart obvious distortion at the mic preamp or the compressor. Both of these options will produce unique analog distortion attributes. Not only do different models of mic pres distort uniquely, compressors do too, and how much distortion you impart will have much to do with your attack and release settings. When distortion is desired on a particular sound source, you should seriously consider imparting that distortion at the analog stage.

Distorting your source signal is not something you necessarily want to do as a matter of course. What's important is that you learn how to use and control the distortion. That's why it's so important to avoid prosumer gear. It imparts distortion whether you want it or not—it can't be contained, and is therefore undesirable. Compressors allow you to control your distortion levels based on attack and release settings in conjunction with the threshold. Limiters are far more prone to momentary distortion than compressors, the level of which can be controlled at the output.

SIDECHAIN

Many compressors include a sidechain function, which allows you to compress a signal based on the input of another signal. For instance, you can cause a synth pad to pulse by running a hi-hat signal into the sidechain of a compressor strapped to the synth. The compressor is reacting to the input from the hat, which results in compression of the synth. If you want a more aggressive pulse, you can use the sidechain of a gate, which can be set to close momentarily based on the input from the hat.

Radio stations often use a sidechain to automatically attenuate the music when the DJ is speaking. Some mixers use the sidechain to compress their bass with the kik drum. I've never been a big fan of this technique. That doesn't mean it's not a valid technique. It just means I don't favor it.

PARALLEL COMPRESSION

Parallel compression is achieved through combining the uncompressed signal with the compressed signal. Aggressive compression will attenuate low end information, which for certain source instruments, like a kik drum, can be problematic. Aggressive use of a compressor combined with the uncompressed signal will provide you the full blossom of your low end, in conjunction with the punchiness of an overcompressed transient. This is a particularly useful trick for hip-hop kik drums, as it can be difficult to get a huge low end while retaining punch.

Some rock mixers are known for their appreciation of parallel compression, especially on drums, but this is by no means a technique that's required. I rarely use parallel compression on rock drums.

Many, if not most, newer compressors include a "mix" knob, which essentially offers you parallel compression right from the unit itself. Essentially, the mix knob will allow you to blend, to taste, your uncompressed signal with the compressed directly from the module itself. The Tonelux TX5C, A-Designs Nail, and the Empress ECM 519 all include this option.

Equalization or EQ

The original intent of equalizers is quite simply to balance the frequencies being imparted by the microphone on the source. That's a fine application for EQ when you're working with an exceptional source. If your experience with EQ is limited, then you might be wise to approach it in this kind of manner, particularly as it relates to the initial recording.

Like compressors, EQs can impart tonal characteristics, particularly analog ones. An API 550 sounds completely different from the EQ section in a Neve 1073, which sounds wholly dissimilar to a Pultec EQP1a3. Although all EQs will allow you to boost and cut particular frequencies, they do so in different manners based on their electronic design.

Cheap EQs are more prone to distortion than high-quality ones, and adding distortion at every stage will severely degrade your options later. Don't be confused. Distortion can be your friend, but when you compound *unintended* distortion upon unintended distortion, you merely exhaust the listener. You'll exhaust yourself too.

Mic placement can effectively be used as EQ, and it's not a bad idea to avoid EQ processing at the recording stage, if for no other reason than to force good miking practices. When your first instinct upon opening up a mic is to reach for an EQ, then you are often abandoning your best option in exchange for the most convenient. A source that doesn't translate in your control room is best addressed through mic selection and placement before you even consider engaging an EQ.

This is not presented as some dogmatic, purist way of recording. Should practicality dictate inserting an EQ because you have a performer ready to go, then by all means, engage an EQ and move on. But don't allow yourself to fall into the trap of routinely employing EQ before you address the source and mic.

All modern recording desks have EQ sections, and you can use this EQ in conjunction with the pre. Desks also tend to have inserts, which allow you to plug your outboard EQ or compression inline before the signal is printed. The order in which you place your processing gear makes a difference. An EQ placed ahead of the compressor allows you to manipulate how the compressor reacts to the source. A strident vocal can be tamped down by sending a low-end boost to the compressor, which doesn't sound the same as adding the low end after the compressor. It's the difference between the compressor reacting to the EQ and the EQ reacting to the compressor.

There are all sorts of myths in regards to processing audio. You may read that subtractive EQ is preferred over additive EQ, and if you're using an exceptionally cheap EQ, that's probably true, given the usual distortion specs of prosumer devices. Somehow, I've managed an entire career without worrying too much about additive EQ, and I'm doubtful that my records have suffered because of it. Barring a radical boost in the top end, it really won't matter whether you're adding or subtracting frequencies with a quality EQ. The method you choose will vary depending on the situation. I mean, if you feel a source could use a bit more top end, then the easiest way to accomplish this is by adding some top end. Right? There's no need to be precious about this.

Plug-in EQs don't tend to distort the same way as analog models, and they also don't seem to have quite the same variance in personality. If you like the API plug-in, that's great. By all means use it. But the analog API EQs have a very unique and inviting sonic characteristic about them, that has not, to date, been accurately modeled by a digital plug-in. In other words, analog EQs can add flavor.

For instance, ribbons can be exceptionally good overhead microphones, but they tend to be dark in nature. I very well may want to open those ribbons up considerably, and given this, it's important to choose an EQ with minimal distortion properties. Even if the intent is to distort the ribbon-miked overheads, that function is best served by the pre and compressor, not the EQ. High frequency distortion caused by an additive EQ boost at 16 kHz is not necessarily preferred, as it will only serve to exhaust you, and ultimately the listener.

While you may find the rather grating distortion of your EQ to be perfect for your purposely irritating track, in general, this is not the stage you want to use to introduce distortion. Which is why the myth was born in the first place, because additive EQ does add distortion. It's just that some EQs distort far less than others.

The Pultec EQP1a3 is a tube EQ that was manufactured in the 50s and 60s. There are a number of companies that make a proprietary version of a Pultec, but there is only one company that makes a perfect clone, and that's Pulse Techniques. I know it's exact, because I was sent prototypes as it was being developed, and I'm familiar with the long process that Steve Jackson went through to stay true to the original.

Given the electronic design of the Pultec, they impart almost no audible or irritating distortion, and you can boost the high end excessively without the usual repercussions. Pultecs also deal with the low end in an inviting way, and they are, in my view, the best-sounding EQs there are for broad shaping of the high and low end information. Ribbons tend to do beautiful things to the cymbals, and you can maintain that overall sound, without losing clarity, by inserting an analog Pultec EQP1a3. There are several other Pultec models worth investigating, including the EQP1s3 which has a shelf, and the MEQ5, which is a midrange EQ. And no, there is no such thing as a Pultec plug-in that sounds anything close to the analog model.

Your typical prosumer EQ, like what you might find on a Mackie or Behringer mixer, will add copious amounts of distortion, and you're far better off using a plug-in over a prosumer-grade analog EQ.

The most common EQ that we use in the studio is a parametric, which offers you the ability to boost or cut a specific frequency bandwidth of your choosing. Bandwidth represents the width of the frequencies you're manipulating, and is indicated as "Q." The wider the bandwidth, the more frequencies you're affecting.

The fundamental frequency that you select on an EQ will fall directly in the middle of a bell curve. The Q widens the scope of the frequencies you're affecting. A boost at 2 kHz with a broadband Q will affect many frequencies above and below that 2 kHz frequency selection. The narrowest setting on the Q is basically called notch, and is used to deal with an ultra-narrow frequency problem.

In general, parts in need of slight EQ do well with broadband adjustments, and parts that have unwanted resonances are best served by a notched cut in frequency. The more aggressive you want to get with an EQ, the more likely you are to use ultra-narrow bands. In general, narrow bandwidth Qs are used to fix severe problems, or to mangle parts, as a notch will often produce a rather unnatural sound on a problem-free source. You can produce a "radio" effect using aggressive high- and low-pass filters in conjunction with a notched EQ boost in the midrange.

The number of EQ bands available for processing with any given parametric EQ varies greatly. Some analog parametric EQs have only three bands. Many plug-ins offer up to seven bands of EQ unless they're designed to model a specific analog EQ. An API 550 plug-in has three bands of EQ, just like the analog 550. Frankly, I find that slightly baffling. It's not like the digital version is identical in tone or reaction to the analog EQ.

Every EQ band added to an analog EQ reduces the overall sonic clarity. There is no such limitation on a plug-in as they are designed to model the tone of an EQ, and a disengaged band in a plug-in can be coded to have no effect on the sound. As far as I'm concerned, there's no valid sonic argument for limiting the bands to three on an emulation plug-in. It's the tone of an API 550 that is so appealing. If that tone can be modeled convincingly for the three existing curves of the unit, additional bands will have no effect until engaged.

Of course, An API 550 with seven bands of EQ would no longer look identical to the original. Plug-in manufacturers count on the graphic representation to produce confidence and good feelings. If it looks identical, you will be far more likely to believe it sounds identical. And if you think that doesn't work, think again. It works a like a fucking charm. Talk about expectation bias!

Most EQs, whether analog or digital, include shelving. There are two shelves—high frequency and low frequency. A shelf primarily affects the frequencies above or below a set point, the quick slope of which peaks at the selected frequency. A high shelf essentially affects all information above your selected frequency, and a low shelf affects all frequencies below the set point. A high shelf boost at 10 kHz will essentially bring up all frequencies evenly from 10 kHz and up. A low shelf set at 100 Hz will affect all frequencies evenly from 100 Hz down. The slope of a shelf is affected by the Q function, which will result in a more radical "S" curve at the point of the slope. This is visually represented in your stock DAW EQ.

Most EQs include high- and low-pass filters. A high-pass filters out low frequencies (thus allowing the high frequencies to pass), and a low-pass filters out the high frequencies from the signal.

Filters, unlike shelves, can only be used to cut frequencies. The Q of a filter affects the severity of the slope, which can be gradual or steep. A low-pass filter set to 10 KHz (depending on the Q or slope of the cutoff) filters out all frequencies above 10 KHz, thereby allowing frequencies below that point to pass unabated. A high-pass filter set to 500 Hz filters all frequencies below that point, thereby allowing anything above 500 Hz to pass.

Filters can be useful to fix problems of unintended capture, such as the low rumble of an uncoupled air conditioner. Other than that, I recommend that you rarely use filters for recording unless it's for purposes of a radical production decision. Even then I would be reticent to record using a filter, as once you remove those frequencies, you can't readily get them back. It's impossible to boost a frequency that doesn't exist because it's already been filtered out of the sound.

Shelves are also good for addressing high and low end problems, albeit in a slightly less radical way. Still, I would dissuade you from using them while you're recording. They're great mix tools. They're dangerous when used for recording, and you would do well to have a bit of practice with them before you start engaging in them for that purpose. You can just as easily insert a filter on the return without any disadvantage.

Just so we're totally clear here, you can be as aggressive as you like within the comfort levels of your clients, to the point that you leave yourself no options upon completing the recording. So long as you've worked towards the agreed-upon vision and accomplished it in an effective manner, I'm all for it. Unfortunately, most of us aren't clairvoyant, and as much as I encourage aggressive techniques, it would be imprudent to leave yourself absolutely no room to maneuver later. You can literally record yourself into a corner if you're uber-aggressive in this regard.

It's smart to aggressively compress using an analog compressor that might not be available come mix time. It's foolish to remove sonic information that can just as effectively be processed on the return. Yes, you can't undo the compression either, but that decision has more to do with availability than any other factor. If your access to analog compressors goes away come mix time, you should use them at the recording stage.

Don't confuse aggressive compression with aggressive EQ processing. A compressor is used mainly for dynamic control, which can't necessarily be dealt with by mic position—not without placing the mic some distance from the source (which will increase the level of ambient information in your capture). EQ is useful for minor tone shaping, and in general that's about as aggressive as you want to get with EQ at the recording stage. The preponderance of your capture tone is best accomplished through source adjustments and mic positioning.

Aggressive EQ decisions at the time of recording are an indication that you haven't done the first part of your job—to get the source sounding as it should in the room. Even if the room has some problems, like a bump in 700 Hz, your mic choices and placements in conjunction with your acoustic manipulations are your first line of defense. Then insert your EQ to deal with room deficiencies and mic coloration.

Use EQ. Use it all the time on every session. But get yourself in the habit of considering your other options first.

Graphic EQ

Graphic EQ employs sliders with set frequencies and bandwidths. Graphic EQs are not commonly used in recording as they offer limited control over bandwidth and frequency. You will see this kind of EQ on some people's home stereo systems. The API 560 is a graphic EQ.

Effects

I think the number one recording myth, or at the very least one of the longer-standing ones, is the idea that one should never record with effects.

Wrong, wrong, wrong!

Okay, admittedly, that's not bad advice in general. It's the "never" part that's wrong. Effects, like tremolo on guitar, or delay on a Wurli, can influence the performance. Any effect that is part of the overall tone should be recorded that way. At the very least, the effect should be recorded to a separate track, although that's not really an option if your effect is generated from the source itself.

Guitar amps have tone and gain knobs, and sometimes include reverb and tremolo options. If an effect generated from the amp makes for a compelling component of the tone, there are few reasonable arguments for excluding that effect from the capture. If you want your tremolo effect in perfect time with the track, then you might prefer to use a plug-in for the job. However, tremolos and delay timings are often most effective when they aren't quite exact, nor do they react quite the same as a tremolo coming from an amp.

Vocals, being front and center to any given production, are best recorded as neutrally as possible. The vocal carries the song. Given this, in all but the rarest of cases, you should leave your options wide open by limiting the introduction of room information returning to the mic. Most recording spaces won't offer the kind of ambience that you want on a vocal, as medium rooms are neither grand nor intimate in nature. More often than not, you will seek one or the other, making a medium room an awkward choice.

Modulators

Modulation means an inflection of the tone or pitch, and we have a number of ways to modulate tone including flangers, phasers, choruses, wah-wahs, tremolos, Leslie cabinets, and countless whacky (and fun) envelope filters, useful for frittering away countless hours of time.

Modulation adds motion to a sound, which can make it more interesting and pleasing.

FLANGERS

Flangers are used to create a frequency-sweeping motion. An electronic flanger is modeled from the resulting effect of syncing two tape machines reproducing the *identical* audio. Once synced, the engineer can cause a frequency sweep to occur by lightly alternating thumb pressure to the two flanges (the reels themselves). This will cause the audio to go through various stages of frequency cancellation as the machines drift from the engineer's speed manipulations. Organic analog flanging is considerably more random in reaction than any digital model, which results in more variance of the effect. Not that it matters—you probably don't have two tape machines.

Flange effects processors are a little less random than the original method, and recreate the effect by modulating a delayed signal with an LFO. You can also introduce the delayed foldback of the signal, which will offer a more complex reaction.

PHASERS

Phasers are basically flangers with a generally less radical sweep. The analog version of the effect is performed the same way as flanging, but rather than altering the playback speeds with a thumb, the slight variations in machine motor speed are wholly responsible for the sweep. This produces a much tighter frequency sweep.

Phaser effects processors tend to use an all-pass filter in combination with the direct signal to mimic the original effect.

CHORUS

A chorus offers motion through pitch and time discrepancies between two or more *similar* signals (as opposed to identical). Therefore, chorus is a naturally occurring effect caused by recording and combining multiple tracks of the same part. This provides enough variation to cause the frequencies to beat due to naturally occurring, mild tuning discrepancies. The more parts you record and combine, the more obvious the chorusing, and the less obvious the tuning discrepancies, although if you record enough of them, you will start to cause an interesting phase effect.

Chorus processors mimic the natural chorus effect by detuning and delaying the signal and combining that with the direct signal.

TREMOLO AND VIBRATO

Tremolos, which can be found on some guitar amplifiers like the Vox AC30 or the Supro Big Star, act as automatic volume control allowing you to pulse the tone. The depth and speed controls allow you to set the severity of the pulsing along with the timing. The speed of a tremolo is typically set based on the tempo of the track, although not necessarily at ¼- or ⅛-note intervals. Triplets can be extremely useful tremolo settings, as can more random settings.

Some guitars include a tremolo bar, or whammy bar, which allows the player to physically pulse the pitch, rather than the volume. The whammy bar will lift the bridge, thereby elongating the strings. This effect comes off as more of a vibrato than a tremolo. Either way, motion is being introduced to the tone.

Vibrato control on a guitar amp is just a more subtle tremolo. You will have less precise control over the timing of a tremolo or vibrato at the guitar amp than you will with a plug-in. Variations in tempo can cause a set tremolo speed to sound out of time. Given the option, I much prefer a natural amp tremolo over a virtual one.

REVERBS

Other than springs on guitar amps, reverbs are generally undesirable while recording. They only tend to obfuscate, and recording is the time that you want to be able to hear every detail. Reverbs are used to create a feeling of space in a mix. It's perfectly reasonable to engage reverb if you want to get a sense of the track as a whole. Beyond that, they're best left off for purposes of critical listening.

If you ever find yourself in a room with a real EMT 140, do yourself a favor and plug that bad boy in. You will never listen to a digital plate the same way again. A plate reverb is nothing more than encased sheet metal plate suspended by springs. A transducer excites the plate, which then returns through pickups. There is nothing quite like a good plate, and I routinely print the return of the plate on certain parts so that I have it available come mix time.

DELAYS

Delays also tend to obfuscate and mask tone, but not nearly to the extent of reverbs. Just the same, unless the delay is an integral part of the tone, it's really best to leave them off while you're recording. That is, unless the delay is part of the tone. Guitar and electric pianos are good candidates for this treatment.

Tape delays like the Echoplex and the Roland Space Echo can sound considerably more inviting than any digital replication, and if you have one available to you, try it out. You just might end up printing some of those effects. Tape decks also make for great delay units.

Chapter Three

The Source and Capture

Now that we've discussed the recordist's tools and phase coherency, it's time to deal with capture techniques. Let's start off with some broad concepts, and then we'll discuss the specifics as they relate to unique source instruments.

Microphone Placement

Aside from the source itself, your most powerful tool is microphone selection and placement, and that's not even a tool, that's a process. The microphone you select will have some bearing on its best location, the initial placement of which is nothing more than an educated guess based on the nature of the instrument and the properties of the microphone. It's still just a guess, and if the microphone you've chosen seems inadequate for the job, you should swap it out for another. Don't hesitate for a moment to remove a mic if it's clear you've made the wrong choice.

The actual physical placement of the microphone is crucial. A placement difference of less than a centimeter can cause a dramatic change in how a mic picks up the source. This is especially so with close-miking techniques, in which the proximity effect can greatly skew the low-end properties of your capture.

Dynamic microphones are sensitive to minute adjustments, and require evaluation by ear in order to locate the most effective placement.

One-Mic Techniques

When it comes to placing a single microphone on a source for purposes of capture, there is one technique that will all but guarantee your success. You'll need an assistant for this, and it can be just about anyone you can trust to handle your most fragile and expensive microphone.

Ready? Here's the procedure.

After placing your microphone in the area in which you believe it will sound best, direct your assistant to deliberately adjust the placement of the microphone, starting first with broad movements. As the sound begins to focus, stop your assistant, and have him fine-tune the placement with more refined movements. Once the sound comes fully into focus, lock it down.

Seriously. That's how you place a microphone.

Of course, I'm certain that some of you don't understand what I mean when I use the term "focus" as it relates to sound. When you hear it for yourself, you'll know it. There will be a sweet spot in which the microphone is picking up all that's good about the tone and surrounding space. Given that your goal is to capture the tone as it sounds in the room, you should have a pretty good idea as to what you expect to hear.

Now, you might have to repeat that procedure more than once depending on the source. You could very well find a decent macro location only to reject it upon implementing micro adjustments. Still, there is no better way to find a good mic placement than by ear.

Once you locate the sweet spot, you can typically alter the tone at the source without having to readjust the microphone. A microphone that sounds good on a guitar amp should translate as you alter the tone. You can typically adjust the drum tone at the source to your heart's content without ever having to change the microphones, that is, unless you've also managed to change the physical makeup of the drums. Replacing a piccolo snare with a deep brass snare will force you to raise the snare mic given the size differentials between those two drums. Any time you move a microphone, you must check its relationship to the other mics in close proximity. Otherwise, you could end up with phase coherency issues.

If you have copious amounts of time available, and you'd like to take the technique of locating the sweet spot to its extreme, you can do so by completely disregarding the source location in relation to placement. This can offer nothing short of surprising results, to the point that the visual location of the microphone could leave you in a state of disbelief. Trust your ears.

On those occasions when a placement seems outside the bounds visually, be sure that you have sufficient isolation for the task at hand. An amazing guitar tone is useless if the mic is picking up some other source information louder than the guitar itself. A snare drum mic that sounds fantastic in isolation two feet off the drum could be quite problematic once the drummer starts crushing his cymbals. The further your mic is from the source, the more likely you are to pick up unwanted, if not problematic, information. There's a reason why we close-mic drums. Placing a mic two feet off the snare ignores the need to make compromises for the purposes of the whole.

Should you find yourself without any assistance, you can use headphones to place a mic yourself. This takes some practice, and is ineffective when dealing with the high SPLs of a blaring guitar amplifier. The best way to place a mic using headphones on a guitar amp is to compare the tone of the line noise coming from the amp, to the tone in the headphones at volume. Just make sure the guitar player isn't plugged in, or you could find yourself plastered to the ceiling. Once the tone of the line noise matches between the amp and the headphones, your mic should be in a relatively effective position. Adjust from there.

You can place your drum mics with headphones too. You have to crank them up, but you can easily find the sweet spot of the close mics by moving the mic as you strike the drum. You can certainly get close enough that you will only need minor adjustments from there.

I swap out mics frequently when I'm recording, particularly when tracking. Once I've determined that I don't like how a mic is influencing the tone, I won't waste my time trying to make it work. Rather, I'm going to evaluate the tone in the hopes that I can identify where it's falling short, and then use that information to make a better second choice, followed by the third, and then the fourth. And yes, I've swapped out mics as many as four times (maybe more) to get the capture I seek.

As an example, I might start with a pair of Neumann U87s as my overheads on a drum kit, only to decide the tone captured is too aggressive in the context of the arrangement. At that point, I may swap out the 87s for a pair of Coles 4038 ribbons, and there could very well be a pair of AKG 451s waiting in the wings. This procedure continues until I can narrow down my selection to a clear winner.

Neumann U87s, which are LDCs, tend to capture and accentuate the biting midrange of the cymbals, making them a great choice for straight rock productions. The Coles 4038s, which are ribbons, will tend to soften the more aggressive tone of the cymbals. A pair of AKG 451 SDCs will produce a detailed stereo image.

Given those unique attributes, you'd think it would be hard to pick the wrong mic. Which is a good point. But there is more involved in the mic decision than just their overall tonal characteristics. There's strategy involved in recording a drum kit, and your room mics can come into play. More on that later—I just don't want you to beat yourself up for swapping out mics while you're learning. What matters is that you get the capture right. And if I can swap out overheads four times before choosing a pair, then so can you.

Stereo Techniques

As much as I prefer to simplify matters by keeping to one mic on a mono source, there is no getting around the need for two capsules when capturing a stereo image. A stereo mic is the easiest solution, as the capsules are housed specifically for phase-coherent stereo capture. Stereo mics also happen to be rather expensive, and aren't always available, at which point you will need two microphones to capture your stereo image.

I might point out that two microphones can be equally as expensive as a stereo mic, seeing as you have to buy two of them. Furthermore, you can use a single capsule on your stereo mic, but you can't record a stereo image with one capsule. Just saying.

There are some tried and true stereo mic placement configurations that will greatly reduce the chances of phase coherency issues.

X-Y

This is probably the most fail-safe of the stereo miking techniques, particularly when employing SDCs, which are superior at collecting off-axis information. An X-Y miking technique is achieved by placing your microphones with the capsules one above the other, facing each other at an angle of 90 degrees (or higher, depending on the physical width of the source). This technique works well because the sound that's emanating before the mics will reach them at same time, which will greatly reduce phase coherency issues. Stereo microphones like the Shure SM69, AKG C24, or the Royer SF-12, have their capsules set in an X-Y position, and you can rotate the relative angle of the capsules in the SM69 and the C24.

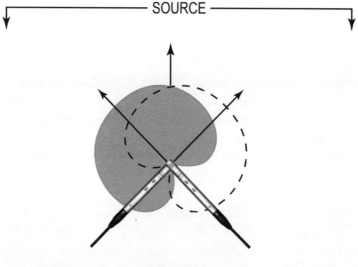

X-Y Diagram

Blumlein Pair

The Blumlein Pair technique is similar to X-Y, except it uses two figure-8 microphones (often ribbons) so that the tops of both microphones are aligned vertically. Essentially, one mic should hang upside down above the other. The capsules are then rotated so that they face 90 degrees relative to each other. Because the capsules are figure-8, they capture four quadrants of information. The first mic captures the front left source information along with the back right room information, and the second mic captures the front right source information and the back left room information. Given the rear pick-up patterns of figure-8 mics, this method will capture considerably more ambience than an X-Y technique. The Royer SF-12, which is a stereo mic, is configured as a Blumlein pair.

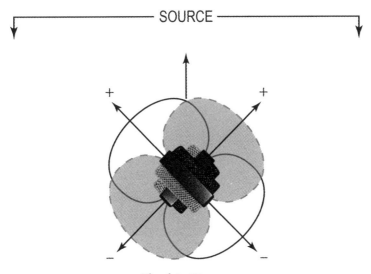

Blumlein Diagram

A-B

This is a parallel miking technique in which two omni microphones are placed between three and 10 feet apart from one another. This placement differential, along with the capsules being perfectly parallel, will reduce the likelihood of phase issues. Make fine adjustments by ear.

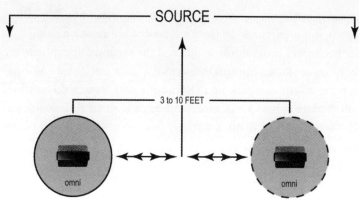

A-B Diagram

ORTF

This technique requires specific measurements. Place the capsules of two directional microphones so that they are facing away from each other by 110 degrees with the capsules exactly 17 cm apart.

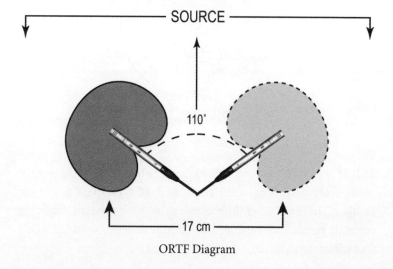

ORTF Diagram

Spaced Pair

Two cardioid microphones spaced out from one another and pref-erably equidistant from the sound source can, and will, often require some slight microphone placement adjustments in order to avoid phase coherency issues.

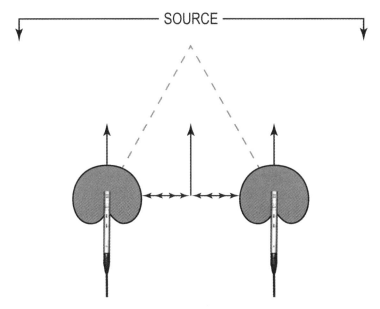

Spaced Pair Diagram

Mid-Side or MS Technique

This technique offers the most flexibility, in that you have some control over just how wide you'd like the source to appear within the sound field. Place a directional mic facing the source above and perpendicular to a figure-8 mic placed such that the capsules face the sides. The mics should be as close as possible to one another, one on top of the other, and recorded on their own separate channels. The resulting audio from the figure-8 mic should then be multed to another track. The two identical signals are then panned hard left and right, with the polarity reversed on one of them. Once you blend in your mid signal, you can control the image width by its relative level to the side signals. This is an exceptionally useful technique for miking a B3 Leslie cabinet.

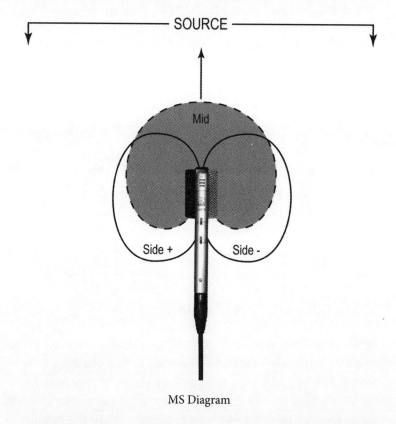

MS Diagram

As you can see, we can go through great lengths to place two mics in close proximity to one another. It only gets more complicated the more mics we add to the equation. Therefore, the overall rule of thumb is: use as few mics as you can, as many as you need.

Trap Drums

I'm not sure anyone under 80 calls them trap drums anymore. "Drum set," "drum kit," or just "drums" seems to be the more common vernacular these days. Still, they are indeed trap drums, and are without a doubt, my favorite instrument to record. They also happen to be the most difficult to record well.

Source Instruments

Of all the instruments you could record, drums require a good acoustic space more than any other source that I can think of—particularly *loud* drums. There is no better way to expose the deficiencies of a room than to bombastically perform on an instrument that covers the full spectrum of the frequency range. The kit's rather large footprint certainly doesn't help matters.

Look. If you want to record a violin in your apartment with a condenser mic, I'm sure it'll be fine. Certainly the violin will sound better in a proper recording space, as will any source instrument, particularly once we bring isolation into the equation. But a violin requires neither the sonic nor physical space of a drum kit.

When you attempt to record drums in an inadequately sized room, the tone of the room will fold right back into your microphones. You will never capture a decent drum tone this way, but rather the usual and typical indie drum sound I would just as soon mute completely, were that an option. Should your main goal be to achieve a shitty drum tone, an undersized room is often a great way to achieve it. On the other hand, should you wish to capture a beautifully open kit, you would do well to place yourself in a room appropriate for the job.

It doesn't matter whether a room has significant ambience or seemingly none—sounds with the kind of SPLs generated by a drum kit need space to travel. If you don't have the space required to accomplish your recording goals, then you shouldn't record there. Even if it's your own room. Subcontract a proper drum room. It'll be well worth the investment, even if it means you take a hit on what you can charge for the project.

Drum kits come in all shapes and sizes, and often reflect the personality of the player. A relatively small kit might include a kik, snare, hat, rack tom, floor tom, (or no toms at all), hi-hat, a crash, and a ride. A large kit could have two kiks, two snares, too many toms and cymbals to bother counting, and any number of percussion instruments attached either to the kit or the sticks themselves. Super-drummer Jim Keltner often attaches a shaker to one of his drum sticks.

Given the generally modular nature of drum kits, you have significant control over the tone. Changing out the kik and the snare alone will alter the feeling imparted by the drums as they relate to the production. A wide-open obnoxious brass snare will produce an entirely different feeing from a dead snare, piccolo snare, wood snare, so on and so forth until we've managed to list every variety of snare ever made, each of which will generate its own particular feeling.

You have way more control over the drum tones through source manipulation than you do by any other means. Tuning has a major role in the quality of drum tone, as do your choice in heads and the measure to which you dampen them.

For instance, if you seek a vibrant tone from the drums, you would be wise to have them skinned up with new heads and professionally tuned. Not all drummers can tune their drums worth a damn, which I can assure you doesn't bode well for your pending session, since tuning one's drums is kind of an important part of the gig. If any of the tuning lugs surrounding a drum are out with the others, it can cause all sorts of strange phenomena like frequency beating and pitch dives. On those occasions when you find yourself recording a drummer incapable of tuning his drums well, hire someone for the job. Or better yet, learn how to do it yourself.

Band drummers are notorious for carrying less than stellar instruments. Many studios carry their own drums just to deal with this reality, and you can always rent or borrow a set. What you don't want to do is record a poorly maintained drum kit, complete with lug buzzes and rattles.

That's not to say an old beat-up kit is unacceptable for purposes of recording. It just means it's going to sound like an old beat-up kit, and should be reserved for those productions in which such a tone is desirable. Attempting to capture a brilliant tone out of dusty kit is an exercise in futility, and you're only wasting your time. And should you mistakenly hire a drummer who couldn't be bothered to bring a useful kit to your session, send him home. Band drummers, of course, are not so easily replaced. Changing out the source instrument is far easier than replacing a band player. Drum kits don't care whether you use them or not. Drummers often do. Besides, that's not your call. You're the recordist.

Drum Heads

The heads are your first consideration when evaluating a kit. Old heads are far less vibrant than new ones, which provide a softer attack with less ring. The heads should be considered and discussed in advance of your tracking session. Dead heads are useful for more mellow drums, and if you're not sure whether that's the sound you want, you should probably check them before the drummer installs new heads. The tone of months-old heads can't be recreated in a reasonable time frame. Once you remove an old head, you really can't reasonably put it back on, and a change in heads on one drum pretty much requires a change in heads on them all.

There's a famous story that's gone around for years, about a producer who spent an entire day working on the snare tone. Supposedly the band was popular and the budget expansive, as one might expect on a session in which it's acceptable to take a day to dick with the snare and its mic. Upon achieving the desired sound, the producer ended the session for the day, and called the tech in to change the heads for the purposes of making takes.

Apparently the second day went similarly to the first, as the producer still found the snare tone displeasing. This happens. He spent another 12 hours slaving over the tone, and once again called in the tech to retune the drums for a morning downbeat. By the end of the third day, as the producer once again called for the drum tech, the engineer piped in, "Maybe you just prefer the tone of a beat-in head," at which point, they began making takes.

New heads are more vibrant, have a more definitive attack, and offer you more range in pitch adjustments. Dead heads, particularly months-old ones, won't be as responsive to pitch change, particularly if you want to lower them. Detuning a fully stretched and worn head would be tantamount to shedding 400 pounds of excess weight—the result of which would be flabby skin. Once you bring those old heads down in pitch, you might as well keep loosening the lugs, because it's now time for new heads.

Drum heads come in many varieties. The drum head that is struck is called the batter head, and the other is called a resonant head, although some players might choose to go without resonant heads—a tone I generally abhor. They lack resonance. Go figure.

There are two main types of heads: white-coated and gel. White-coated batter heads tend to emit a richer tone, and given the thickness of the coating will produce shorter resonance times than a single-ply gel head. When it comes to recording drums, coated heads will often make your life easier, but genre does come into play. The metal hard rock drummers seem to really love the gels for their sharp attack.

Fully resonant heads on a drum kit can be overbearing and subject to obvious overtone interaction. Toms in particular are notorious for interacting with the rest of the kit, and this can result in excessive and obvious frequency beating. Although that's partly (if not mostly) a tuning issue, these maladies tend to appear more prominently during the decay of the drum. The longer the decay time of the drum skins, the more likely they are to negatively interact. While this sort of issue can be addressed partly through tuning, some dampening may be needed as well.

How much overall tonal decay you want out of the drums has more to do with production aesthetics than any other consideration. As difficult as it can be to deal with tuning issues of long decays, if you seek to capture the sound of a wide-open resonant drum kit, dampening would seem to work counter to your goals.

Of course, it's rare that you're going to want a four-second tonal decay on a tom, as it will likely be swallowed up by the rest of a track anyway, and all you're doing at that point is filling valuable space with superfluous low-end resonance. You can keep your decay in reasonable control through dampening without sacrificing the illusion of resonant drums.

There are all sorts of ways to dampen drum heads, including the style of head itself. Rings, gels, two-ply heads, paper towels, gaffer tape, tampons, and of course, dampers found inside the drum are all exceptional tools for controlling excessive ring.

A wallet on a snare drum is a great way to achieve that dead snare drum tone that was so popular in the 70s. Of course, that iconic Al Green drum tone is best accomplished in a room with minimal to no ambience. If you want a dead drum tone, record them in a dead room, which should not be confused with a small room. You still need space when it comes to drums. "Dead" only describes the overall absorption attributes of the room.

The size of the drums will also factor into your decisions. Drum size, as it relates to recording, has gone through all sorts of fashions. In the mid-80s, Yamaha tried to convince everyone that small drums were better for recording than big ones. Had Yamaha had their way, everyone would be recording with their undersized recording series drums, which were touted as the best way to get a "big" drum tone. While it may be easier to tune a kit of what I can only call miniature drums, I don't agree that a smaller kit will produce a bigger tone. That has everything to do with how the player tunes the drums, and small drums means high-pitched drums.

Accessories

There are all sorts of accessories one can use to alter the sound of a kit. Bali sticks are made of reeds glued together, which makes for an almost splintery attack on the drums. Brushes, which are often used by jazz drummers, produce a much softer and warmer drum tone in which the drag of the brush against the head is a staple. Rivets on a ride cymbal (and there are rivet chains that can be draped over a ride) offer an extended ring to the cymbal as the rattling modulates and perpetuates the decay time. You will come across numerous accessories that alter the way a drum kit sounds, and none of them should really affect the process of recording a kit.

Gating Drums

A noise gate is an easy way to automatically mute and unmute audio, but it's just as easy, if not easier, to just strip silence the unwanted audio in your DAW. Gates can be inserted on the individual drum channels in order to remove unwanted cymbal information bleeding into the close mics. But you don't ever want to record with a gate as they are prone to mistriggers, and anything you can gate as you record, can be processed just as effectively afterwards.

For some reason, there seem to be a great many neophyte recordists who use gating techniques as a matter of course on drums, mostly because they believe this is how the "pros" do it. In reality, well-recorded drums are not in need of gating. Removing all resonance of the kit produces a disjointed and disappointing overall tone. When you seek a natural and organic drum tone, gating, or strip silencing, should be a measure of last resort. Besides, if you go into your drum recording with the expectation that you will be gating them later, you will slough off problems that could have prevented such a decision in the first place. All of that said, Ken Scott (Beatles, David Bowie) uses gates on drums as a matter of course. My friend Wyn Davis loves to use U87s on toms, which I've already suggested is a mistake. There is nothing I can advise you on, in which some other, more decorated engineer might have a completely different viewpoint.

Toms emit a sympathetic ring as the drummer plays, and if that ring is overbearing, or if there is an excessive amount of cymbal leakage, the drums could be well served by riding the offending information down between strikes come mix time. The more toms there are on a kit, the more likely this will be a necessity. When you eradicate all of the ring from the toms, you remove much of the tone from the drums themselves. This highly unnatural tone will almost require the addition of digital reverb, at which point one has to wonder why you gated the drums.

If you want great organic drum tones, you should avoid gating techniques.

Top-Down Recording

The best way that I've found to record acoustic drums, really, for just about any genre, is a top-down approach. This means you start with an aggregate stereo sonic image and then use close mics to supplement the sonic information and balances. The aggregate is captured either with your room or overhead mics, and the decision as to which depends mostly on how the room itself sounds.

Overheads

Overhead mics used for purposes of the aggregate stereo capture must be placed high enough, and perhaps back enough, to capture all the kit information. Of course, the more distance between your overhead mics and the drums themselves, the more aggregate room information you will collect. Your overheads could sound more like room mics should you place them too far above the kit.

A ceiling height of eight feet or less is insufficient for a good stereo image. The early reflections returning to a mic just a foot off the ceiling will smear the image and accentuate harsh high-frequency information. Absorptive treatment of the ceiling will only serve to make the tone of the drums boxy. Like I said, drums require space.

As we discussed earlier, baffling is a good way to control the ambience folding back into the microphones, thereby allowing you some control. Just make sure you don't over-baffle, as you could choke out all of the room's positive attributes. By adjusting the number of absorptive baffles in conjunction with their distance from the kit, you can attenuate the amount of ambience returning to the mics.

When placing baffles, you should be mindful of sight lines. Musicians tend to perform better when they can see each other, and communication is easier when you can make eye contact with your players. A baffle shifted two feet in either direction shouldn't compromise the recording. The exact placement of the baffles will have less significance than the amount of absorptive material you've introduced to the space. If you've added too many baffles, you can remove one at a time, and/or pull them further off the drums.

It's often preferable to place a drum kit a few feet off a wall or corner rather than in the middle of the room, and that really has more to do with your ability to control the room than any other factor. Whenever I find myself in a room for the first time, I seek the counsel of the studio personnel, who can usually tell me where the drums tend to sound best. A poor source placement will make for a poor recording, and the staff will likely know the sweet spots as well as the positions to avoid.

The goal with top-down recording is to capture a convincing stereo image of the drums in balance. The better the drummer and the room, the better the balance, such that you could conceivably record perfectly balanced drums with nothing more than a stereo pair of mics.

Oh, I realize that statement probably just made you shake your head in disbelief. And I know why too. Because if you haven't heard one of the top players in one of the best rooms, you can't even fathom how good the capture will be, nor how simple the procedure. I'm telling you, I could easily record a well-balanced drum tone in certain rooms with certain players, with nothing more than two mics.

Of course, that leaves little room to maneuver later, and as much as I don't mind working without a net (relish it, even), I haven't completely lost my mind, thank you very much.

SDCs are particularly good at capturing a balanced stereo aggregate of the kit. AKG 451's, 452's, B&K 4003's, and Neumann KM84's are all good choices, although there are a great many SDCs that will do the job outside of that rather abbreviated list.

I'm much more likely to use LDCs on a straight-ahead rock kit, as they tend to offer a feeling of aggression. Neumann U87's, U47's, M49's, AKG C12's, 414's, the C24, and the Shure SM69 are all common LDC choices for overheads. Once again, availability comes into play.

Ribbon mics can be superior for overheads when you're looking to smooth out the more aggressive frequencies of cymbals. They're also a great choice for capturing an aggregate drum image. My absolute favorite ribbon mics for drums are Coles 4038's.

Sometimes, either due to space restrictions or the lack of a weighted mic stand, you could have no option but to approach your overheads from behind the drummer, which means those capsules could be facing the opposite direction of your close mics. This will put the overheads 180 degrees out of phase with mics that approach from the front of the kit. The interaction between your reversed overheads and close mics will result in a significant loss of low-end information. Therefore, you must either mind the direction in which your capsules are facing, or reverse their polarity.

Overhead compression is best performed with either a stereo compressor, or two linked mono compressors of the same variety. You're going to have all sorts of whacky reactions if you use compressors with different properties and reaction speeds. The Fatso Jr. can be an exceptional choice, particularly if you don't have ribbons available, as the "warmth" function does similar things to the top end. The API 2500, Urei 1178, Neve 33609, Crane Song STC-8, and A-designs HM2 Nail are all stereo compressors I'd consider for overheads. It's very easy to overcompress overheads (especially with the 2500 and the 1178). Copious compression will tend to extend the ring of the cymbals and the ambience of the room, depending on your attack and release settings. You can't undo that compression later, so be sure the tone suits your recording.

X-Y is probably the easiest method for miking overheads. However, X-Y methods can get a bit tricky with LDCs given their general size and bulkiness. It's far easier to use an X-Y stereo miking technique with a pair of SDCs, and easier still to use a stereo mic. If the kit is particularly sprawling, a spaced pair might be desirable over an X-Y technique.

There will be times that you may prefer to primarily capture cymbal information with your overheads, either because you're using room mics to capture the aggregate, or because you seek to maximize immediacy by relying on close-miking techniques. A ceiling height of eight feet or below will virtually force this decision. A spaced pair of LDCs just a foot or two off the cymbals should help with the maladies caused by a low ceiling.

Be careful about how close you put the overheads to the cymbals. You don't want to pick up the rush of air from a flailing cymbal. Those mics also become susceptible to a strike from an errant stick. If your mics are in danger (and that depends on the overall motion and dexterity of the drummer), then you might consider a compromise placement.

When monitoring drums in isolation, the balance of the cymbals will often sound too loud outside the context of the track. Even knowing that, I get uncomfortable without hearing other instrumentation. I don't care how exceptional your vision, you put yourself in a tough position attempting to make mic placement decisions on drums without context for balance decisions.

Rooms

The overall usefulness of your room mics has mostly to do with the quality of the room itself. Once again, an insufficiently sized and treated drum room will render room mics virtually useless, as the ambient information will contain an inordinate amount of early reflections, which results in phase coherency issues being caused by the room itself. Further, not all drum tones call for room mics, and if you have bleed from other instruments seeping into the drum room, those mics will act as an ensemble-room rather than a drum-room capture.

On those occasions when room mics are a nonstarter, you can always re-amp the drums later in a more appropriately sized room. Whenever I mix in a commercial facility, I ask the assistant to set up two mics and a PA for purposes of a makeshift chamber. I've re-amped to create a usable room mic on many occasions, and while it's certainly not ideal, it can be considerably more organic in tone than a digital reverb.

On those occasions when I use my room mics to capture the aggregate, and the overheads to capture cymbals, I'm likely to record a mono room mic for purposes of ambient smack. Actually, who am I kidding? I almost always record a mono room mic, unless I know for certain I'm not going to need it.

One of my favorite mono room mics is an SM57, particularly for rock drums, and especially in large ambient rooms. Room mics are susceptible to excessive cymbal information, depending on their placement and the overall aggression of the drummer. In order to accentuate the beautiful room action caused by the skinned drums, you need to be sure that you're not also introducing overbearing cymbal information into the balance. Place an SM57 behind a short baffle as distant from the drums as possible, and face the mic away from the drums towards the back wall. Both the distance and the baffle will greatly reduce the cymbals within your mono room mic capture, providing you with the warm ambient slap off the wall. The natural midrange boost of an SM57 accentuates the crack, and minimizes the wash of the room tone.

Compressors are quite useful for room mics, as you can extend the size of the room by bringing up the apparent ambient information in the capture. Compressors can also help you balance your aggregate image, and if you set a VCA compressor to a fast attack and release setting, you can easily distort your room as you simultaneously extend its apparent size. Distorting rooms adds all sorts of goodness to rock drums. The Urei 1178, API 2500, and Neve 33609 are all useful analog room compressors.

How aggressive you want to be with your room compression on the initial recording is a matter of taste and production needs. However, if you seek to smash the room mics, you should do so at a time when you have access to analog compressors. You can always use bussing to record both the smashed and natural rooms at the same time.

If you find that the delay of the room capture (due to distance) is causing the drums to feel out of time, you can use your DAW to slide the audio files back in order to reduce the flamming effect. The room smack is naturally delayed given its distance from the source, but sometimes it's preferable for the tail of the room to occur nearly simultaneously with the hit. That's an artistic decision. In general, the room mics should be far enough away to avoid any overt phase coherency issues with this technique—but always verify.

Once you have a well-placed aggregate image, you can analyze the balance issues by bringing up your close mics. It's fine to work in isolation when you pull your initial close mic tones, but you also need to constantly check them within the context of the aggregate. You don't necessarily want to accentuate the sound of the beater hitting the head if you've already got plenty of that information contained in the overheads, and this could affect your close mic placement decisions. Besides, it's typically the low-end information that needs to be supplemented in your aggregate picture.

Kik Drum

There are a number of ways to dramatically change the overall tone of a kik drum. Many drummers prefer a hole in the resonant head, which allows a rush of air to escape the drum. The hole is placed offset from center so that the air is still given an opportunity to compress and resonate the heads before escaping through the port. A hole in a kik drum head will reduce the overall resonance of the drum. It also gives you access to the inside cavity, which can be handy for miking and dampening purposes.

A kik drum with a hole will likely still require dampening. A pillow pushed up against the beater head, and held in place by a heavy sandbag, will go a long way toward dampening the drum. Some kind of weight is a requirement, otherwise the pillow will migrate, and your kik drum tone could change over the course of a take. Sandbags are exceptionally useful for this purpose.

A rug under a drum kit is a common decision. For starters, it reduces the early reflections coming off the floor. It also prevents the drums from migrating, although you still might need a sandbag or two. If you prefer the tone of drums placed on a wood floor, you can tie the drum throne to the kik drum with string in order to prevent the drums from migrating.

Kik drums sans the hole in the front head tend to resonate more, and can sound as funky as a circus drum or as signature as John

Bonham's kik drum tone on all your favorite Led Zeppelin tracks. Given the lack of a hole, any internal dampening must be achieved by removing the head. The problem, of course, is that you don't want to keep installing and removing a head from a drum, as it will gravely shorten its lifespan.

You can also dampen the resonant head from outside the drum, using a sandbag pressed against it. The more surface area you cover with the sandbag, the more dampening you'll achieve. Keep in mind you're best to allow yourself some measure of resonance, as this is where the tone lives.

Kik drum beaters and their corresponding pads can also have a dramatic effect on tone. A hard plastic beater will produce far more attack than a soft felt beater. Most attack issues can be solved by changing the material makeup of the beater.

Microphones placed inside a kik drum sound highly unnatural, as they tend to collect far more beater information than tone. To make matters worse, the tone can get kind of funky inside the drum itself, to the point that it could sound like a bouncing basketball. That said, I've miked countless kik drums with internal mics, particularly if the kik drum is meant to be placed prominently within the track. Given the sound pressure levels inside a kik drum, dynamic mics are typically best for the job, the most common choices being the AKG D12, or the tried and true classic Electro-Voice RE20.

The RE20 is a ported microphone, and if you'd like to get more low end out of your capture, you can cover up one side of the ports with some gaffer tape. The D12 is a bullet mic designed for kik drums, and tends to sound a bit more modern than an RE20 given its frequency scoop in the lower midrange.

In recent years, dual-capsule kik drum mics have come into vogue. The Lewitt DTP 640 REX, for instance, employs both a condenser and a dynamic, which can be recorded individually.

An inner mic is best offset from the center of the drum, which is where the beater strikes. The hole in the front head is naturally offset. That is, unless someone cut their own hole in the middle, which would have me chuckling for many hours were I ever to witness it. A hole in line with the beater will only manage to allow the air to escape the drum directly. You may as well have no resonant head at all.

Placement of an interior kik mic will often require some adjustment by ear. If you enjoy running back and forth between the rooms because that's how you get your exercise, you can do this yourself. If, on the other hand, you'd like to actually use your ears to determine where the tone best comes into focus, then you'll need an assistant to maneuver the mic as you listen.

An interior mic must be threaded through the hole, which can make maneuvering difficult. Sometimes it's best to locate the placement by removing the mic from the stand. Adjusting a mic in a kik drum attached to a boom is often similar to Snoopy wrestling with a lawn chair, only not quite as funny. You could very well find the best location for the mic is in a spot that you can't actually get to with the mic on a stand. Isn't recording fun?

This is about the time you start to come up with ways of mounting microphones using whatever materials happen to be available, like pillows or gaffer tape. I can tell you, I've recorded more than one kik drum by laying a mic on a roll of gaffer tape inside the drum. When it comes to getting tone, and placing mics in tight places, you do whatever you have to do. And you get a good story, to boot.

An external condenser mic can be exceptional at collecting a more natural kik drum tone. They're also problematic, as they tend to pick up scads of cymbal and snare information. Therefore, it's not necessarily a bad idea to record both internal *and* external kik drum mics. Combining an internal with an external mic in a phase-coherent manner can provide you both a solid attack and a full natural tone.

I often call for an internal and an external mic to be set up on a drum recording session, and I could very well use one, the other, or both, depending on how it's working within the aggregate picture. A large diaphragm condenser mic is a good candidate for the outer kik mic, and you will often find a 47 FET in that position on my sessions—mostly because they reproduce an exceptional low end.

I've even been known to use ribbons as external kik drum mics, as well. Most ribbon mics (other than Royers) can't take the typical SPLs coming from an aggressively played kik without frying the ribbon itself. So this is typically an option best reserved for drums played with finesse as opposed to pure aggression. Make sure that you warn everyone on your session. It doesn't really matter whether that ribbon mic is plugged in or not—if someone sits down at the kit and really socks one, you'll be selecting an alternative mic.

There is another alternative, and that is an SPL filter. This is a very new device, and as far as I know, there is only one being produced, and that's The Blast Pad by Pete's Place Audio. This filter will allow you to place your more sensitive ribbon microphones in front of your kik drum (or guitar amp) without putting the mic in danger. The Blast Pad also happens to be the most impressive pop filter I've ever used. Best of all, you can run it through your dishwasher to remove the usual buildup of mouth smegma.

When recording with an outer kik mic, you can limit its exposure to the rest of the kit with a tunnel. Some engineers build their own. Or you can just do what I do, which is throw up two mic stands and drape a blanket over the booms to form a rather large tent-tunnel.

Blankets are the quick fix, but they do tend to muffle the air around the kik. This can force you into a tough decisions, as the negative side effects of each choice could be equally undesirable in their own unique ways. At which point you might want to design your own tunnel using less absorptive materials.

Speaker mics can be exceptionally useful outer kik mics, as they offer sub-frequency information (60 Hz and below) without capturing the high end from the cymbals. Anything from an NS10 woofer to a large 18" woofer can be used for this purpose. You're not going to need very much of that speaker mic information in combination with the inner mic, and you could very well end up filtering it out later. Not all productions call for a kik drum bloom to live that low.

When recording with both inner and outer mics, it's important that you check for phase coherency between them. You do this by bringing up your intended primary mic, and then introducing your secondary mic methodically as you evaluate the changes in tone. Reverse the polarity on one mic, and compare.

This would be a good place to discuss what you're listening for when it comes to phase coherency between two mics combined to mono. When you flip the polarity on one of the two blended mics, you will likely notice an obvious sonic shift in the low end frequencies, although it will affect the overall tone as well.

A frequency shift is often a result of time-based coherency issues. Given that the outer mic is further from the drum than the inner, you may want to delay the inner mic to match the millisecond or so differential between the mics. The problem is that it's the outer mic that is slightly late. Not the inner. I almost never try to time align the kik drum mics, because I can use that frequency shift and cancellation to my advantage. It's okay if two mics have a phase coherency issue, so long as the issue remains consistent (as it will on a stationary instrument), and so long as they work together to form the totality of your desired tone.

In practical terms, flipping polarity on one of those kik drum mics can offer the difference between a kik drum sounding punchy from a bump in the upper low-end information, or deep from the bloom of sub information.

Given the time differentials between the capsules, reversing polarity will tend to manifest as a shift in the low-end cancellation properties. To make matters worse, you might not be able to place the two kik mics in a way that is fully phase-coherent. At some point you will have to dump a mic, or accept the frequency cancellation that occurs as part of the tone shaping.

Whether you choose the deep kik or the punchy one is an artistic decision, and you will need to fine-tune your mic placements if neither option is working for you. That said, no matter how diligent you are, it's unlikely you can pull them fully into phase coherency without some kind of phase alignment tool like the Little Labs IBP. Offered in both hardware and virtual forms, the IBP will allow you to alter the phase relationships between two mics electronically. You can slide the external mic capture a small measure of time (under 2 ms), to help with the cancellation.

I've recorded a great many drum kits without a phase alignment tool, which is best reserved for problems that you can't overcome through mic placement. Again, it's okay if there is some cancellation occurring. It really can't be avoided. What's important is that all the mics are working together to produce the tone you seek. If you reverse the polarity on one of your kik mics, and you like the tone, then there's no reason to spend further time dicking around. Just be sure that your kik drum mics are playing nice with the rest of the mics on the kit.

Compressing Kik Drums

The difference between a great drummer and a good one, really, is the difference between using many compressors and none.

Let's not confuse purposeful aggressive compression used purely as an effect (like on many of the early Radiohead recordings) with compression used to maintain some dynamic control over an erratic source. It doesn't matter how consistent a drummer is at striking the drums, if you're looking to achieve the heavy breathing artifacts of overcompression, you need compressors in order to pull that tone. Once again, that's an artistic decision.

There's a big difference between a tastefully dynamic performance and an inconsistent one. A drummer who accents the downbeat kik after a slightly rushed sixteenth-note pickup is performing a musical dynamic, which requires musicality and control. When a player isn't fully in command of her instrument, the sound suffers. This describes 98 percent of players, regardless of the instrument. I'm one of them, so don't take offense. Why do you think I record others?

In general, fast compressors are preferable for dealing with inconsistent kik drums. Fast response compressors (like VCAs) can grab quickly after the initial attack, and release in time to allow for the final low-end bloom. If the ring of the kik is overbearing, you can set a release time that's longer than the duration of the sound in order to tamp it down. Commonly used compressors on kik include the dbx 160, Urei 1176, and EL8 Distressor.

Given that compressors tend to bring up ambient information, be sure to check your kik in isolation, especially after the first take. Drummers are notorious for digging in once you start making a take, which could negatively impact your capture. The moment a first take is undoubtedly falling apart, you should adjust your compression threshold levels on the fly. Given the predictability of players performing with more aggression during takes, you may want to back off your compressor input levels in advance of recording your first take.

It would be unusual for an internally placed dynamic mic to pick up an overbearing level of bleed from the rest of the kit. It's the external mic that you need to be mindful of, as it can be quite problematic given its location outside the drum. Even if you've built a tunnel, make sure that you're not getting so much external information that you're rendering that mic permanently problematic. And while gating techniques can be used to remove much of that bleed, doing so kind of defeats the purpose of the exterior kik mic in the first place.

When recording both interior and exterior mics, you have the option to combine them to a single track by bussing the mics together. This allows you to compress the signal as a whole on the path to the recorder. This is standard procedure on my recordings, as I don't want to be dealing with two kik drum tracks throughout my session.

Double kik drums can present themselves as either two kik drums on one kit, or one kik drum with a two-beater pedal. Typically, whenever there are double kik drums, the intent is for them to be somewhat pronounced within the context of the production. Given this, interior mics are often preferred, as two exterior mics can get a bit overbearing given the usual excess cymbal information. Drummers who use double kik drums tend to adore cymbal crashes.

The kik and the snare will most readily define the overall drum tone, and it's worthwhile to invest the thought and time into how they make you feel in the context of the production. On those occasions when you're recording a collection of tunes, whether an album or EP, you can dramatically change the overall feeling of the drums by changing out your kik and snare, even if you touch nothing else on the overall kit.

Snare Drum

Snare drums offer the most tonal context to a track, as they often hit the musically important backbeat, and sit right in the heart of our hearing frequency curve. This also happens to be where the vocal lives. Fortunately, the transient nature of the snare drum strike doesn't fully compete with the vocal. If it did, we probably wouldn't tend to put it in the center of the stereo image.

Snare drums are probably the more challenging piece of the puzzle. The snare is the most insidious of all the drums, given its designed propensity to rattle and their close proximity to the hi-hat. Tuning issues between toms and the snare can exacerbate the obnoxious rattling of snares between drum hits. There is a natural amount of rattle, regardless of how well you tune the drums, but the line between acceptable and overbearing can be thin.

Most snare drums are close-miked from above with a dynamic mic, which would be the absolute worst way to mic a snare drum were it in isolation. The bright cracking tone of the drum is all but lost using a dynamic mic placed inches from the head. Unfortunately, the snare drum is nestled between all sorts of other drums, and if you want control over how immediate your snare sounds, a dynamic inches from the drum is often your best option. The most common top mic used on snare is the Shure SM57.

Every professional recordist has experimented with alternatives to the 57 for the snare drum, and I have yet to find anyone who has found the answer. For a while, I was using a Sony C-55P, and while that produced great snare results, it also presented the same problems that are always associated with miking a snare drum with a condenser. They don't reject cymbal information—in particular the hi-hat.

Even a 57 placed on a snare drum will reproduce an excess of hi-hat information if you don't take some measures to reduce it. The problem is that most drummers, for whatever reason, don't play their hat in balance with their kit. The hat is typically played with far too much aggression, likely because it's difficult to play it with finesse as one whacks the skins with authority. Of course, some drummers have it all completely backwards, and will crush their cymbals as they practically tickle their skins. Your best option is to point this out to the drummer. That's also your worst option, as you are asking her to correct what is likely a lifelong habit in a matter of minutes. Good luck with that.

Hats tend to be exceptionally bright, and the 57 on the top head of the snare quite dark, which could require brightening. To make matters worse, the high-frequency bleed that makes its way into a dynamic microphone tends to be brutally bright and distorted. The moment you begin to compress the snare drum, and/or compensate for the darkness with EQ, you will also bring up the most annoying frequencies of the hat. This would be a good argument for compressing your snare at the time of recording, as then you can judge whether or not you're capturing too much hat information.

The most effective way to capture a snare in isolation is with a condenser off the drum, often pointed at its shell. This too is a technique that just about every recordist attempts at some point in her career. Unfortunately, placing a condenser some distance from the snare will also capture excessive and overbearing bleed. The cymbals could appear louder than the snare itself. Which brings us right back to the 57 inches from the top head.

The way around the dark capture of the 57 is to place an additional mic on the underside, typically an SDC facing upwards with its polarity reversed. This will brighten the overall tone of the drum significantly. It will also introduce snare rattles, which requires balancing your brightness needs against the level of snare buzz introduced.

Since the snare drum itself shields the bottom mic from much of the cymbal information, you can successfully use a condenser, which will offer you a much more open and accurate snare tone without necessarily bringing out excessive and brittle high-end information from the cymbals. Some recordists can't stand the sound of a bottom mic, and will even suggest they have been unable to do so successfully. You could very well come to the same conclusion, but I have yet to find an acceptable way of capturing a kit without implementing a bottom snare mic.

Even after introducing a bottom mic, the high end from the hat can be oppressive. You can reduce that high end bleed by facing the 57 away from the hat, but even that isn't always sufficient. Therefore, you may want to physically block the space between the snare mic and the hat with some foam (or even cardboard) attached to a boom. This should reduce the hat bleed sufficiently, which will also provide you more leeway with your mic positioning. You can also always put some gaffer tape on the hat to knock down the high frequency information at the source.

Some drummers play rim shots on every snare hit because it offers a more aggressive and solid crack. If you find the snare hits lacking a powerful attack, you might suggest the drummer play rim shots.

Different snare tones elicit different responses from the listener. There's the rude snare, which often has an obnoxious overtone that sings on every whack. There's the Al Green snare, which is big, deep, and dead with no ambience. There's the piccolo snare, which is high-pitched in nature. The brass snare, which is brighter than your typical wood snare. Then there is the marching snare, which sports especially tight skins, and requires some amount of finesse. Of course, it would be unusual to include a marching snare as part of a drum kit.

The more snares you can have available for a session, the easier your job becomes when tracking drums. I mean, if a drummer comes in with just one snare drum, and it happens to sound perfect for the production, then that's all you need. The problem comes when you try to make a snare do something it's really not built to do. So if the drummer or producer has radical ideas for varying snare tones over the course of a project, you're going to need several snare drums with their own unique sonic properties in order to achieve this.

Toms

Toms are really a major pain in the ass. For starters, they often sit just below the cymbals, and some drummers place their cymbals with the minimum amount of clearance possible. This can make threading a microphone impossible. If you can't get a mic to a tom, aside from abandoning the close mics, you really only have two choices. You can either ask the drummer to raise the cymbals, or you can mic the bottom of the toms.

As much as I really hate to fuck with any musician by suggesting they physically alter their instrument in a way that makes it unfamiliar, it's sometimes the only viable option. Miking the bottom resonant head on the toms is rarely the answer. Let me put it this way: If you've never miked the resonant head of a tom, you should definitely try it. Frankly, it's been so long since I first and last tried it (they were the same event), I've forgotten what it sounds like—beyond unusable, that is. This leaves raising the physical placement of the cymbals as your only viable option.

While there are a number of clip-on mics that can be used for toms in these situations, they aren't commonly available in the studio.

Toms can be slightly dangerous to compress at the time of recording, given their proximity to the cymbals. As it is, toms will have a sympathetic ring to them that will affect the overall tone of the drums. Further, if you're compressing the overheads, you may not need to compress the toms. Regardless, the most important consideration, besides phase relationship, is the level of cymbal information picked up by the tom mics. Even well-recorded toms can collect an overbearing amount of cymbal and sympathetic shell ring, and this may have to be dealt with later.

Dynamic mics are usually preferred on toms within the context of an entire kit, particularly if you're using them to supplement an aggregate stereo capture. Placing a dynamic close to the skin will reduce the level of cymbal leakage, and provide you with the necessary boost in low-end information for the aggregate picture.

Toms can really sing when they're distorted slightly. A good mic pre is a great way to give the toms a little edge, as the distortion tends to thicken the sound somewhat. Of course, the quality of the distortion really depends on the mic pre itself.

The larger the footprint of a kit, the more toms, kik drums, snare drums, and cymbals, the more strategy involved. I can tell you, I'm not likely to put eight mics on eight toms. It's too many mics! It's far better to put one mic on every two toms in that situation.

Hi-Hat

Many recordists capture the hi-hat with an SDC just above it. I rarely use the hat mic, it's often superfluous to the capture. Given that I work in genres that are suitable for compression, I'm often only managing to make the insidious nature of the hat worse.

When placing your hat mic, you want to be certain that you aren't picking up the blowback of the hat closing, as you will render that track useless later. This will manifest as a surge of low end every time the drummer closes the hat. Pay special mind to how the hat mic is working with the rest.

Be sure that the capsule on the hat mic is facing in the same general direction as the snare mic. This will help reduce phase issues, which won't be a problem once you mute that useless fucking hat mic anyway.

Compromise

Recording a drum kit is an exercise in compromise, as is any recording in which there are multiple mics required. Placing two mics is relatively easy to deal with. Every mic you put on the drums after that is complicating matters significantly, and getting what you deem the perfect tone on each individual drum in isolation is a recipe for failure. Given the tight spaces that we must deal with when threading microphones on a kit, we can't always place them in the ideal position. The mics have to work together as one unit.

This is why I recommend the top-down approach for recording drums, as it forces you to work on the overall tone of the drums. It's certainly not a requirement to use an aggregate capture technique when recording drums. If your goal is immediate, in-your-face drums, then you might want to close mic your cymbals, rather than to capture an aggregate. Of course, that still leaves the room mics for that purpose.

The mere fact that I won't use a condenser microphone on a tom is an immediate compromise. One that has come from experience. That doesn't necessarily mean I won't ever use a condenser on the toms, but I would only consider this approach on a well-balanced drummer.

As you pull your drum tones, it's important that you're checking the phase coherency on each mic in relation to every other mic. You can do this quickly by using polarity reversal buttons as you solo different combinations of mics. Be sure that each individual tom mic is working properly and phase coherent with the overheads. Make certain that mics facing each other are coherent with each other. Check that the snare is in phase with the kik, and the kik with the overheads, etcetera etcetera. And remember, how mics interact will change based on the internal balances, so be sure to manipulate the blends as you check for phase coherency issues.

Bass

Electric bass responds well to distortion, and as such, is best recorded through a bass amplifier. That said, much like drums, recording bass requires space.

Once again, low-end sound waves are long and require an inordinate amount of space in which to fully develop. To make matters worse, low end is not easily absorbed, and as a result, will tend to resonate and interact within a room of insufficient size. Which makes you wonder why so many people stick bass cabs in closets.

Oh, I understand that recordists would prefer to avoid even low-level bass bleed coming through the drum mics. Nothing can cause tuning issues more readily than bass bleed. Any missed notes, or changed part, once fixed on the bass track, will cause a rub in the lower register, which is the most obvious and disturbing rub there is.

A rub is either a tuning discrepancy that causes frequencies to sonically beat against each other, or a note that falls outside of the key. There is nothing worse than low-end frequency beating, as it can be somewhat volatile in nature. You can literally rattle everything in a room from the beating caused by two low notes a semitone apart.

When you record with bass bleeding into other microphones, you risk rubs, especially if there's a mistake. Discrepancies in tuning between the bleed and the fix can cause a rub. This has the unfortunate side effect of causing discomfort in the listener. Depending on the level of bleed, you could be far better off editing together a take of the bass and drums as they were performed naturally, than to punch in the bass mistakes.

Given the choice between recording the bass amp in the drum room and isolating it in an undersized closet, in most cases I'll probably take the closet. But that really depends on how proficient the band is, in particular the bass player. If neither solution seems to work, I might just turn off the amp in favor of tracking the DI for re-amping later, although that's far from ideal.

Most recordists print a DI track as a matter of course, and I'm no exception. Given the prevalence of the overdub process in modern recording, we often lay down the bass at a time when there is limited sonic information. This makes it far more likely to screw the pooch, as it were, where your bass tone is concerned.

While a bass DI tone is generally not preferable, it happens to be usable. Further, virtual bass amps make for rather believable simulators, particularly in the context of the track. In fact, as a third-party mixer, I won't hesitate to dump a problematic amplified bass track in exchange for a DI through a virtual amplifier. Of course, the player can cause resonant and dead notes, as can the instrument itself, all of which will be evident in the DI track. So the DI isn't always the solution.

It's not uncommon for many engineers to use the DI in conjunction with the amp. An amplified signal will be milliseconds behind the direct, which will cause some measure of phase cancellation.

Flipping the polarity on the DI signal will manifest as a shift in the lower frequencies just like I described on the kik drum. Should you seek to put the overall frequency of the bass in the sub territory, you can use this shift to your advantage, but make no mistake, you're dealing with a phase relationship issue.

You can also line up your amp and DI tracks, and then nudge the amp signal by samples until the tone comes into the desired focus. Just keep in mind that the balance between the DI and amp will affect the nature and measure of frequency interaction. Frankly, there's no need to worry about the time alignment while you're recording. That's mostly a mix decision.

You would be well advised to use a quality powered DI, like a Countryman DT85 FET, a Demeter VTDB 2B Tube DI, or the A-Designs REDDI for bass (which is a jewel of a DI that I have just recently discovered). Frankly, I typically use whatever a studio has available, as this is often the least of my concerns. So long as there are no ground-hum issues or a need for extra gain, a passive DI box should be fine. You can also use the DI input of an external mic preamp.

There is no doubt—I much prefer to use an organic amp tone when possible, mostly for the distortion it imparts. The level of audible distortion you record is program- and genre-dependent, but in general you can introduce an exceptional level of distortion before it's obvious within context of the track. Distortion can be handy for bringing out bass motion within a dense track. It also tends to toughen up the tone.

The most commonly found production basses are likely the Fender Jazz and Precision, although there are scads of boutique basses around, many of which I've come across just once. The Hofner bass, which has a definitive hollow midrange that can't be matched, is the signature tone of Paul McCartney. Given its identifiable sound, there are times when a Hofner is the most effective bass for a production. Of course, that requires having one around.

The bass is often the foundation of the track, and a weak bass part or performance that doesn't sing will cause your track to crumble. A sloppily played bass full of inadvertent double notes and pickup clacks will significantly weaken the overall integrity of a track. Even if you have to work one measure at a time to get a bass part that offers a rock solid foundation, it's well worth the time, as it could be the difference between success and failure on any given track.

Obviously, there are productions without bass, and some tracks in which the kik drum delivers the low end harmonic informa-tion. There will also be productions in which the bass is almost inconsequential—otherwise known as holding space—a quality I find less than endearing. In most modern music, however, the bass is an integral part of the production and you would do well to capture a solid and compellingly performed bass part. Whatever that takes.

As a Designated Recordist, studio politics will determine just how involved you are with parts. And since this is a recording book, we're not going to go fully into production decisions. You can pick up *Zen and the Art of Producing* for that. Make no mistake, the bass *part* is equally as important as the bass performance.

There are a number of heads and cabs that are tried and true. The SVT-Ampeg combo is one of the more commonly used recording rigs. The Ampeg cab is often called a "fridge," as it's similar in size and shape to a refrigerator, and I'm talking about the big one in your kitchen. Given its size, the unit requires some space. When recording as an overdub, you can put the head right in the control room with you, which puts the tonal adjustments within reach. You can run a proper speaker cable a long way before you start to lose high end. It's the unbalanced lead line that you need to keep relatively short in order to avoid high-end capacitance.

The Ampeg B15 flip top is a classic bass head and cab combo. There's also a whole plethora of cleaner rigs (a tone I generally abhor when it comes to bass), often preferred by modern R&B and funk players for purposes of a popping bass (one that is played with the side of the thumb in combination with finger plucking). The worst is when you get an R&B rig on a rock session. Clean popping bass tones are not generally the goal in rock productions, although The Red Hot Chili Peppers might have something to say about that.

The five-string bass is also a favorite in the R&B genre, given the addition of a lower string. The fifth string sounds as a low B with a fundamental frequency of just above 30 Hz. That's quite low. Although the five-string bass is more prevalent in R&B than rock, the song key has much to do with the decision to inject a B string into a production, regardless of genre.

The bottom note of a bass and guitar in their natural tuning is an E. This means a song in the key of C puts the player very high on the neck, which results in less low-end information. It can also force the bass player to move in a downward motion from the root position, which is not always musically ideal. A five-string bass allows the player to sound the root C and move up throughout the progression.

There are times when it's effective for a bass player to be in the higher registers. So you don't need a five-string for every track in the key of C. The low B on a five-string is really fucking low. Performing a more melodic bass part in that frequency range is going to manifest as pure mud. If a five-string isn't an available option, you can always drop the bass tuning down to C, at which point you'll get a valuable lesson on intonation problems caused by excessively loose strings.

Basses often have multiple pickups and tone controls. The pickup will make a significant difference in the tone of the bass. Like guitars, there are a variety of pickup styles and placements, and you could get pretty deep into it. As a recordist, I encourage you to research anything and everything that will make you more knowledgeable, but let's be real here. You're not going to pull and replace pickups on your client's bass.

Almost all basses have some sort of tone control that allows you to adjust the overall brilliance of the instrument. Some basses have variable tone controls that allow the player to combine the pickups. Others offer graphic EQ controls.

The tone control on a bass can be quite handy for quick adjustments at the instrument rather than at the amplifier. Unfortunately, bass players (and guitar players) often absentmindedly turn their knobs to the fully closed position immediately upon completing a take. You can mark the tone knob with a piece of tape to protect against this, but the bass player will also automatically turn the knobs up to full before the next take, which kind of negates the whole purpose of the mark. Given this tendency, you're probably better off adjusting the tone at the amplifier.

When dealing with an overt 60 cycle (Hz) hum, the ground switch on the DI box or the amplifier will often fix the problem. Buzzes typically occur when there's a single-coil pickup involved, which are highly susceptible to interference, and we'll discuss those when we get to guitars. Physically turning the direction of the bass player will often reduce the buzz to acceptable levels. Of course, then she has to remain in that position. A double-coil pickup will likely eradicate that buzz, but you could be compromising between tone and noise at that point.

String choice will also significantly affect the tone of a bass. Stainless steel roundwounds are the most common bass strings, which tend to be brighter than the nickel strings. Then, of course, there's flatwound strings. It's the flatwound strings that will offer you the most significant change in tone.

Flatwounds sound almost dead, as they are much darker in tone than rounds and don't sustain the same. You can hear an example of a bass played with flatwounds on Sheryl Crow's "All I Wanna Do," which was performed by Dan Schwartz. There will be productions in which flatwounds are ideal, and you should be aware of this tone, as it can be quite useful.

Most recordists are inclined towards new strings, although there will be times that old strings could be the better option. Old strings serve to reduce both the brilliance and sustain of the instrument, which increases the likelihood of dead notes. If you want the tone of old strings without the maladies that go along with them, flatwounds could be your best option.

A pick used with a bass provides a much brighter and aggressive tone in which the second harmonic (an octave above) is accentuated. Picks are quite useful for aggressive and fast-moving parts. If you find a bass tone needs some grit and growl, a pick is an option worth investigating.

Some bass players are guitar players filling a void, and could require a pick in order to perform. Should you find yourself in a situation where you need the tone of fingers with a player who requires a pick, you want to avoid bright new strings. Try flatwounds. Fortunately, bass players that routinely play with picks typically write parts designed for them.

Compressors shine at controlling low end. For an aggressive bass, a VCA compressor like the dbx 160 can be a good choice. In general, however, I'm much more likely to gravitate towards an 1176, or a leveling amplifier like the Teletronix LA2a or Gates Sta-Level, both of which shine on bass. And if you can ever get your hands on an RCA BA6A, strap that bad boy on your bass track immediately.

Pedals can be loads of fun when recording bass, particularly fuzz bass. The ultimate bass distortion tool is probably the original Sans-Amp, as you can get a beautiful sustaining sawtooth buzz among other useful flavors of distortion. But there are all sorts of pedals for this application. When it comes to bass tone, the denser your track, the more distortion you may want in order to cut through.

I would advise against using high-pass filters during the recording process in general, but especially on bass. The instrument's main purpose is to supply low-end rhythmic and harmonic information to the track. Low end is not information you want to remove until you have the full picture.

It seems there are some territories, Australia for instance, in which high-pass filters are inserted on the mic pre as a matter of course. I even had an Australian studio assistant ask me why I reset all the filters to the off position as I pulled my tones, and I responded with a question of my own.

"Why would I want to get rid of that information?" He didn't seem to have an answer for that.

Low end information is good information. Besides, anything you can high pass before you record, you can easily filter after you record, and it's unlikely you'll have an analog filter the sound of which can't be beat. Therefore, there's really not much point in recording with HPFs. Low end is the easiest frequency to deal with later.

Remember, you're attempting to capture the source. If you think the source has unwanted sub frequency information, then change the pickup, the bass, the amp, the tone controls, the mic, the compressor, or the pre. That's seven places that you can adjust the low end without ever touching a filter.

There are a number of mics that work well for bass, including the 47 FET, RE20, and Beyer Dynamic M160. I've just named a condenser, a dynamic, and a ribbon, respectively, so you have a wide variety of miking options available for bass.

In a good room, you can place a mic several feet from the cabinet. An undersized room will force close miking techniques, and lower overall levels coming from the amp. Keep in mind that bass requires some volume in order to properly move air. The overall high-end and midrange information that supplies the upper harmonic definition of the bass can be adjusted by how you place the mic in relation to the tweeter (if there is one) or the center of the cone (if there isn't). Neither the Ampeg cabinet nor the B15 have a tweeter, so there you go.

I rarely use two mics on a bass cab, although you can certainly introduce a speaker mic in order to capture the sub information.

Acoustic Bass

Acoustic bass (sometimes called a stand-up or double bass, and not to be confused with a guitarrón, which you'll find in your typical mariachi band) can be an absolute nightmare to record, mostly because a high-quality instrument is out of the price range of all but your most successful (or independently wealthy) players. As if that's not enough, it can be challenging to find a good player, as the acoustic bass is a difficult instrument to play well, and the pool of players relatively small.

Most acoustic double bass players will install a pickup that you can record as a DI track. This can come in handy later, as it tends to offer more pluck than low end sustain, not that acoustic basses sustain all that much without a bow.

A tube LDC like a U47 or M49 placed in front of the acoustic bass can work great, especially for bowed bass, which is often performed in a seated position. A plucked double bass is typically performed standing, and this can be more challenging to mic, particularly if the bassist is a twirler. An acoustic bass sits upon a six-inch peg, which can make it nearly irresistible for some players to spin the instrument.

Twirled or not, the acoustic bass is susceptible to motion by a performing player, which can negatively affect your capture. In order to combat this, you can lay an SDC between two pieces of foam with the capsule fully exposed, and then wedge the foam into the bridge of the instrument. This way, as the acoustic bass player moves, so does the mic. Too easy!

Acoustic basses can be plucked or bowed, and once you have a good tone it shouldn't make a difference which. I'm more inclined to use an LDC out in front for a bowed acoustic bass, but I'm not going to waste too much time with that if I already have an SDC wedged in the bridge.

Electric Guitar

Whereas a drum kit is probably the most difficult instrument to record from a technical perspective, electric guitars are easily the most problematic from a musical perspective, mostly due to the mind-boggling range of tonal options available. Further complicating matters is precedent. There are some rather identifiable electric guitar tones that require certain combinations of guitar and amplifier, and if your amp selection is limited and outside of the production needs, you could have a difficult time pulling your desired tone.

When I choose a studio for tracking a rock band, or any band in which electric guitars are an integral part of the sound, one of my main considerations is the availability of certain guitar models—

mostly vintage. There's a reason for this. Instruments made from organic materials, such as wood, tend to improve with age.

That's not to say I wouldn't record a non-vintage guitar. This isn't about snobbery. It's about speed. I know what certain guitar models sound like from various eras, which translates directly into speed. Since vintage guitars are coveted by definition, they are commonly found in studio and player arsenals alike. Given that I see certain coveted guitars on regular occasion, I know what they sound like.

There are certain guitars that have a reputation for a superior tone, which is what defines a guitar as vintage far more than its age. Barring a dud (and much like children), the quality of a vintage guitar is affected over the years by its environment and care. A poorly maintained guitar of any status will make your life more difficult.

A vintage guitar with fucked-up intonation can be a nightmare to record. Intonation is the relative tuning of the instrument to itself. A guitar with intonation issues will have frets that are out, causing tuning problems on some chords but not others, regardless of how well-tuned the open strings are. This is problematic, and if swapping out the guitar isn't an option, you could find yourself recording the guitar parts by the chord. Uy yuy yuy. Been there, done that. A guitar tech could be your best friend in these situations.

The value of a vintage guitar has to do with how the market reacts to certain models and years. A 1958 Gibson Les Paul can cost more than most U.S. houses, and although that's one of the exceptions, it's not uncommon for a vintage guitar to cost in the thousands, if not tens of thousands, of dollars.

Clearly, if you're somewhat isolated, vintage guitars might not be as readily available as they are here in LA. This would be the time to make friends with every guitar player in the area. You'd be surprised what kind of guitars you might find nearby, and you can always trade recording time for a guitar loan. If you're having trouble finding guitar players near you, call the lawyers in your area. They love expensive vintage guitars, and would be thrilled to loan them to you. As funny as that may sound, I'm quite serious.

On those occasions when there's not a vintage guitar to be found, use a non-vintage guitar. Der. There are plenty of great non-vintage guitars. A guitar is evaluated based on the guitar itself, not its model and year. The safe bet is to hire a well-regarded guitar player. Then you can get an inexpensive lesson in guitar tone, and a great performance to boot.

Amplifiers

If you want that identifiable Marshall tone, you kinda need a Marshall amp. If you want the sick uber-distortion of a Mesa Boogie Rectifier, you need a Rectifier. I mean there are so many amps (and lines) that have their own characteristic sound, it's absurd. Just to name a few, there are the Vox AC30, Fender Deluxe, Fender Twin Reverb, Fender Bassman, Fender Bandmaster, Fender Champ, Fender Princeton, Supro Big Star, and Gibson GA-79. There are also the Hi-Watt, Orange, Matchless, Marshall, and Mesa Boogie lines. Don't let size fool you. The biggest guitar sound I ever got was through a Fender Twin with a Gibson SG (Gibson's answer in the early 60s to the popular Stratocaster body design).

In other words, you don't have to have a high-gain amplifier in order to capture a big sound. The Gibson GA-79 amplifier has a midrange that won't quit, and the Supro Big Star can sound enormous. The Fender Twin, GA-79, and Supro are all combos. That means the amplifier and cabinet are contained in one housing, and therefore aren't quite as powerful as a high-gain amplifier, which implements a separate head and cabinet. The kids just love the high-gain amps.

Once again, we find ourselves confronted with the issue of availability. If you don't have a Marshall amp available on a session in which that's the desired tone, you're going to be in a world of hate as you spend hours dicking around with oppressively loud guitars. Unfortunately, you need some volume in order to evaluate the tone of an overdriven electric guitar.

Given the enormous variances in electric guitars, finding the appropriate tone can be nothing short of a maddening hit-or-miss process, particularly with a relatively inexperienced guitar player and/or recordist. There's nothing quite like the amusing scene of a clueless guitar player and a neophyte recordist pummeling themselves with volume for hours in order to come up with a suitable tone. Admittedly, I may be reminiscing.

Many of you won't have access to certain amplifiers, and as such you may be tempted to use amp simulators. While there are certain genres and productions in which an amp simulator could do an adequately convincing job, I haven't found any that actually sound like the amps they model. Besides, sims just don't distort the same as amplifiers. Oh, I'm sure there are all sorts of people who think the amp sims currently available are amazing, and they're great for those times when you find yourself in a pinch. But amp sims pale in comparison to the appropriate analog amplifier, and this is especially true for straight rock.

Obviously, if all you have are amp sims available, then use them. The overall effectiveness of a sim will be determined by the quality of the player, as the performance and the part will outshine the tonal deficiencies. A hack player on a proper amplifier is problematic. A sim will tend to compound problems.

A great player, on the other hand, shouldn't require a sim in the first place. Fortunately, most guitar players whom you could accurately describe as "great" would have at least a few amps and guitars available for your session. So be sure to ask your guitarist to bring everything she's got to the session. I'll warn you now, the definition of "everything" often seems to get lost in translation.

The biggest issue I have with amp sims is their overall versatility. That may sound strange, since when is versatility a bad thing? When you never lock down a tone, that's when. I touched upon this earlier, but I think this point bears repeating.

It seems young engineers and producers commonly record a DI guitar and insert the simulator on the return. This only serves as a temptation to avoid commitment. Hey, if you have the discipline to leave that amp sim relatively untouched on your production—forever amen—then I suppose it's a reasonable approach. Just keep in mind that players react to the amplifier, and the amplifier reacts to the player, and if you don't commit to a tone, to some degree, you're not committing to a performance.

I always find it fascinating when someone sends me a session with DI'ed guitars for a mix. My first question is always the same: "What were you monitoring as you recorded?" There's rarely a coherent answer.

Yes, I realize it seems like a great advantage to have the option to change your core electric guitar tone come mix time. And if you absolutely feel that you need to alter the sound that late in the game, then so be it. But if you've built the track through the overdub process, all of your subsequent tonal decisions have been made based within context of the track. And if you tracked everything together, then you had all the information necessary to make a tonal decision in the first place. A guitar-driven track is practically defined by the tone. Why would you defer such an important decision?

Even if you ignore my advice and choose to leave your options open with your amp sim, a commitment to guitar tone should most certainly be made before the vocal is performed. How can a vocalist deliver an inspiring performance on a track that's not making her feel the intended way? The vocalist is trying to deliver a lyric, and she feeds from the feeling provided by the track. You don't want to leave this to the vocalist's imagination. You want her in a position to perform.

Far be it for me to criticize anyone for changing their mind, but you can't work towards an end game if you refuse to lock in your guitar tones, especially before you overdub a vocal. And while there are times I'll ask a singer to perform on a track that isn't fully realized, that decision is often made due to extenuating circumstances, and it's far from ideal. At that point, I'm pulling the tones based on the vocal, which is both backwards and undesirable.

If you're recording a remix, in which part of the fun is to create a certain disconnect between the vocal and a known song, then you can change your guitar tone anytime you like in the process. A remix is a completely different art form in which its derivative nature defines it. Success is what puts an original track in the position to be remixed in the first place.

Recently, I was challenged in a thread on the Internet by someone who was absolutely convinced that there was no good argument for neglecting to print a DI'ed track for "safety." A safety for what exactly? Bad decisions? Or maybe no decisions? Anytime you defer decisions, you're leaving the results to chance.

We all get lucky, but once you have success, you'll be expected to repeat it. So if your accomplishment is based purely on happenstance, you could find yourself way out of your league in short order. Therefore, it's best to learn how to record towards an end goal, aggressively and decisively.

Clearly, your guitarist is going to want to hear some kind of tone as she records. It would be absurd to record a guitar without monitoring some kind of amplifier tone, even a simulated one, as your player will have no idea what the hell she's playing. A DI guitar tone offers no distortion, no sustain, and no vibe. Given that the tone will affect the performance, you may as well pull one with intent, just as you would with an analog amplifier. This can be a difficult discipline to develop because leaving yourself nearly infinite options is so fucking alluring. But then so are Sirens, which according to mythology, will often result in your boat crashed up against rocks.

I imagine some of you might question why I suggest you defer certain processing, like high-pass filtering and gating, when I'm so adamant about committing to a tone. Quite simply, a tonal decision affects performance. Clean-up processing doesn't.

Choosing to high-pass filter the guitars slightly so as to open up the low end for other areas of the track is a mix decision that does not inherently alter the tone of the guitar, and can be dealt with first through mic placement, pickup selection, and tone adjustment. Any processing decision that affects performance should be recorded. A decision that doesn't affect performance, and permanently removes sonic information that you might need later, should be reserved.

I also recommend you record a bass safety, and not a guitar safety. There's a reason for this. The bass DI can actually be used, and requires far fewer amplifier artifacts to set it off. A guitar DI offers you nothing, other than a performance that has no bearing on any tone whatsoever.

I will spend far more time selecting an electric guitar tone then I almost ever do recording it. Even armed with years of experience, discovering the right tone often involves some measure of trial and error. If you've ever sat in front of your computer switching between guitar amp simulators, then you have some idea of the process, it's just that you don't have to get up from your chair. No, that's not an argument for using amp sims. Get some exercise!

Tone

When it comes to electric guitar, your main consideration is overall distortion properties, as this will have the most significant effect on tone. Not only are you evaluating flavor of distortion, but also level of saturation. If the goal is sustain, a slight breakup is unlikely to inspire, no matter how good the guitar player is.

The nature and saturation of your distortion is dependent on both the part and the feeling you wish to pull from the track. For instance, if you have a guitar part with some intricacies that include licks, it wouldn't make much sense to distort the electric guitar past the point of clarity. A purposefully bright and grating tone is far more effective for a wall of sound on an angst-ridden song, much like Radiohead's "Creep." The guitars in that track are insanely bright and overdriven to the point of instability, which just so happens to mirror the lyric. That's not by accident.

Blues licks are more often just slightly overdriven, as it allows the player plenty of room to use dynamics. A fully overdriven guitar lacks any kind of dynamic, as the gain acts like compression, both electrical and acoustical in nature. As a result, you can put your guitar in a near-steady state.

A good player can use dynamics to control the overdrive, which may include leaving some room on the volume knob or the insertion of a volume pedal. This way, your guitarist can use natural amp overdrive to help build some excitement through the performance. Sadly, not all guitar players have practiced this maneuver enough to pull it off. Most guitarists use gain pedals to make radical switches in distortion over the course of a performance. You can always overdub a sudden gain change.

By the time you're distorting an amplifier, you're pushing the electronics beyond their capabilities, and this has the result of compressing as well as distorting the signal. It's the preamp volume that determines how hard you push the electronics, and the master volume that increases the output level of the amplifier. Once you're pushing the air sufficiently from your amplifier to fill the room, you will introduce acoustic compression. A blaring amplifier in a small room will offer the most obvious and clearly audible example of acoustic compression.

The further the mic is from the source, the more you're using acoustic compression to your advantage. Unfortunately, it's at the expense of a direct tone. Excessive room information is often undesirable on electric guitars. When roomy guitars are desired, you might consider a separate room mic in order to capture the ambient information.

Your frequency curve is yet another consideration. The overall balance of the part within the context of the track will directly affect the perceived EQ curve. An overly bright electric guitar part that is designed to sit within the track could sound like a high end wash due to masking effects by cymbals in the midrange. An overly warm guitar won't cut and can obliterate bass movement.

Since it's typical to monitor an overdub prominently in the monitor mix, you should be sure to check your tone within its intended balance. This will reveal the effectiveness of the tonal frequency curve. Obviously, you have the power to shape the tone later, so don't go crazy seeking absolute perfection. It's the fundamental sound that matters. Get it close if time is becoming a factor.

Some guitar pickups have a higher output than others, and therefore distort the amplifier more easily. This means the overall sound of the amp and its distortion properties will change significantly depending on the guitar itself. A Fender Stratocaster through a Vox AC30 is not going to sound anything like a Gibson 335 through the identical amp, even if you were to match the output levels of the guitars. There's a very good reason for this, and that has to do with the physical makeup of the guitar in conjunction with the nature of the pickups.

For starters, a Gibson ES-335 is a hollowbody guitar. Unless you're a guitar player, or have experience recording a 335, you may not have even known that. Hollowbody guitars are much more prone to feedback than solidbody guitars, and that can work for or against you. Further, the Gibson ES-335 comes with humbucker pickups that have a considerably higher output than the single coil pickups found on a Stratocaster.

Humbucker pickups have two coils, which helps to prevent hum, hence the name. Single-coil pickups, like those found on a Strat, are far more susceptible to noise issues than humbuckers. A high-pitched buzz is often a result of interference with the pickup, but even a humbucker can be susceptible to noise. I've been shaken off a single-coil pickup more than once because of noise issues, and it seems that there's no rhyme or reason as to when such problems arise. You're never safe from noise when you're recording electric guitars. Just as with bass, you can physically turn your guitar player to reduce it, but if that fails, you may have to address your pickup or amp choices.

If you're feeling overwhelmed, don't. No one can be an expert in everything, and although I can recognize a great guitar tone when I hear it, finding the right tone for a recording still requires some participation from the talent. Otherwise, I'm left to my own devices, and I will be limited by my own expertise in such matters. Twenty years of recording guitar is not the same as twenty years of playing guitar. And although I may have a pretty good starting point where an electric guitar tone is concerned, if I find myself in over my head, I won't hesitate to seek help.

Problem-solving is a skill, but it can be difficult to identify solutions to problems you haven't come across before. No matter how long you've been recording, you will encounter situations that are outside of your experiences. You'll often work it out for yourself, but at some point you must factor in time and the destructive forces of frustration upon your session. Without some experience, you might not know to offer a capo when a player is having an issue playing certain voicings. It's way easier for an inexperienced guitar player to perform in the E position compared to the more awkward F position (for example), and a capo allows the guitarist to play in a higher key using the physically familiar positions one might find in the keys of E, A, G, and D. You also wouldn't know that the capo clamped to the eighth fucking fret would explain the lack of low end you're pulling from the guitar. Drop tuning is one way around this.

Guitars are designed to be tuned for the key of E, which keeps the strings in their optimal tension. A song in the key of C, C#, D, or D# can benefit from dropping the tuning of your guitar.

A drop C tuning, which is really the maximum you can reasonably bring down a guitar, will result in floppy strings and intonation issues, just as it will on bass. The floppy strings will manifest as audible buzzes and scrapes, and the intonation issues will force you to tune certain chords to the fret positions for punching. Or you could try to use the polyphonic tuning capabilities of Melodyne, but there's no guarantee Melodyne will be able to track the notes in an overdriven tone. Of course, you could record and tune the DI signal, but then your player isn't monitoring his amplifier, which I advise against. Plug-ins can help you when you have no other options, but generally aren't something to rely on.

I personally like recording in drop tuning for certain productions, as the recording comes off much darker than those in the key of E. The low E on a guitar sounds at a frequency of 82.41 Hz. The low C on a dropped guitar sounds at a frequency of 65.41 Hz, which is significantly lower, and will result in a much deeper-sounding record.

The less you drop, the fewer problems you'll have with tuning. Therefore, drop D is much easier to deal with than drop C. Don't let the inherent maladies dissuade you. Drop tuning can be a worthwhile decision.

Oftentimes, a tonal struggle will result in the brilliant idea to reference other material in search of the tone, and yes, I'm being sarcastic. Referencing other material is typically an exercise in futility, as there is rarely a reasonable comparison to be made. The only real value in this kind of reference is to demonstrate the type of distortion, conceptually speaking. Referencing for purposes of matching a tone is enough to drive any recordist batty. The part, the player, the room, the instrument, the amplifier, and any pedals that may have been used make such comparisons dubious at best.

How are you going to match a tone in which you have absolutely *none* of the original Source Components available to you? Do you really think you're going to come close to a reference tone that works on a completely different track? Even if you could, it's likely not worth attempting, as more often than not, the parts don't even come close to aligning.

Attempting to match the tone of a slightly broken-up, arpeggiated guitar in comparison to a rhythmic funk guitar will be about as fruitful as matching a snare to a kik drum. That's how closely those two tones will correlate given the nature of the parts. More often than not, references presented by clients tend to reflect a feeling rather than a literal example of how they envision a part to sound. Unfortunately, your client will often confuse the two and have you chasing a tone that has no relation to the recording. Your best tool for combating this is to ignore the reference, and pull the tone you think sounds good. That's all your client really wants.

When it comes to music and recording in general, comparisons to finished records in regards to organically produced tones are just about useless. Your overall EQ curve of a track will be dictated by the arrangement and recording decisions over any other factor. If your recording matches up perfectly with a reference such that it provides a veritable sonic roadmap, then it would put into question the uniqueness of your own recording. You're the recordist. Not the duplicator.

There's a ton to learn when it comes to guitars and amplifiers, and it takes time and experience. Given that this is a written medium, I can't go nearly in the kind of depth that you or I might like regarding the characteristics of specific amps and guitars. The challenges inherent in describing something as abstract and subjective as sound can't be overcome. Our adjectives won't necessarily align. Worry not—you will learn all of this over time as you gain experience.

Miking Electric Guitars

Dynamic mics are often the call for overdriven guitars. The most common choice is the workhorse Shure SM57, as it has a pronounced midrange that we like from guitars. A 57 is all you really need to adequately capture an electric guitar tone, although it's a bit limiting. Personally, I much prefer a Royer 121, although I'll certainly use a dynamic at times.

Placing your average ribbon on an amplifier blaring at over 110 dB is generally inadvisable, as you will surely blow out the ribbon within milliseconds of the guitarist's first strike. The Royer 121 is anything but average in this regard, as it can handle outrageous SPLs. As a result, the 121 is often cited as a go-to microphone for electric guitars by many recordists—myself included.

There are certainly times that I prefer a 57 on electric guitar, as it tends to reject everything but the guitar amplifier itself. Given that ribbons are figure-8 by definition, the Royer will pick up both the direct and rear signal, which can be problematic when you're looking for an ultra-dry distorted guitar tone. Placing the amp and mic on a rug and perhaps bringing in an absorptive baffle can offer a bit more isolation from that returning ambience. Turning the brighter rear side of the Royer to face the cab is also a good way to reduce the ambient information collected. But if the ambience is fucking up your tone regardless of modular acoustic treatment, then you might be better served with a dynamic mic.

Rugs are a consideration regardless of the mic you choose. An amplifier sitting on the floor will result in reflections, which might negatively affect your tone. I generally don't put amplifiers on a rug unless there's a problem, and I'm far more likely to bring in a rug when using a Royer. You can also place the amplifier up in the air, or mic the top speakers of a four-cone cabinet, which will reduce the level of early reflections from the floor.

The Royer is far easier to place than a dynamic, because much like a condenser microphone, it's not quite as sensitive to position. This saves me from dicking with a microphone by millimeters, only for some asshole to kick it later—a devastating blow, even when self-inflicted.

My point is, you might find it easier to use a mic that delivers a relatively accurate sonic image of what's coming out of the amplifier, as opposed to using the dynamic mic to help boost the apparent midrange. You should experiment with this in order to form your own impressions. I swear, some recordists are almost allergic to Royers placed on guitar amps, particularly in the hard rock arena. Subjectivity is in full play.

The most commonly used microphones (in no particular order) for electric guitars are as follows: AKG 414, Neumann U87, 67, Electro-Voice 609, Sennheiser 421, Royer 121 and 122, and as mentioned, the Shure SM57.

As much as you want to adjust most of your problems at the source, microphones do influence the tone, and you certainly shouldn't rule out any possible mic choices, particularly in times of struggle. There's no such thing as "exact" when it comes to capturing a source in practical terms—only "effective." Both your mic and pre will influence the overall nature of that translation, as will the mic placement. But frankly, capturing the guitar should be the least of your struggles once you get the tone in the room.

Time is always a part of the equation when it comes to record-ing, and although your primary goal is to get the right tones for the production, there are limits to how far you can take this. It's fairly easy to recognize when you're pushing boundaries in this regard; it manifests as frustration from everyone in the room—including yourself.

There is no better weapon for killing the forward progress of a recording session than frustration. You would do well to deal with this eventuality in a preemptive manner, by explaining the process to your clients and requesting their patience. I do this as a matter of course, so as to buy myself some measure of time. Once a session breaks down to frustration, it's compromised.

Players perform better in the right headspace. Shit, everyone performs better in the right headspace. Struggle begets more struggle, just as success begets more success. I get very nervous when frustration sets in on my session, and will do anything to pull us out of that potentially destructive loop. Getting a good tone quickly is one way to get out of a jam, but that's a rather simplistic solution to what can be a difficult problem.

An uninspiring tone will generate a lackluster performance, just as a lackluster performance will generate an uninspiring tone. Therefore, it's critical to prevent the entire team from falling into the depths of debilitating frustration, even from the position of recordist. As the recordist, you never want to be the cause of problems. You want to be the solution.

The Two-Mic Technique

Some recordists prefer to use two mics to capture a guitar tone, and often record the mics to their own discrete tracks. As a mixer, I will usually dump one of the mics shortly after I listen to them combined. And if there was some sweet magical blend that could have been achieved with the mics, I have to wonder why anyone would ask me to recreate "magical." If you have the key to the best blend of two microphones, then combine the mics so it's no longer up for interpretation.

It's one thing for you to leave yourself options. It's another thing entirely to leave those options to a third-party mixer. The thinking that the mixer is better qualified to make those kinds of balance decisions is by its very nature defeatist. Why would a mixer, no matter how successful, be more qualified to determine the best fundamental guitar tone for *your* recording?

Self-doubt can be just as debilitating as a delusional ego. As someone who beat himself up relentlessly in the early stages of my development, I understand all too well the wild fluctuations that occur in the constant battle between ego and insecurity. It's far better to be wrong than it is to be timid. Your mantra should be the same as the musician's: if you're gonna play it, play it loud. When you metaphorically play it loud, no one will ever doubt your intent.

You learn from your mistakes, and if you're constantly trying to avoid mistakes because of what you read on the Internet, or in this book, or anywhere else, you may just avoid success. You have to trust yourself. And even if your confidence is shaky in regards to recording, then trust that you're going to figure it out. It's a long slog learning how to record, and self-doubt, while important for keeping the ego in check, can be a destructive force if allowed to dominate. A tone that leaves you wanting more, needs more. A tone that leaves you feeling good is right. Believe that. Lock it down.

Please pardon my digression. We now return to our regularly scheduled discussion on miking electric guitars.

I've heard great guitar tones captured with two mics in close proximity. To date, none of them have made it on anything that I've recorded. Barring a designated room mic, I much prefer a single point of collection.

I can assure you, were my good friend Slipperman writing this book, or perhaps this section, he would tell you that he has no problem recording distorted guitars with two dynamic mics. Yet somehow, we both successfully record electric guitars on regular occasion.

Miking technique is personal. I once joined a session as a recordist midstream and found myself completely lost. The producer, wishing to be efficient, requested that we stick with the miking decisions of my predecessor. I was so far out of my comfort zone that I couldn't operate—certainly not quickly.

The whole point of the setup is to speed up the recording process. Unfortunately, I was not the architect of this setup. As a consequence, the session was anything but efficient. Once the producer realized how hamstrung I was (I had recorded several albums for him at this point), he released the shackles and allowed me to use the techniques that made sense for me. Things went much faster after that.

Were I to hire Slipperman as a recordist (or vice versa), there would have to be some give and take between us. He would have to adjust to me as the producer, knowing that I prefer to record aggressively. I would have to adjust to him, knowing that he's going to choose to record using mics I'd never even consider. So long as we both worked together towards the same goal, there wouldn't likely be any problems.

As a learning recordist, you need to try any and every technique you can in order to discover what works for you, and this will change throughout your career. I had tried and failed at a two-mic capture of guitar many times before I came to my conclusions on this technique. You should too.

Whether seasoned recordist, neophyte, or anywhere in between, there are times to experiment, and there are times to get a mic up and record. You have to pick your moments. It's fine to try new techniques in the heat of battle, and a creative recording idea can have a significant impact on a production. Still, you should be prepared to abandon those beautifully whacky ideas if your attempts are getting in the way of forward progress. This too is all a part of the learning process.

Although I don't prefer the sound of two mics on an amplifier, it's not because I don't understand how to do it. Learning how to place mics in close proximity is as easy as learning the sound of an incoherent phase relationship. Once you know what you're listening for, you have the tools necessary to use this technique on any sound source.

My issue with the technique is that two mics on a guitar amplifier makes life exponentially more difficult where capture is concerned, since the distance between the mics, the distance of the capsules from the cabinet as they relate to each other, the distance of the capsules from the floor as they relate to each other, the location of the capsules within the circumference of the cone, and the relative balances between the mics themselves will all affect how they interact.

Now you're getting some idea why I prefer a single point of collection. It's way fucking easier. I would much rather spend my time getting the tone at the amp, and collecting it with one mic, than to spend my time trying to generate the tone by moving two dynamics by millimeters along three planes in order to achieve a great tone that's also phase coherent.

A two-mic technique all but requires assistance, as the interactions must be evaluated by ear. The best approach is to get the first mic placed in a manner that gets you 80 to 90 percent there, and then to have your assistant maneuver the second mic until the tone comes fully into focus, such that any cancellation that occurs benefits the guitar tone. Lock it down. Then bus them to a single track.

Oh, I'm sure you just got very uncomfortable at my concept of bussing the two mics to a single track. But you have to remember, that tone you're monitoring is not just a function of where those mics are placed, but also the relative balance between them. Changing that balance will cause obvious shifts in tone. I suggest you bus the two mics together and be done with it.

At the very least, print the mics so that the magic balance between them is represented by the two faders at unity gain. This way you can always get back to the blend you had at the time you recorded.

You can also get creative with that second mic. The back of the amplifier can offer some interesting results (don't forget to flip polarity if necessary!) You can use a second mic as a room mic. And of course speakers are an excellent choice for capturing the sub frequencies.

I've even been known to mic the strings of the electric guitar, like it were an acoustic, which can be combined with the amplified tone. This can provide you a bright string attack in conjunction with your amplified tone, and it's a technique that can prove useful at times. I wasn't even going to bring up this technique, until my friend Aardvark mentioned it in a recent conversation. To which I responded, "I thought I was the only one who ever did that."

Apparently not. I'm not sure whether the belief that I was alone was a result of delusional ego or self-doubt. Regardless, there's no such thing as a technique that is yours alone. If you think of it, chances are someone else thought of it before you. So you're neither unique nor alone in this regard.

If your goal is to become a Designated Recordist, then you should experiment with placing two mics on the guitar amp, and you should develop strategies where mic selection and placement are concerned. If, on the other hand, recording will remain your secondary job as either the producer, musician, or artist, you should keep your techniques as simple as possible, and as complicated as necessary. You have bigger fish to fry.

Overdubbing Electric Guitar

When recording electric guitars as overdubs, it's not a bad idea to put the guitar player in the control room with you. It's considerably easier to communicate with a player sitting right next to you than it is through the talkback system. It's also more pleasurable to perform using monitors as opposed to headphones. The biggest hurdle to this are your cable runs.

An amplifier head can be put in the control room with you and your player, and you won't lose top end from a proper speaker cable, regardless of length (within reason). It's the combo amplifiers that make life difficult because long guitar leads will result in high-end loss. The shorter the guitar lead, the less lossiness. This malady will be quite obvious when your guitarist gets her tone at the amp with a short lead, only to plug into a 50' lead in order to reach the combo from the control room.

There are solutions for this, one of them being the Little Labs Mercenary Edition STD, which is an instrument-cable extender and splitter. This sub-$150 box will allow you to make long cable runs without the consequence of high-end attenuation due to capacitance issues. Generally, you're good with cable runs under 20 feet. Anything longer will likely be problematic. Just don't sacrifice your guitarist's general mobility for cable length. You could very well buy yourself top end at the expense of her ability to perform.

An unstable guitar that is prone to feedback is caused by the sound coming from the amplifier returning into the pickups. You can cause this interaction in the control room too. All you have to do is sufficiently turn up your monitors, although you might want some ear plugs. Guitarists just love it when you put earplugs in while they play! You can even help to induce feedback by adjusting the volume during the take.

Some guitar players might prefer to perform their more unstable tones near the amp, as they can induce the feedback by physically approaching it. If that makes your performer more comfortable, I'm all for it. Most players, however, end up right back in the control room, as it's kind of hard to hear through the headphones when you're standing in front of an amplifier emitting 110 dB of earsplitting electric guitar and its corresponding feedback.

Pedals and Effects

Whereas there are probably hundreds of guitar amps, there are easily thousands of guitar pedals (aka stomp boxes), and as a recordist, you likely won't hear (or at least remember) more than a few dozen in your career unless you're a collector.

Although many distortion pedals offer a quick, hands-free way to kick in overdrive, there are also any number of distortion pedals that offer a unique tonal quality, making them useful in the studio. Distortion pedals can help if you're dealing with a short supply of amplifiers. You're not going to achieve that classic Marshall tone with a pedal, as they aren't designed to mimic tone as much as to quickly alter its sonic characteristic. On those occasions when you can't seem to get enough sustain from your amplifier, pedals can save the day. A generic Tube Screamer can be quite helpful for pulling sustain from a guitar.

Unfortunately, at up to a few hundred bucks a pop, it's unlikely you'll have an enormous collection, and I'm not sure why you'd buy a whole shitload of pedals when you could just as easily purchase a few good amps. Amps tend to be more versatile and useful, as there are all sorts of pedals out there that I would describe as nothing more than one-trick ponies. It's just that sometimes it's a great trick.

Many guitar players carry a pedal board with a variety of pedals from distortion, to modulation (phaser, chorus, flange, tremolo), to delay. Most pedal board rigs are a clusterfuck, and unless the pedal board is an integral part of the guitar player's sound and versatility, you would be wise to disconnect pedals that aren't in use. The jumper cables used to connect pedals are often the cheapest ones available, and while I'm not much of a nut about cables, cheap jumpers certainly don't help matters. Neither does running your audio through bypassed pedals.

Some guitarists have effects rigs that they consider part of their sound. These rigs can include tabletop and rack-mountable digital processors, some of which are often nothing more than simulators.

Rack mount and table top multi-effects units are often set up to pull quick, easy, and versatile tones, prepared well in advance of your session. And while that's a great time-saver when working with a sideman, or a live player, it's kind of lame from a recording perspective. Why would you want to record a simulation when a rather small investment in your time can give you the real thing?

"Why, that's a fantastic tone, it reminds me of a Rockman, can we plug into this GA79 now please?"

I mentioned the GA-79 before, and really the only reason I'm familiar with this amplifier is because they have one at Echo Mountain Studios in Asheville, North Carolina. I've produced and recorded several albums there over recent years, and I have fallen in love with the sound of this amp for its definitive midrange— much like a Rockman, only good.

Of course, getting a GA79 in your room is probably more trouble than it's worth, given their rarity. I can get just about every amplifier known to man in LA, and that one could be difficult to find. The point is, it kind of defies logic to try to simulate a tone in which the tools are available to capture the real thing. Who knows? The processed tone could win the day, but you'll never know if you don't compare within the context of the part and production.

When evaluating an obviously processed tone, genre is certainly a consideration. I would be nothing short of horrified to record a simulated guitar tone on most straight-ahead rock bands. I'd certainly protest such a suggestion, even in the position of Designated Recordist. I might even ruffle some feathers in the process, but I can't sit idly by as someone performs a pale imitation of a tone that can be achieved with just a little bit of effort. There is a time to be a purist, and recording a straight-ahead rock production is one of those times.

There are some genres in which a simulated and/or processed tone is almost a prerequisite. This has much to do with sonic fashion, and even more to do with the relative importance of the guitar tone in relation to the production. There is likely no point in hunting down a vintage amplifier to record what amounts to a single distorted guitar hit occurring in the bridge of a pop song. That would be a poor use of your time, and this would bring purism to new and impressive levels of wank.

Frankly, I fucking hate the sound of digital processing on guitars. Even on records where it's appropriate to have that plastic 80s tone,

I can't help but cringe. I'd sooner get that processed tone using an amp with pedals, but I'm admittedly a bit of a purist when it comes to guitars—wank or no.

I recorded a guitar player recently for one of my productions, and he, like many guitarists, would occasionally kick in a digital delay. Now, there's nothing wrong with a digital delay pedal for certain tones, particularly pop. This band harkened back to a more classic rock sound, and to me the digital delay stood out like a sore thumb, particularly since we had a plethora of vintage guitars and amps available to us.

I use digital delays frequently, so don't get bogged down by my overt claims of disdain. This was purely a case of matching the appropriate tone to the record. It seemed to me that this would be a good time to bring out a Roland Space Echo, which is a modular analog tape delay the size of a small breadbox.

When I make suggestions in a recording session, even when I have acquired the full trust of my performers, I sometimes feel as though I'm speaking Chinese.

"Hey, let's try a Roland Space Echo instead of your pedal."

"But that's my pedal, man."

Then we plugged it in.

That digital delay pedal never came up again on that session. Whereas an analog tape delay is cumbersome and wholly inconvenient in a live situation, it was nothing short of magical for a recording. The guitar player now recognized the digital delay pedal for what it really was, an easy way to mimic what an analog tape delay does better. In the studio, it's no more difficult to use a tape-delay simulation pedal than it is to plug in the real thing.

So how big a difference would it make had we recorded all the delays with the pedal? That would be impossible to measure, really. The nature of that delay will certainly have an effect on how the track feels, and this will have an effect on how the singer performs. Since the goal of this album was to produce an organic feeling, it was reasonable for me to do anything and everything to work towards that goal. When it comes to art, the finest details can make a big difference.

Honestly, sometimes when I bring out old analog gear I feel like a dinosaur. But the thing is, even the youngest players become believers upon hearing the results for themselves. A guitar and an amp that's twice the age of the performer shouldn't be dismissed as archaic kit. I have yet to meet a young guitarist who couldn't wrap their head around the tone (and feel) of a great vintage guitar through a killer amplifier.

Pedals and digital effects processors can easily make a guitar tone dated, especially for a rock production. You'd think that the Vox AC30, popular in the 60s, would sound dated, but they are still used regularly for modern recordings. Organic tones never go out of style.

Even dated tones could be desirable, and I leave those decisions to you. But we can't ignore the fact that we go through definitive sonic fashion trends when it comes to productions. The SPX90, one of the most god-awful digital reverbs ever produced, can be heard on nearly every major production from the mid- to late 80s. If you want a dated sound, it only makes sense to use the gear that achieves it best. If you want a tone that will never go out of style, use good instruments and good amplifiers, regardless of their age.

There is no piece of gear that I won't use, given the right circumstances. I would use a fucking Rockman if that's the kind of tone I wanted. It's an atrocious tone. But it evokes a feeling nonetheless. It's a tone that has precedence in popular music, and you've heard it on countless records. That fact in and of itself makes it a viable tone for purposes of manipulating the listener through your recording.

Of course, we're talking about pedals, and I've managed to completely digress to tape delays, SPX90s, and Rockmans. Welcome to my world of non-linear thought processes, brought on by years of recording. Perhaps that's why I'm so attracted to it in the first place.

Acoustic Guitar

There is nothing I find more annoying than two mics on an acoustic guitar. I find it baffling as to why anyone would want to put two mics on a mono source point that isn't fully stationary, especially for the stated goal of a "stereo" acoustic guitar.

Two microphones in close proximity to a rather compact collection point for stereo capture makes absolutely no sense. Remember, you need time differentials in order to properly record a stereo signal. Drums take up a large swath of real estate, and so when you stereo mic the drums, you have all the time differentials that you need to create a coherent stereo image. An acoustic guitar isn't large enough to offer a significant time differential for a phase-coherent image, and so the guitar will tend to wrap around your head within the stereo field.

Any time the listener can notice what you've done in a recording or mix, you're greatly reducing the effectiveness of the production. If you want stereo guitars, you're far better off recording two mono guitar passes, as they will be absolutely phase coherent within the stereo field, and will offer you the full width of the stereo spectrum.

I'm not a fan of using two mics on acoustic guitar combined in mono either. Many recordists put a mic on the bridge and another on the 12th fret (which is in the middle of the neck). I would argue that if you like the sound of both positions, then just place one mic between those two locations. If the two mics aren't coherent in stereo, they certainly aren't coherent in mono.

It's pretty rare for me to use two acoustic mics in a mix. They almost always have obvious issues when combined, and I don't understand how anyone could record with two mics when they are quite obviously negatively interacting.

There's a big difference between placing two mics on a stationary source compared to a shifting one. An amplifier sits on the floor motionless, and once you lock down your mics on the amp, the phase relationship doesn't change. An acoustic guitar either sits on a player's lap or hangs in front of her torso. Even a slight turn in position will change how the sound reaches the two mics. That will result in obvious comb filtering.

An acoustic guitar can be a powerful rhythmic and harmonic force in a production, and you weaken its effectiveness when you attempt to record it with two microphones. I've literally recorded hundreds of acoustic guitars with just a single point of collection. There's absolutely no reason to complicate matters, especially if you're not a Designated Recordist.

If you really want an acoustic guitar to appear stereo in the production, you can place a mic in the room, giving you the kind of time differential necessary to accomplish a stereo image. This may or may not be useful depending on how much is going on in the production. Obviously, the room mic won't sound nearly as immediate as the close mic, and the room could be swallowed up quickly in a track that also includes distorted electrics.

When it comes to recording acoustic guitars, condensers like an AKG 451, Schoeps CMC5-U, Neumann KM 84, AKG C12, or Neumann U47 are all good choices. Overall I prefer SDCs (especially the 451), but there are occasions that an LDC might prove preferable, particularly if you're struggling with an SDC. Condensers are exceptional for capturing the full brilliance of an acoustic guitar. Ribbons also make a good choice, especially if you want to mellow the top end of the instrument.

Be mindful of the sound hole when placing your mic. This is where the low end emits, and a mic placed directly in front of the sound hole will result in a boomy and volatile tone. You can deal with this malady by placing the mic off the sound hole either towards the bridge or the fret board. The bridge placement does start to get a little honky in tone, which can be useful or not. You can also back the mic off the guitar, but be aware of how much room information you're collecting.

It's really important that you actually listen to the acoustic guitar in the room before you try to capture it. That goes for any source, really. For starters, it's not uncommon to have more than one acoustic guitar available, and it's kind of helpful if you know what they sound like before you go picking one. Further, if you listen to the guitar, you can actually use your ears to locate the sweet spot. Imagine that, using your ears to find the location in the room where an instrument sounds best. Who woulda thunk?

Dynamic microphones on acoustics can offer an interesting and effective tone. While a dynamic like a 57 sounds atrocious on an acoustic guitar in isolation, it can provide just the kind of mid-range presence needed to cut through crunch guitars. A brightly nuanced acoustic guitar in the midst of distorted electrics can be rendered to nothing more than high-end finger slides in context. This occurs due to frequency masking effects. Essentially, the electrics will tend to obliterate the shared frequencies of the acoustic, leaving only the less-desirable artifacts to appear in the mix balance.

You can only place acoustic guitars so loud in a mix before they dwarf everything. They are generally broad instruments that take up an inordinate amount of sonic space compared to their relative size. A 57 will capture with a pronounced presence and limited brilliance, which can allow you to place them audibly in the mix without dwarfing the other instruments.

Some of you might get quite uncomfortable at the prospect of using mic selection to mangle tone. Such trepidation is understandable as you may feel you'll be judged based on your capture in isolation. This is something that every veteran recordist has grappled with early on in their career, and the ultimate conclusion is the same. Get over it.

Your job is to capture the tones in a manner that best serves the recording, and there is no good argument for recording a full-range acoustic guitar that clearly should be knocked down in fidelity. You make yourself far more valuable as a recordist if you record for the situation, and not for the glory of a gorgeous tone that's essentially useless for the production at hand. Your perfect acoustic guitar tone is anything but when it doesn't work within the production itself.

Of course, you won't always have absolute clarity on this, in which case, you're best to leave yourself room to maneuver. It's easier to dumb down a brilliant tone than it is to pull air from a dynamic mic.

Acoustic guitars can be exceptionally dynamic instruments, and as a result, compressors and limiters are often desired. Fast VCAs like the dbx 160, 165, and 165a are all reasonable choices. The Neve 2254, Neve 32264a, Inovonics 201, and almost never to be left out, the FET-based Urei 1176 are all exceptional for compressing acoustic guitar. The aggressiveness of your compression has most to do with the overall arrangement. A sparse track may be better served by the full dynamic of the performance.

Acoustic Guitar/Vocal

Some players find it far easier to play as they sing, which often translates into better performances. The decision to record an acoustic guitar and vocal at the same time is most commonly made on sparse tracks, which means your recording is fully exposed.

A microphone on the vocalist perched two feet above the acoustic guitar mic will produce swirly results due to comb filtering under the best of circumstances. This problem becomes far worse with someone like Ben Harper, who is nothing short of animated when he performs—even in the studio.

Sometimes Ben whips his head so violently in the midst of a performance, that I wonder how it manages to stay attached. And you know what? I have never, ever, not once, ever suggested that he limit his motion. This would significantly and negatively affect his performance for the worse.

There are ways to mitigate the swirliness between the two mics. For starters, you might want to use a dynamic on the vocal, since it will tend to reject far more of the acoustic guitar than a condenser. You can also insert a pickup into the sound hole of the guitar. Unfortunately, even the best pickups produce a rather undesirable plucky and distorted tone. This can be tamped down slightly by combining the pickup with a condenser mic, but then you're dealing with swirly vocals again.

Really, vocals with momentary comb filtering and motion in the sound field aren't a big deal. I've mixed countless tracks recorded this way, and yeah, it's not a pristine way to record, but it sure is raw. And if you're going to try to capture a raw inspired performance of a guitar player singing his song, a raw recording would seem completely appropriate.

There is one other solution I should tell you about, and that's the Mag Mic, which is an insertable pickup with a condenser microphone as part of its design. A thumbwheel on the unit allows you to adjust the blend between the pickup and the tiny internal mic. The result is a much less plucky tone, and given the tiny mic's location directly under the strings, its rejection qualities are exceptional. You might record the acoustic with a condenser too—this way you can figure out the best combination later rather than flogging your artist for an hour just to pull a tone.

I received a track once for mix that was recorded with a single microphone capture of the singer and his acoustic, and it was completely balanced. In this particular case, the artist was the recordist, so he was willing to spend the time necessary to find that perfect placement and keep himself motionless in the sweet spot. In general, this is a tough proposition. Most performers don't want to be hamstrung in this way, and even this particular performer might have been better served with a rawer treatment.

Sidechaining can be a useful tool for dealing with a vocal that's coming through the acoustic guitar mic. Insert a compressor on your acoustic guitar track, and feed the sidechain with the vocal. This way, anytime the singer belts, the vocal compressor will attenuate the vocal bleed on the guitar mic. Voila!

It'll still be swirly.

Creating Guitar Textures

When it comes to electric guitars, texturing can be an effective recording technique. The most common texturing technique is the doubling of guitar parts so as to pan them to the sides. This gives you a bigger sound, and a more symmetrical sound field. I don't bring up symmetry as though it's somehow always desirable. It's not. Contrast is an important tool in music production and you reduce contrast when you work at all times in symmetry. Without asymmetry there is no symmetry.

Doubling guitars and panning them hard to the sides (don't be afraid, you can use the full width of your sound field), offers a much larger sound than a single panned guitar. The big chorus is often a desirable time to fill up the sides with your electric guitars, offering you both symmetry and contrast for purposes of lift.

When you double blaring guitars from top to bottom of a track, you greatly weaken the overall contrast of the production. Some recordists lay down doubles of everything as a matter of course, and then dump what they don't need later. This is not only a waste of time, you risk your "safety" doubles making the mix, especially if you and your clients get used to hearing the track that way.

One of the more common doubling procedures is to record the identical source twice, with little to no variation in part. You will achieve an obvious natural chorusing effect using this technique. While there's certainly precedence for this, it produces a rather one-dimensional sound. Natural chorusing obfuscates tuning issues. It also softens tone. In general, distorted electric guitars aren't chosen for their softness of tone, and polyphonic tuning issue aren't so easily veiled as that.

In order to pull some texture and width from your guitars and simultaneously reduce the chorusing effect, you should consider recording your double with its own discrete tone. This is most easily achieved by performing the double with a unique amplifier and guitar pairing.

Keep in mind, and we discussed this, copying a guitar part to another track and panning them to the sides will manifest as a mono guitar up the center. You would have to delay one side by about 20 ms in order to throw the guitars to the sides, and there will be frequency cancelation caused from this. While you might be able to convince me that this is a reasonable concept with a mono string pad (which it really isn't, although I did it early in my career) you will never convince me that this is anything but madness when it comes to electric guitars. If you want coherent stereo guitars playing in time (musically speaking), you *must record two discrete guitar performances*. There is no way around this.

The more you alter the source for a double, the more texture and width you will get from your guitars. Just changing out the guitar alone will greatly improve the width and texture of your doubled parts. A second player will produce the most dramatic results, as technique-induced timing discrepancies are far more significant between performers. Unfortunately, there isn't always a second player up to the task.

Frankly, I find the concept of doubling the identical guitar source as nothing short of aggravating. A blasé attitude is a cancer upon the process, one that may not fully metastasize until it's all but too late. Don't be a cancer to your session.

Should you choose to record an identically sourced double for artistic purposes, I can't possibly criticize. More often than not, this technique is used as a way to keep the session moving. As much as speed is a consideration, it should never, ever be at the expense of the production. If you want to experience for yourself what electric guitar texture can bring to your life, then I would suggest you record both a strict double and a nuanced double, and make a direct comparison.

I can assure you, mangling the tone of an identically sourced double is an exercise in futility. You will never be able to overcome the fact that the two parts are nearly sonically identical aside from the timing discrepancies. No matter how you process that double, you can't alter the sonic fingerprint produced by the same player, with the same guitar, through the same amplifier, captured by the same mic, in the same placement, through the same mic pre, into the same converter, onto the same DAW. The apparent width of your track will be compromised.

The layering of guitar tones is also a useful and common production technique, one you should certainly explore. The problem with layering is that you once again risk introducing a natural chorusing effect. Layering guitars is a technique commonly chosen by neophyte recordists for a big sound. Your results will often be the opposite.

If you record six distorted guitar parts of the exact same source material for the purpose of building the most massive guitar tone ever, what you will achieve is a phase- and chorus-riddled mishmash of guitars, the result of which will be a complete loss of power. Now, if you're recording the same part repetitively for purposes of creating a fucked-up, phase-induced abortion of a tone, this is a really cool way to achieve it, and I recommend you record the part 10, 20, 30 times or more, if only to experience the effect for yourself.

In order to get a really big guitar sound you only need two guitars: one for the left, one for the right. So if you've been wondering what the secret is, that's it. Yes, there could be three guitars at times, even four or five, but the main power of the track need only come from two. Layering comes into play when you seek an interesting and textured wall of sound.

The closer in tone and part the layers are, the more obvious the natural chorusing. While a chorus effect from a plug-in can be useful for making a part pop through a dense mix, it's the distortion properties and the frequency sweep that cause this effect. Natural chorusing doesn't tend to introduce these properties, but rather tends to obfuscate tuning and blur definition. It's like the sonic equivalent to airbrushing.

The key to successful layering has as much to do with arrangement as it does tone. Variance in part and tone is what makes a layer most effective, although it's the unique motion of the part that make this technique shine.

Distortion properties are probably your most significant consideration when adding layers, as combining excessive breakup will result in nothing more than an undefined mess. If your primary guitar parts are overdriven, consider layering a cleaner, more defined part in order to accentuate the undefined melodic top note movement of your distorted guitars. You can also layer in a clean part containing countermelodies to the original. The result will be a distorted tone, with internal motions that couldn't possibly be performed in a single pass. Most listeners won't know this.

Acoustic guitars can be exceptional doubles to overdriven guitars, and even if recorded cleanly, can produce a massive guitar sound. In fact, you often can't tell that there's no overdrive on the acoustic side. I tend to record acoustics for this purpose with a 57 for the apparent midrange and reduced top end. Amplifying the acoustic is also quite effective for this technique, although I don't generally gravitate towards the effect.

Piano

Piano is probably the second most difficult instrument to record well, after drums. It's large and unwieldy, and occupies a substantial footprint in its grand form.

As source instruments, pianos come in all different shapes and sizes, each of which will require unique recording strategies. Further complicating matters, no two pianos sound the same. You will come across good and bad specimens of any and every type of piano there is. While I could tell you that Steinways are typically warm in tone, and Yamahas generally bright, that doesn't change the fact that one of the warmest pianos I've ever recorded was a Yamaha. Brand and model is mostly irrelevant. You have to *hear* a piano in order to judge it.

Unless you're recording Elton John, who will bring in pianos that he's personally selected, your supply of available pianos is likely somewhat limited to geography. If you have your own piano, then I would assume that's what you'll record most often. The fact that you only have one piano puts a bit of a dagger in your ability to alter the source for purposes of capture. It's not like you can just swap out pianos at will. They're basically furniture.

Of course, some of you are thinking, piano tone? I can get lots of piano tones!

Yes, sample pianos are quite convenient, and can provide a totally appropriate piano tone for certain productions. Just recognize that as of this writing, I've yet to hear a piano sample that sounds convincingly like a real piano. I imagine that will change one day, but the interaction between piano strings makes sampling a piano far too complicated, and the computer processing required to account for this is currently prohibitive.

An acoustic piano can offer you a richness that you're not going to get from even the most convincing sample, although an amazing player can mitigate the problem slightly. If you find yourself recording a sample piano, and it leaves you somewhat wanting, then you should consider recording an appropriate analog piano. Most commercial studios will have a piano, and if there's a particular tone you have in mind, then you may have to go on the hunt. So if you seek the tone of an acoustic piano, you should record one.

Pianos are full-range instruments, with loads of string interaction and overtones. Given their size, they're often recorded to fill the entire stereo field. Such a treatment eats space. This is not a knock, it's a fact. If the piano part is sitting within a rather dense and wide track, you don't necessarily want a stereo piano. When you find space to be an issue, consider a reduction in the piano's overall sonic footprint.

Stereo pianos placed within a guitar-driven rock production can be particularly problematic as they reside in the same frequency range as the electrics. This causes a masking effect, which occurs between two instruments covering the same frequency spectrum. You can combat the masking effect by recording a mono piano internally panned away from hard-panned guitars. An overcompressed mono piano on the opposite side of your overdriven guitar is another interesting technique. There is no point in recording a stereo piano if the part is best served in mono.

Pianos have sound holes, and if you want an accurate capture, you should avoid placing a mic anywhere near them. Should you seek a more radical representation of a mono piano, you can stick a 57 just above one of those sound holes and crush it with an analog compressor, preferably one with relatively slow response time. Vari-mu and tube compressors are ideal, Distressors work great if a tube compressor isn't available.

Setting a relatively fast attack, a super slow release, a high ratio, and a radical threshold can offer you the iconic Beatles piano tone in which the overtones are just as prominent as the fundamental frequencies. This is very effective for cutting through a big rock production, although even in mono, the compressor-induced steady state will still eat significant frequency space in the production.

When it comes to piano of any variety, you can't name a mic, nor a placement, that I wouldn't consider using, and while that may be partially true to recording in general, pianos are an instrument that you can't so easily swap out for another in times of trouble. There's rarely more than one piano available in any given room.

Therefore, mic selection and placement become your most formidable tools, and mangling might be your best option.

This is a decision of practicality. If the piano is crucial to a production, particularly the tone of it, then I will seek out the right piano for the job, even if that requires going to another room for a few hours. If the piano is secondary in nature to the production, then I'm likely to use what I have available, within reason.

When you hire a room specifically for a session that includes piano, then make sure it's placed where you want it ahead of time, and then request that it's tuned the day of your piano session. Moving a piano will knock it out of tune, so make sure you have it placed appropriately first. Lock it down!

More often than not, recordists tend to reach for LDCs to mic a piano. AKG C12's, C12a's, 414s, Neumann U87's, U67's, and U47's are all reasonable LDC choices for piano. Stereo mics like the AKG C24 and Shure SM69 work brilliantly for stereo piano. Ribbons such as the Royer 121's or the stereo SF-12 can offer a warm tone. Even SDCs like AKG 451's, 452's, Neumann KM84's, and Mojave 100's are good choices. Your mic selection is wide open when it comes to a piano because this is the only reasonable way to alter the tone.

Some recordists prefer a matched stereo pair on piano, but I've never really bought into this, even if it may reduce phase coherency issues. I don't discount the concept either, but matched stereo pairs aren't all that common, and even the better studios don't typically have more than one or two matched pairs available. Any of the stereo miking techniques we've discussed can be useful for miking a piano, and I encourage you to try them all.

The mics and the technique that you use to record a piano have as much to do with the part as they do the physical realities of the piano itself. An aggressive and intricate piano part designed to cut through a dense arrangement is often best miked within close proximity of the hammers. A part that's meant to fill significant low-end space is best miked off the hammers. Pulling the mics back and out of the piano will offer a mellower tone, but you begin to introduce the room, which could be a sum negative if the room is insufficiently sized.

Some recordists like to use three mics on a grand piano, with two LDCs approaching the hammers and a third LDC at the end of the piano. This way you can to get a more robust low end to work with the hammer mics. Be mindful of phase coherency by comparing the phase relationships between all three mics.

Upright pianos can be the perfect candidate for a recording. They're also a little trickier to mic up, as the player is sitting directly in front of the vertically mounted sound board. Many upright pianos have a trap door on top allowing you to approach from above, but you may choose to remove the panel covering the sound board and place your mics there. A spaced pair works well on upright.

There are also a number of piano variants that can be great fun for the right recording. The barroom honky-tonk piano is achieved with a significantly out of tune upright. Tack pianos have little tacks that you can engage on the hammers.

Lastly, pianos make exceptionally interesting reverb chambers for other instruments when miked from underneath with the sustain pedal down. Place a speaker on the edge of the piano facing the strings, pump through your signal, and record. Try it!

Piano/Vocal

When recording a vocalist who prefers to play as she performs, you once again will have to deal with vocal bleed into your instrument mics. Unlike an acoustic guitar, a piano lid can be shut and covered with blankets. Many grand pianos have a short stick, which allows you to reduce the opening without closing the piano completely. While pianos don't sound as good with the mics shut inside of them, it can be better than the alternative.

You can also close off a piano by placing it across the threshold of sliding glass isolation doors. This way you can isolate the keys from the soundboard, by putting the player in one room, and the piano strings in another. This will require some construction on your part, as you literally need to build a wall. I would reserve this solution for a project that featured a piano-vocalist.

Rhodes, Wurli, Electric Pianos

Electric piano samples can be a bit more convincing than piano samples, especially within the context of a production. A little distortion can go a long way towards improving a sample if that's what you need. As instruments, electric pianos are rather mellow in nature, and are often used to fill in the lower midrange of an arrangement. As a result, they can be quite haunting.

When it comes to the real thing, electric pianos are acoustic instruments that require some kind of amplification. They have physical strings and hammers, and must be tuned, preferably by someone who knows how, and if you own one of these instruments, you might do well to learn how to tune it yourself. They're also prone to broken hammers and dead notes when in disrepair.

Rhodes pianos come in a variety of configurations, the grand-daddy of which is the 88-key "suitcase" model. This behemoth sits upon a large stereo speaker cab, and offers a panned tremolo effect, with speed and width adjustments available. Two microphones in front of the cabinet speakers set as a spaced pair will offer you the full beauty of the panning (which is optional). If you'd like to hear an example of this effect, you can listen to the track "Brother Sister" by The Brand New Heavies.

There are a number of smaller Rhodes piano models that don't come with any kind of amplification, and therefore you must either record them direct, or run them through your own amplifier. If you're looking for a radically overdriven tone, then you may want to use a high-gain amplifier. Typically, Rhodes parts do well with mild breakup distortion. I usually just use the amp that's closest and already miked up, unless it somehow requires more thought than that. The Fender Twin Reverb is always a good choice.

A Wurlitzer electric piano is very similar to a Rhodes in tone, but has a bit more presence and attack in the initial sound of the note. They also don't include a built-in panning function. Wurlis have their own amplification, but the speakers are small, and are placed on each side of the chassis just above the keys. These speakers are often blown, distort easily, and are inches from the audible keyboard action. That shouldn't necessarily prevent you from using a mic on them. I do. Sennheiser 421s and Shure SM57s work well.

Dynamics tend to be a good mic choice as they accentuate the midrange of the instrument, and reject more external information—like fingers striking the keys. More often, Wurlis are dealt with in the same manner as a Rhodes, either recorded through an amplifier, direct, or both. Miking an amplifier for a Rhodes is no different from a guitar, although a dynamic goes a long way towards reducing an overbearing low midrange tone.

Electric pianos tend to be somewhat dynamic, and often require a little help from compressors as you won't tend to push the amplifiers to the same kind of SPLs as you would an overdriven guitar. In general, they're dark instruments, particularly when played in the lower registers, and you would do well to clear some of that frequency muck if it's masking the motion of your bass. A compressor can help to rein in some of that low-end information.

Many times electric piano parts are best monophonic in nature, and will most easily cut through a dense production when put in a steady state. There are certain analog compressors that absolutely shine for electric pianos, and they tend to be what I call binary compressors, which is a term of my own making. A binary compressor either barely affects the signal or absolutely crushes it. There is seemingly no in-between. The API 527, Valley Dynamite, and Inovonics 201 all fall into this category.

The dbx 160x, the Neve 2254, and 32264a are also great compressors for electric piano, and of course, you will rarely go wrong using an Urei 1176 or Distressor.

Organ

There are all sorts of organs that provide their own unique tonal quality. B3s have drawbars which are basically sliders (like faders) that you use to adjust the balance of set octaves and overtones. Pulling out all of the sliders provides you the full range brilliance of the instrument.

Pipe organs have stops rather than drawbars, and are generally monstrosities that require their own building, like a church. As a result, you're unlikely to record a pipe organ unless you go to it. Miking a pipe organ would be similar to miking an orchestra in a hall, as it's far too large an instrument for close-miking techniques.

Farfisa organs offer that identifiable 60s sound of The Doors, as this was Ray Manzarek's keyboard of choice. All you have to do with a Farfisa is plug it in to a DI box, just as you would any other keyboard. The tone of the organ is manipulated by the player using the drawbars. Vox and Lowrey organs were also popular in the 60s.

Hammond B3 and C3

The most famous and often used organs for recording are the Hammond B3 and C3, which are commonly run through a Leslie cabinet.

A Leslie is a large wooden speaker cabinet designed specifically for the Hammond organ in the aftermarket, and they are revered for the way they both distort and modulate the tone. There are a number of Leslie models, each with their own particular setups. The most common configuration includes a large speaker at its base a horn at the top of the unit. While it appears as if there are actually two horns facing opposite one another, one of those is a dummy horn that emits no sound. I would imagine that was used as a counterbalance, as both the top and bottom speakers spin. This modulates the tone. The rotating speakers have two speeds, slow and fast, and the performer will often switch between the speeds for purposes of dynamic excitement.

There are a number of setups available on Hammond organs, including a pedal board that allows the performer to play bass notes with her feet. Some have internal spring reverbs, which are very handy and can be exploited for effect with a swift and aggressive strike to the top of the organ itself. Some Hammonds have a "perc" function, which supplies a harder attack, but it's variable, in that the perc function doesn't reset so long as there are notes being sustained. There's also a volume control pedal, which allows the player incredible dynamic control, which can require some rebalancing if implemented too aggressively.

B3s are difficult to play well because they require the use of all your limbs. That shouldn't necessarily prevent you from recording them with lesser players, but your average keyboardist won't be able to perform that instrument anywhere near like a real B3 player could. As a consequence, this instrument can render even a quality keyboardist somewhat ineffective.

I've recorded the best on this instrument (Jimmy Williams), but I've recorded a number of somewhat convincing players as well. Most people don't use the pedals in productions, as that's often covered by the bass. That frees up the player's feet for volume control and speed selection, leaving the hands for drawbars, perc, and reverb implementation over the course of a performance. Oh yeah, and your player also has to perform the part. This can be nearly impossible for someone who hasn't had quite a bit of time with the instrument.

I'll often go in the room with an inexperienced B3 player and help her perform the parts by taking care of some of the speed and drawbar action. The speed is far easier to deal with when there's a foot switch, but not all B3s have this. Some switches are mounted on the front side of the organ, which merely adds one more thing you have to do with your hands.

The speed is useful for building up excitement and offering internal dynamics through motion. The change in speed is not immediate, and it can take more than a second to fully ramp. B3s are extremely expressive instruments when played well, and with just a little practice, two people can do a relatively convincing job, so long as it's not the featured instrument. At that point, you should seek an appropriate sideman for the job.

Leslies distort, which along with their motion is what makes them so compelling. They're also massive space-eaters, much like pianos, and special attention should be paid to the drawbar settings where tone is concerned. Your performer has vast control over the tone, and there are presets that can help with transitions. Leslie cabinets are also useful for guitars, and many will include an input for external instruments.

There are a number of ways to mic a Leslie. Many recordists put a mic on each side of the cabinet facing each other, which pick up a stereo representation of the spinning horn. Unfortunately, the horn is offset from the center of the cabinet; therefore the mics are not equidistant from the horn using this technique. To prevent this, you can place one mic on the slatted side of the cabinet at a 45-degree angle, which faces directly towards another mic placed on the open back. Be sure to check polarity between the two mics. Mid-side techniques can be also be exceptionally effective on Leslie speakers.

Typically, I use LDCs on organ, and often it's based on what mics I have left available over any other factor. AKG 414's and Neumann U87's are good choices. Given the nature of the spinning horn, you're probably best using the same model mic for the two top positions.

It's also common to mic the bottom of the Leslie. This is especially useful if you want a fuller tone. You can certainly bus the three mics to stereo, but I much prefer to print the bottom mic separately as it's not always needed, and sometimes not preferable. Occasionally, I'll bring the bottom mic in and out based on the needs of the sections when mixing. While the full range of the instrument sounds lovely, the broad low end can be problematic in masking bass movement. In general, I treat the bottom mic as a way to EQ the overall tone at the time of mix.

Since B3s shine as dynamic instruments, compression is typically not advised. Organ samples can be effective, but you'll never get the unique sound of a real Hammond B3.

Synths

Synthesizers can be a whole world unto themselves, although in most cases, you'll merely be recording tones from MIDI patches. Learning to program synth tones on the fly is inadvisable. That's a rabbit hole that must be ventured into well in advance of a recording session.

Many keyboardists will choose to layer synth pads for purposes of texture, and often there is a magic blend between the textures that will form one unified sound. At some point, you should consider combining them to a stereo track before sending them to a third-party mixer. Don't leave synths blended with intent to the mixer's imagination. If the blend is designed to form one basic part, commit to it.

Soft synths and MIDI are a part of most DAWs, and at some point, you should record any MIDI synths as audio files. As MIDI files, you will be able to change patches throughout the production, but at some point you should commit. By the time you deliver a session, everything on that session should be recorded as an audio file.

Stand-alone synthesizers often have mono and stereo outputs. Stereo keyboard patches appear as a soft stereo, sufficient enough to fill the sound field without totally mucking up the middle. Much like pianos and organs, synths can also eat space in your soundfield. To record a stand-alone synth, you should use a direct box or a mic pre with a direct input.

Strings

String samples are used regularly on productions, and for good reason—average to below-average string players can bring one to a very dark place of disturbing thoughts. It's a normal reaction when you hear the unrelenting screech of an out-of-tune violin. Even here in LA, where string players abound, you can pay good money for some rather underwhelming players.

That said, the difference between the feeling a string quartet can offer and what you can accomplish with string samples is nothing short of significant. The overtone interactions between the instruments can't be adequately mimicked in samples. Not at this time.

String samples are much more believable in the form of an ensemble pad. Given the expense of recording a large string section, samples are almost a requirement for such an arrangement decision. That said, a bona fide maestro will have a far easier time programming convincing strings than your average musician.

Then, of course, there's the fiddle, which is a violin played predominantly using Irish folk modes. Given the Irish settlements that took place in the Appalachian Mountains, the fiddle has become a staple in many southern styles of music. The frenetically aggressive and inflective style of fiddle would be exceptionally difficult to pull off convincingly on a keyboard. Even if you could come up with a high quality sample, most keyboard players wouldn't be able to pull off this kind of performance. It's far too nuanced.

When recording a string quartet, you don't necessarily have to mic each and every instrument, although you can, and should, if your room tone is problematic. Some productions call for a string quartet in a more intimate setting, at which point you should knock down any unwanted ambience with baffles. Digital reverbs are fairly convincing on strings in the context of a modern production. Typically, a quartet is meant to be prominently placed in a somewhat organic production, at which point digital reverbs can sound rather apparent, if not downright disturbing.

Strings are often recorded with LDCs, especially if you're going to put a mic on each instrument. Ribbons don't tend to capture the grate of the string, and are often best reserved for annoyingly whiny violins. If you're starting to get the idea that I've had bad experiences with this instrument, that would be an understatement. Of all the instruments, I would be hard-pressed to name one that can be more maddening than a poorly played violin. Although an atrociously played banjo would be a close second.

It's far easier to record a quartet than it is to write the parts for one, and I say that as someone who can do both. Four-part voice-leading requires adherence to strict musical rules, all of which can be broken under the right circumstances. (Sounds a lot like recording, doesn't it?) A string section as small as a quartet can, and will, be a disaster without a proper chart written by someone who knows what they're doing. Therein lies the rub.

I was mixing for a producer once who sent me a production with what I can only describe as some very suspect string parts that did absolutely nothing good for the track, to the point that I actually suggested he dump them from the production. His reaction?

"My client paid 25 fucking thousand dollars for those strings, and we're going to fucking use them."

That track never went anywhere.

The expense of strings on a production can put the producer in a bit of a predicament later. Therefore, unless you can read charts and hear the music in your head, then you should have them mocked up with MIDI strings first. Mark my words: I have dealt with many string quartets, and I can assure you, there are few more effective ways to completely fuck up a production than to introduce a lame string arrangement.

The more players you attempt to record at once, the more space you'll need, not only to house them, but for purposes of room tone. Typically, large string sections are recorded either in a hall, for purposes of classical performances, or in a large studio complex with an enormous mic collection. You need a ton of mics to record a 60-piece string section in a studio, and you also need some experience. I've set up numerous string dates, and I've watched the best orchestral engineers in the world record them. I can assure you, this is the kind of job best subbed out to an expert. A three-hour full-scale string session in LA will cost tens of thousands of dollars, and an expert recordist will add nothing appreciable to the budget. Consider it a really inexpensive insurance policy.

For the large majority of recordings, budget restraints can make an ensemble any bigger than four a prohibitive expense. Many producers and recordists will choose to double-track the parts for the illusion of a more substantial section. This is not a convincing illusion by any stretch of the imagination, but you may have few other options.

Bolstering your real strings with samples certainly isn't unreasonable. But the larger you make the section, the less important it was to use real string players in the first place. It's really easy to mimic a big lush string section in a support role, and no one is going to expect a full orchestra on anything but the most outlandish production. What's nearly impossible to simulate is a smaller, more intimate section.

Fiddle players are typically close miked because they tend to play fast moving parts that require the scrape of the instrument. Any good LDC will do a superlative job of capturing a fiddle or a violin, and compression is rarely needed nor desired. You're more likely to increase the dynamic range of a string part using automation than you are to limit it.

As with anything we discuss here, mic placement depends on the role of the part. Intimate parts are best recorded with minimal room information, but if your mic is in close proximity to a mediocre player, you're going to pick up every nuance of that bad playing.

In general, you should avoid recording each string part as an overdub. You might as well use samples, as you are removing one of the main benefits—that is, the string players interacting and blending with each other as an ensemble.

Horns

Horn sections can be equally as frustrating to record as strings. Any time you put together a section, you're hindered by your weakest link. The best protection is to seek out a section that plays together regularly, although there are no guarantees this will quell the issue.

Horns are often served best by ribbons like Royer 121's, Beyer Dynamic 160's, Coles 4038's, Sony 44's, and RCA 77's, all of which make for good choices, so long as they are well-maintained. Condensers like the Sony C37a or C38b, which have a rather mellow nature to them, are especially good for woodwinds, like saxophone or clarinet.

As with strings, double-tracking four horns is not the same as recording an ensemble of eight. The most common issue with horns is tuning. Weak horn players are notoriously out of tune. Even decent players go out of tune, especially when monitoring through headphones.

Unlike strings, a good horn section doesn't necessarily need charts, but you better have a producer around who can work on the fly. You still must work within voice-leading rules, but horn parts are typically delivered in short phrases, which simplifies matters tremendously. I would much rather record a group of players that perform routinely as a section than to attempt to organize one piecemeal.

When recording a horn section, you can line the players up in a row, and the players will have a preference to their order. The typical arrangement from left to right is bari sax, tenor sax, trombone, and trumpet. You can place a mic in front of each player, and then place a room mic (or two) to capture the whole ensemble. Strings are arranged similarly. Horns typically stand, strings usually sit. Rugs are optional for horns, and not recommended for strings.

When setting up for a string or horn section, be sure to give each player a music stand, a pencil, some paper, a headphone box, and water.

Percussion

When it comes to rock productions, I typically don't record percussion until last. For starters, this prevents tambourines and shakers from bleeding through the headphones during a vocal. Surely you can just mute them, but you can just as easily forget, and underdubbing tambourine could prove problematic as it may be audible in the headphone bleed. You can deal with bleed to some extent by muting the vocal mic when the singer is tacit. And that's a reasonable fix if it's critical to remove the part. Why put yourself in that situation in the first place? Any percussion parts that are designed to offer rhythmic lift, or to increase the high-end information within the track, are best recorded last.

R&B tracks are much more sparse in the midrange, and most of the high-end information tends to come from percussion—often canned in nature, but not always. When a percussion part is integral to the internal rhythms of a track, it should be recorded early on in the process.

I don't tend to put a ton of thought into miking percussion instruments as overdubs. Bells, shakers, blocks, tambourines, guiros, claves, gourds, etc. can all be recorded with the closest condenser mic available, and can be recorded one at a time. If you have an especially talented percussion player with good taste, it's far more efficient to set up a percussion station for an aggregate capture with a stereo pair of condenser mics. Skinned instruments like bongos, congas, and djembes can be reinforced with dynamic mics.

Once you record a stereo image, you won't have control over the panning later (beyond swapping the left and right channels), as that will be determined by the physical location of the performer. Therefore, your percussionist will have control over where in the stereo field a part will sound as she performs. You should strategize with your percussion player in advance of a take.

Rhythmic tambourines and shakers are often best panned. So you would do well to have your percussionist physically move to the side of the stereo capture field, which will appear similarly in your monitors. Since the skinned instruments and cymbals are all stationary, you can place them as you like within the stereo image.

Recording percussion in this manner practically requires that you arrange as you go. You do not want to record a whole shit-load of percussion in a single take, only to have to try to extract it later.

Organic percussion sounds best in a room with some action. And yes, I've recorded plenty of percussion without ambience, but there is no doubt that room decay responds well to percussive strikes. A pair of SDCs or ribbons should provide you with a nice amount of room information. If you need more, you can always record a designated room mic. Some genres, or even parts, might call for a hall, in which case you are best to keep the room as neutral as possible.

Percussion adds rhythm to a track. This much is obvious. It also adds frequency information, and if your track is already strident with high-end information, you might suggest the percussionist gravitate towards parts that will fill the lower middle of the frequency spectrum rather than the very top. Sonic shaping is within your purview as recordist. Your counsel is warranted when it comes to frequency information.

Percussion is practically a feature in some genres of music. Traditional Latin music often makes such heavy use of percussion that a production couldn't possibly live without it. A solid percussion ensemble will play most convincingly together in one room at the time of tracking. This allows the players to interact with each other musically.

Baffles can be used to provide some modicum of separation, although you may get protests. Really good ensembles like to see each other as they play, and if you barricade the bongo player from the conga player without retaining lines of sight, you will likely have unhappy performers.

It's important that you always keep in mind the needs of your musicians. If eye contact will help improve the ensemble performance, then cutting them off would seem counterproductive. Yes, bleed can be problematic, but baffles will only reduce the problem. They won't eradicate leakage. If the ensemble is relatively tight, or at least vibey, then capture them with an aggregate pair of room mics, and reinforce with close mics. If you have an iso booth with a window, that would be a good place for the bongo player.

Anyone who has ever recorded a bongo player will understand why I just banished him to the iso booth. Bongos are one of the most piercing instruments known to man, and they will bleed into *everything*. Buddha help you should you ever have to record a percussion ensemble in a single room with a spastic bongo player.

Just about anything can be used as percussion. I once made a kik drum by punching a bass cabinet with my fist. There are so many percussion instruments, from all over the world that you are unlikely to see them all in your lifetime as a recordist. Some could even be quite whacky in nature, and your job is to figure out how and where they sound best.

Any time I come across an instrument I've neither seen nor heard, I listen to the instrument in the room so as to evaluate where the sound is coming from. For instance, if you've never recorded a djembe, they are skinned conga-like instruments that emit a beautiful low-end boom from the tapered bottom. Now that I've told you this, you know to listen for it. But you should be able to figure that out just by evaluating where the tone sounds. All the tone.

In the case of the djembe, half the tone comes from the skin slap, and the other half from the bottom, although you could very well choose to abandon the low end boom and use it more like a conga. Typically a dynamic is good on the skins, like a Sennheiser 421, Shure SM57, SM58, or an Electro-Voice RE20. For the bottom, a Neumann 47 FET, AKG D12, or AKG 441 will perform the task well. Be sure to check the phase relationship between the top and bottom mics. It doesn't make much sense to mic the boom of a djembe if all you're going to do is kill it due to phase coherency issues.

Vocals

It never ceases to amaze me how even the most skilled of recordists set up for a vocal session. Recordists who live by the principles of placing mics by ear routinely abandon this good habit when it comes to vocals.

Oh, I understand why. When your vocalist freaks out because the mic isn't where she thinks it should be, you will nearly guarantee an ineffective performance. When this happens repeatedly with every vocalist you record, you begin to adjust accordingly. It doesn't make much sense to upset your vocalist just before a take. And while there are times that pulling your singer from her comfort zone can be an effective tool, you risk the artist second-guessing her tone. Forever.

Artists. They're so damn sensitive. Why can't they be more callous, like bankers?

Of course, the vocals *are* money. The entire song is defined by the melody and lyric, and an instrumental is only defined by the melody. In fact, you can't copyright a harmonic progression. You can only copyright the melody, the lyric, and the sound recording itself (also called the master).

As my friend Fletcher likes to say, "No one walks down the street singing a hi-hat." So it doesn't make a whole lot of sense to view the vocal as anything less than the end game. You can record the most awesome track of your life, and if the vocal is uncompelling in terms of performance and/or melody, the track is irrelevant, as no one will ever hear it. The track is the setup for the vocal.

Of course, if there's no vocal on a track, then there's no lyric, which means the melody defines the song in totality. And at that point, it's the instrument providing the melody at any given time that should be given its due importance.

When it comes to a vocalist, microphone selection will have a significant influence on the tone. You rarely have the option to pick your singer once you agree to the gig in the first place. In the case of vocals, your source is just as important as ever, it's just you don't have the luxury of swapping out your performer or her instrument, seeing as they're attached. All you have control over is the room, and even that's limited. Frankly, the determination that your vocalist isn't up to the job should have been made well before you accepted the gig, and if you take a job purely for the money, well, you'll certainly earn it.

Regardless, your goal is to provide the singer with everything she needs to accomplish an effective performance within her capabilities. The best way that I know to pull a compelling vocal performance out of a singer is to provide a track that inspires her. If you can accomplish that goal, your chances of success will increase exponentially.

Even if your singer is technically atrocious, you can successfully capture an effective and compelling vocal. There have been countless artists who couldn't win a high-school singing competition, yet they are the perfect voice for their own material. Neil Young is an awful singer who should likely never be mimicked, only because he broke the mold. When it comes to his own songs, his vocals are unique, compelling, and perfect for the production, regardless of your personal feelings for Neil Young's music. If you don't like the songs, you certainly aren't going to like the vocals.

Don't get bogged down on a singer's lack of technical skill. Focus on the qualities of your production that appropriately support the strengths of your singer. I mean, if you're dealing with a singer who relies on vibe more than technique, then your best approach is to set her up for what she does best. The track is built for the singer, not vice versa. Therefore, if you can record the right track in a manner that makes her feel the right way, she will most certainly shine regardless of her technical abilities.

I realize these are largely production decisions, but even as a Designated Recordist you're a part of the production team, and you therefore have a responsibility towards the production too. I'll warn you now, I'm going to digress from the topic of vocals for a moment. This is an important concept that we must discuss, and now is as good a time as any.

The producer is in charge of the vision, but your full involvement and counsel are critical to a successful production. You make yourself valuable as a recordist when you work seamlessly towards the vision in conjunction with the producer, and while much of your gig may be to capture, you're not a robot.

There will be times when you find yourself out of sync with the producer or client. You can't be expected to be clairvoyant, and you could very well pull up tones that fall flat. This typically occurs when there has been a failure to adequately express the vision, which leaves it wholly to your imagination. No worries. You have to start somewhere. Besides, sometimes pulling up tones that offend is the best way to get a reaction.

In the late 90s, I was setting up drum tones for Ben Harper's *Steal my Kisses*. J.P. Plunier and I had made a number of records at this point, and it was rare for us to be out of sync, but I was struggling to get a useful description of his vision for the track. So I chose to record drums that sounded country-rock in nature. Apparently, that was just terrible enough to cause J.P. to blurt out the words "New Orleans." We had drum tones within 15 minutes after that.

In this case, I was the Designated Recordist, but I was also the one that knew how to translate a vision into a reality—all that was required was a direction. So as recordist, you are just as important to the production needs as anyone else, it's just that when you're doing your job right, you'll spend most of your time nearly invisible to the process, and that requires attentiveness, thoughtfulness, and a willingness to offer the support needed for a session.

There will be occasions when a producer will struggle. Worse yet, should you be paired with a producer in way over his head, you become more critical to the process than ever. And while it can be tempting to allow a producer to fall flat, you become nothing more than a part of the problem as you neglect to prove your own value. You'll also have your name on that product, and if you choose to fold rather than rise to the occasion, you will have only yourself to blame. In a business in which your most recent discography is king, you can't afford to record duds.

You also can't afford to alienate producers, so don't get too aggressive about taking over the session. Pick up the slack where it's needed and offer your opinion through your actions if you must. It's better to have a producer reject your first tones than it is to debate tone in the abstract—a useless debate if there ever was one.

Believe me, when you save a recording from a lunatic producer with little to no actual experience, it will be recognized. And if your Herculean efforts should somehow produce a hit song, your producer will still be in over his head, and you will be able to parlay that success into more work for yourself without ever denigrating the producer. Plenty of engineers are hired as producers because of their success as recordists. Everyone on the team can benefit from a hit record. And now back to our regularly scheduled discussion on recording vocals.

Vocal Overdub

When recording vocals as overdubs, I recommend you do so to a fully produced track, aside from perhaps background vocals. In fact, you should at all times be prepared to record a vocal take. When a vocalist asks you to stop what you're doing so they can perform, it's usually because they're inspired, and this is the time to strike. I would sooner use a less than optimum mic than to make a singer wait as I get my shit together.

Any time you can record a vocal during the tracking phase (without straining your singer), you should. Now, whether you capture a performance that can be kept, that really depends on the goal. Some groups are candidates for capturing a performance as an ensemble. Of course, you need the space and the gear to do it. More often than not, vocals are recorded as an overdub.

There are two basic strategies to overdubbing a vocal—comping and punching. A comp is a take that is compiled from several full performances. The idea is to record full takes, top to bottom, from which you can harvest in order to create one compelling performance. The advantage is simple. Your singer is performing rather than thinking about performing.

Sometimes you may wish to record the song by punching in on lines or sections after the initial performance, or even after having made a comp. This method allows the singer to concentrate on one section at a time, perhaps even one line at time. The technique is especially useful if there is a challenging section. There's no reason to make a singer perform an entire song just to capture the big note at the end.

Anytime you can capture an entire performance from a singer, you should. This is what the singer's main gig is—to perform. And once you're done the record, she is likely going to perform the song repeatedly live. At some point she will have to perform the entire song, and this would seem an important time to do that. It is, after all, going to be on record that way forever, amen.

At the end of the day, you get a vocal performance any way you can, but if the singer is unprepared, you're kind of wasting your time. Yes, you can punch in one line at time if you have to. You could punch in one word at time if you really want, but that's a tough way to collect a performance. And if you immediately launch into punch-in mode, you don't provide the singer an opportunity to find her best approach. Performers need to get into a flow.

Believe me, if your singer's woefully unprepared, you're better off letting her discover that for herself. That's usually as simple as allowing her to sing the track down three times, although you may have to make an initial comp in order to fully illuminate the problem. If that doesn't work, then bluntness is probably your best tool.

"You're not ready to sing this vocal."

The idea isn't to beat your artist up, but rather to tell her what you expect—her best. And if your singer can't be bothered to bring her best, then how can she expect that from you, since your best is wholly dependent on hers?

Oddly, unprepared singers seem to be more prevalent in the upper echelons of this business, what with young pop icons more interested in their movie and TV careers than putting a full-throated effort into their music. At some point, you can only help those who help themselves.

In general, when comping, you want to avoid working on more than three takes at time if you can. You increase your comping time exponentially with every take that you introduce. Besides, there are benefits to time away from the mic. For starters, the singer gets an opportunity to evaluate her own performance. Secondly, she will have the opportunity to process her thoughts during a break, at which point she might just surprise you. Or you send her home to practice.

If it's the first vocal session of the day, you might record a few takes for warmup (although it's best if the singer warms up before she steps to the mic). Even so, it can sometimes take a moment for a singer to get into the right headspace to deliver a performance.

Some singers will routinely deliver their best on the first take, and if you know this, then you need to make absolutely sure you're ready to record her. It's painful to deal with a self-inflicted fucked-up recording of an amazing take.

You can imagine how annoying it might be for an artist to deliver the performance of her life, only to have it all fucked up because you didn't make sure in advance that you weren't absolutely crushing her with a compressor. And forget about rerecording it. The psychological hit will be far too great to overcome for the large preponderance of singers. Besides, she did her job, which was the harder of the two. You didn't do yours, and now you get to fix it. Fun times.

The best is when you send that fucked-up vocal to me for mix, and I have to split it off into eight different tracks, and ride the living shit out of the automation, because that's the only way I can deal with the heavy breathing artifacts of your overcompression. This means a mix that should have taken six to eight hours is now likely to go into a second day. Thank you sooooo much for that!

If you enjoy it when your clients are pissed off at you, all you need do is drop the ball at the time your services are most important—that is, during the vocal performance of all time. This would be *prima facie* evidence as to why it's critical to get your vocal setting well in advance of recording vocals. Even if you used a mic that you're not pleased with, so long as it's not loaded down with unwanted artifacts, you should be fine. Yes, you'll have to do some damage control, but it's tonal in nature, and you have the tools to mangle it into the shape that you want. While not ideal, it's not a crisis.

Many times, you won't know if you have everything you need for a performance until you attempt the first comp of the vocal. Further, there is nothing wrong with making a comp purely for purposes of giving the singer something to beat. A finished vocal comp can really take the pressure off.

As great as it is to capture 90 percent of the performance on the first take of the day, most singers will require a few just to get into the right headspace, and a good producer will often offer some direction, particularly during the early attempts. While this certainly gives you time to make adjustments along the way, you can't take that for granted, and you must weigh the pros and cons of changing your settings in the middle of a take.

If a singer is performing the take of her life, and there is apparent distortion on the vocal, are you going to leave it or keep it? It's a tough call. If you leave it, and she can't live with the distortion, you fucked up the whole take. If you notch down the pre gain 5 dB, some of the take will be distorted, and the rest will be down 5 dB in level. This in turn will affect the input of the limiter, and thereby affect the tone significantly. Oh yeah, and your singer will hear that 5 db drop in level as she performs, so if you think she's delivering a take, it's probably best to live with the distortion artifacts.

This is why producers get paid the big bucks. That's his decision. But there will be times that it becomes yours. Without a producer, you either need someone in the room that can make that call, or you will have to make it yourself.

Of course, warmup takes are generally atrocious, so you may end up with six takes on your first run at a track. Save yourself some headache, and start by comping from the legitimate takes, reserving the warmups for filling in what you're missing.

Once complete, it's a good idea to let a comp sit a day or two before making a final judgment on it. At some point in the course of recording multiple songs, your singer could set the bar with an undeniable performance, and this gives everyone a basis of comparison. Takes that were viewed as solid can become unacceptable once the singer finds her stride.

Comping a vocal requires an enormous amount of concentration and energy. Further, when a comp is fresh you're far too hypersensitive and oversaturated to evaluate its overall effectiveness, and you would do best to set it aside until you've recorded some vocals on other tracks. There's nothing like a string of successes to bring a performer into the zone, and if you beat her up before she's had a performance she's proud of, you could destroy her confidence for the remainder of the session and beyond.

As much as I recommend comping over punching, and I do, there are times when you will have no choice but to record by section. For instance, if you have six takes in which the first verse doesn't seem to click like the rest of the song, it's totally reasonable to focus on that section of the song. The singer may have trouble finding her groove early in the track, and you would be doing her a service by suggesting she sing the same section repeatedly.

You might also find a problem note, one that is challenging enough that it affects her performance before and after it. If you recognize this as you're making your takes, suggest that she abandon the note for purposes of punching it later. This isn't ideal, but there's no point in having her perform the song repeatedly in order to nail one big note at the end of the song.

Then there are physical considerations. If a certain section is going to blow your singer out for the day, then you may want to avoid that section until you have the rest of the take. And if the plan is to record several vocals in a day, then it would be best to reserve that section for the end of the day.

That said, there can be some tonal benefit to a vocalist who is slightly blown out, as it tends to manifest as a raspy tone. If that's a quality you seek, then letting her rip for a few takes could have a beneficial and desirable side effect. Just make sure you discuss that particular plan in advance, as your singer might get a wee bit pissed after you shred her like that.

Monitoring

The overall quality of a performance also has much to do with the monitoring. Most singers are fairly used to in-ears at this point, and they may prefer them to headphones. Some singers, however, have better pitch when standing in front of studio monitors, which is why I often record vocals in the control room. I can tell you, if you're recording a singer who normally has rock solid tuning and timing, only to find them struggling in this regard, it's usually a monitoring problem.

A singer who is monitoring herself too loudly in her cue balance, what with only a smattering of harmonic information will tend to sing flat. A lack of rhythm in the headphones will cause timing problems. And a vocal that's too low in the cue mix will cause a singer to push, thereby making her sharp. Monitoring with reverb can also cause tuning issues, but some singers are uncomfortable performing without it.

When you find a competent singer unable to deliver the basics, then your first course should be to investigate exactly what she's monitoring. This way, you can make the necessary adjustments to the cue mix. You can also take more control of the cue by sending the singer your monitor mix.

When headphones or in-ears aren't cutting it, try setting some monitors on stands and place the singer in the middle of the stereo field. You can do this in the room, or you can just bring her into the control room, which certainly makes communication easier.

Some recordists will flip the polarity on one of the monitors when recording vocals this way. The thinking is that the center information will cancel, and you can put the mic in the null spot. In my experience, this doesn't buy you much more than the annoyance of listening to an out-of-phase stereo image. I've recorded many vocals with monitors, and there is just as much bleed when your monitors are out of phase as when in.

You may want to use a dynamic mic when recording a singer with monitors, although you certainly aren't precluded from a condenser. If you place the microphone so that it's flush with the front plane of the monitors, you will minimize the bleed. Be sure that the monitors are loud enough for your vocalist to perform, but not so loud that you're picking up copious amounts of bleed.

A healthy bit of compression can work to all but eradicate the bleed during the performance. It's the tacit parts in which the leakage will be most obvious, and you may have to strip the audio between vocals if it presents as a problem. Setting your compressor to a slower release time will help with this as it will give you a little time before that bleed starts creeping back in, but then you will be virtually forced to strip silence the vocal later. Just be sure you don't send parts to the monitor mix that are still up for debate. Monitoring with parts that may be abandoned come mix time can prove problematic.

As much as I'm giving you suggestions for dealing with the bleed from monitors, I record like this all the time with success, and rarely have problems with it come mix time. It just requires a little diligence on your part. If your singer performs better standing in front of monitors, then that's all that matters. Besides, headphone leakage can be just as problematic (if not more so) than monitor leakage.

Miking a Vocal

The vocal is typically the loudest part in the mix, front and center, and as such, you should audition microphones to find the one that best represents your singer within the track itself. Notice I said within the track itself. You could find a mic that does everything you want for a singer in the abstract, only to find it lacking within the context of the track.

The procedure for auditioning mics is simple. Pick five contenders, set them up, and have your singer audition each as she performs to the track. Choose the one that sounds best.

Most sessions are built through the overdub process. This provides a producer the ability to focus on the parts individually, which is a prerequisite for bands in need of some shaping. If you know that your vocal is intended as a scratch, you can audition mics as you track.

LDCs are commonly the first choice when it comes to vocals, and will often be the best choice, but not always. LDCs will offer a broad tone, and some singers need help cutting through, in which case a dynamic may be the best choice, although you will curse me later.

SDCs in omni can be an interesting choice for vocals, as this removes proximity effect. This is going to bring more of the room into the equation, and in general, it's best if you can neutralize the ambience to some degree.

As we already discussed, your singer could very well prefer a mic that you don't favor. Confidence from your singer is far more critical to a good vocal recording than the mic or pre. And if the price of the artist's confidence is a mic that is less than ideal, it's usually a worthwhile cost, and you're likely best to acquiesce.

Not all artists and singers are this sensitive, and if you can shake your performer off a poor mic choice without any ill effects, then by all means, do it. But if your artist or singer likes what she's hearing, there's probably a good reason for it. Besides, you buy yourself so much good will by putting the artist's needs above your own that when it comes time to stand up for your recording technique, you'll have the political capital and trust necessary for an open dialog.

Once you accept that there isn't a single mic that you can use globally for every vocalist you come across, and once you concede that your most expensive mic available could very well be the worst choice, you will be well on your way to the right headspace for choosing the most appropriate vocal mic. Forget about how much a mic costs, and pick the mic that sounds best for the production.

In order to neutralize a room of size, you can use three large gobos to create an open booth. One gobo goes directly behind the singer, the other two gobos flap off at 45 degree angles (or so), and the singer stands such that she's surrounded by the barrier. This will control much of the room ambience from returning into the mic.

For particularly problematic rooms (typically under-sized rooms), you may want to use an acoustic shield, which can be mounted on the mic stand behind the mic. This device will help to keep unwanted room information from hitting the back of the capsule. An acoustic shield is a relatively new concept, and there are a number of companies that make them. I have no specific brand recommendations at this time, as I do all that I can to avoid situations that would make such a device necessary.

Pop screens are often advisable when recording vocals so as to control the plosives. The "P" and "T" consonants will produce a rush of air. This will result in a short burst of low end every time a plosive consonant sounds, which is nothing short of distracting. Plosives could force you to pull out a high-pass filter later, which is always a shame and won't necessarily solve the problem anyway. At that point, you will have to draw out the plosives using automation.

The "S" consonant produces sibilance, and this can be just as problematic as plosives, and the pop filter won't likely help. If the esses are particularly bad, you should consider another mic or placement. You can also attach a pencil vertically against the pop filter, which will serve to diffuse the esses before they reach the capsule. That trick is likely older than me.

Compression brings out esses, and it's not uncommon to have to use a de-esser. However, it is inadvisable to use a de-esser while recording. They are far too dangerous, as it's very easy to make your singer sound like he has a lisp.

De-essers are basically frequency-dependent compressors with a fast response. By selecting a narrow band of the most offensive frequency, you can set the threshold to attenuate the esses. These units take some practice to use, and they are best reserved as a mixing tool.

There are a number of commercial pop filters available. Many of them use material that allows air to pass, and these are certainly acceptable. Others use two metal grates, which I find more effective than the cloth filters. Then, of course, you could use The Blast Pad, which is my new favorite pop filter, despite being marketed as an SPL filter.

Pop screens are also useful to disguise mic placement. Women (in particular) sometimes benefit by lowering the mic toward the chest cavity. This is especially so on singers who are whiny in nature, regardless of gender. The problem is that it can be a bit disconcerting to sing on a mic that looks wrong. The pop screen can be used as a decoy target for the singer, and that usually works like a charm.

Vocal Mic Pre

If you have a solid collection of mic pres available for your session, then you're merely looking for the pre that best pairs with the mic. I'm pretty sure it's not worth comparing five pres in combination with five mics for a total of 25 vocal tests. No singer wants to go through that, and it's totally unnecessary. Any quality pre should be adequate for recording a vocal.

In general, you're best to use compression when recording vocals. And while it's possible that the production calls for an extremely dynamic performance, and while your vocalist might have an absolute command of her dynamics, I have to assume it's rare, since I've yet to come across it.

Analog limiters like an 1176 or an LA2A are exceptional for dealing with vocal dynamics. In fact, more often than not, you will clearly prefer one over the other. If you don't like the sound of an

Urei 1176, change it for a Teletronix La2a. The Distressor also makes for a good vocal compressor. Analog compressors are preferable.

Some of you may not have one of those three limiter/compressor choices, and they are by no means an exhaustive list of good vocal compressors. There are also a whole slew of compressors that I wouldn't be inclined to use on a vocal, mostly VCAs. You just need to evaluate whether you're helping or hurting the tone with your chosen compressor, and you should be sure that you're not doing so in a way that will cause you fits later.

An overly dynamic vocal can be dealt with in mixing through the same compression techniques as tracking. An overcompressed vocal can be nothing short of problematic, especially if your settings are such that there are obvious pumping artifacts due to the compressor.

This doesn't mean you can't be aggressive with your compression at the recording stage of vocals, but you should be careful not to introduce unintended artifacts. The moment you notice any, you would do well to make an adjustment, even if you're already well into your takes. This is one reason why so many of us like the 1176 and La2a for vocals—it's actually hard to fuck up. That's the very definition of making life easier.

Should you find yourself recording a singer so dynamic that she's barely hitting the compressor in the verse and absolutely crushing it in the chorus, you may want to put the vocal mic on a channel ahead of the compressor, and essentially ride the fader into it as she performs. You can do this from the compressor or the mic pre as well, but a rotary knob can be tough to manipulate with any kind of accuracy. This technique comes with its own set of challenges, so don't go crazy with it. In most cases, a single compressor setting during the recording phase is adequate. You can also record by section so as to avoid adjustments on the fly.

Sometimes I'll re-record an overly dynamic comp to another channel through an analog compressor. This technique, however, can compound the maladies of a subpar converter. You've been warned.

Double Vocals

Double vocals can be recorded as an effect, or as a way to deal with a weak vocal. A loose double will flam, which manifests a carefree feeling. A tight double will chorus and offer a feeling of ensemble power. Perry Farrell (Jane's Addiction, Porno for Pyros) frequently sings doubles, triples—sometimes I swear he has seven lead vocals at a time going on in his productions, and each vocal is sung with a slightly different phrasing and timing. Such treatment creates a party-like atmosphere; in this case, all the guests happen to be Perry Farrell. He likely chose this technique to hide the relatively thin nature of his vocals. It also happens to be a pretty cool sound.

Really, all doubling often accomplishes is obfuscation. It's the main purpose for the decision. When you double a lousy singer, you're attempting to obfuscate what's bad. When you double a great singer, you're washing over the nuances that make her compelling. Keep this in mind when you consider doubling a powerful and commanding vocalist.

While the choice and overall precision of doubles (or layers) is a production decision, it's often a telling sign of insecurity. Hey, a double could be wholly warranted, but it's insecurity nonetheless. And while you may think that it's a good idea to double "just in case," it's not justifiable to ask a singer to double herself when she's already delivered the goods.

When recording loose doubles, you can run the track from the top. When recording tight doubles, the singer has to learn the phrasings from the comp and mimic them. Given this, it's best to work tight doubles by section: long enough so that she can get some flow, and short enough that she can remember her phrasings. Make sure that she monitors her original vocal at least as loud as the new one. This procedure could require a few passes. Once your singer starts nailing lines, keep those and punch around them.

Background Vocals

Unless the background vocals are supposed to be as loud as the vocal, there's really no point to auditioning mics. A quality LDC is going to get the job done nine times out of ten. That said, if you're having trouble with the blend between a harmony and a vocal, changing out the mic could be worthwhile. More often than not, this is a source issue, but you may not be able to do anything about that. Mangle at will.

Group harmonies can be sung as an ensemble and recorded stereo from distance. This is far less common than overdubbing vocals, especially with bands. It's also a far less immediate sound, and if you're looking for in-your-face harmonies, similar to what you hear on Queen records, the overdub method is usually best.

Doubling and tripling harmonies will introduce natural chorusing, which can be wholly appropriate or not, depending on the genre and the fashions at the time. You should pay special attention to background vocals that are meant to be nearly as loud as the lead. They should be equally as fine-tuned as the lead if you're going to place them that loud in context. Crowd vocals for the purposes of a party atmosphere can be recorded with an LDC in omni. This way, you can surround the mic with the group, and physically adjust the performer distances based on the blend you hear in the control room.

Chapter Four

The Business of Recording

Fair warning: I may at times come off as a grumpy old man in this chapter. Good. Who do you want to learn from? A happy-go-lucky kid? Or someone just jaded enough to give you a healthy dose of reality based on years of fucking experience? Exactly.

The music business is currently in shambles.

Oh, it's way better than it was in 2008, when the bottom fell out on all of us. But it's a shadow of its former self—back when CDs reigned supreme and the Internet was just a fledgling fascination.

In recent years, I've watched friends with great discographies drop out of the recording industry. The business changed, and they didn't adjust. Not that it matters—my friends chose not to adapt, and I don't criticize that decision. I understand it. What's the alternative? Work twice as long for half as much? That's a bitter pill to swallow. Your income is supposed to go up, not drop by 75 percent. Meanwhile, as seasoned professionals drop out to pursue other careers, audio schools all over the world have been pumping out graduates at an alarming pace into a contracting industry.

To be perfectly blunt, audio schools are predatory in nature by definition, as are all trade schools. The job market in this industry is already completely saturated, yet audio schools continue to rake in massive profits as they sign up students at a breakneck pace. Between the constant influx of audio school graduates, and the remarkable number of startup recordists, the content facilitator is forced to operate in a similar business model to that of today's artist. Get famous, capitalize.

Save a few dozen or so individuals, you are currently in direct competition with every recordist, mixer, and producer in this business, regardless of the size of their discography or yours. This is a relatively new development, as it was never this way before. Ever. In the entire history of this business. The result has been a deep and unsustainable suppression of prices from the top down.

The good news is, there's still opportunity as a musician, recordist, studio owner, songwriter, producer, or mixer. All of these creative careers still exist. It's just considerably harder to make good money doing it.

I'm fortunate in that my discography has such longevity. That has to do with diversity, which prevents me from being dated or pigeonholed. That was no accident.

It was fairly evident to me early on that this was a fickle business, one in which "what you've done lately" is far more important than skill. It was clear that in order to be successful in the short term, I should focus on one genre, and in order to be successful in the long term, I'd be better off working across a diverse cross section of genres. For me, the decision was easy. I couldn't fathom working on the same record day in and day out. As much as I wanted to be financially successful in this business, it wasn't going to be at the expense of my soul.

Long term it was.

That early decision worked out well, and I wish that I could claim there was some genius at play. There wasn't. I just chose the path that fit my personality. So long as you follow your personality, no one will ever criticize you for it. Not anyone that matters.

When you're aggressive as a kid, you're criticized for it. When you're aggressive in high finance, you're heralded for your boldness (until you lose it all; then you're mud). When you're over-emotional as a child, you're criticized for it. When you're over-emotional as an actor, you win awards. When you're an introvert able to spend hours upon hours alone in a room as a child, you're taken to specialists. As an adult, you're a mixer, which, of course, makes you a specialist. Go figure.

There is no reasonable personality trait that can't be an asset in your work, so long as you choose the work that fits you best. Clearly, you've already chosen recording as an interest. I won't second-guess that decision. However, recording is a rather broad category, and you would be wise to follow your predominant traits when making decisions regarding your path in this business.

If you're the kind of person that has to run the show, then you have one of the key components for working towards a career as a producer. If you're a risk-taker, and you can handle owing hundreds of thousands of dollars at all times, then you're the perfect candidate to own a commercial studio. If you can't stand being cooped up in the same city for more than a few days at a time, then the road is likely your calling.

You have to evaluate yourself, and determine who you are as a person in order to make good decisions where your career is concerned. Take my advice: do not compromise what makes you happy for what gives you work in this business. Recording music is one of the top ten most competitive fields—as is writing books. Ahem. It's a grind at the best of times. There is nothing rewarding about working on music that you don't like, and I would argue that if you don't like it, you can't possibly understand it.

Do you really want to work 12 hours a day, five to seven days a week, making music you don't love? You can't settle. You should set your goals based on what lines up with your personality, and manifest these goals through determination and perseverance. And I apologize if I sound like your father, but my son recently turned 18, and as far as I'm concerned, young adults are all walking into an extremely fucked-up world in which uncertainty abounds and a job is hard to come by.

As if that's not bad enough, you're trying to get into a business that has been annihilated, first by the atrocious long-term business decisions of the major distributors, then by the predictable backlash of music piracy which had the result of greatly devaluing music, topped off by an influx of streaming services and video sites that pay artists nearly nothing for hundreds of millions of plays. The technology industry has pretty much taken over the music industry, and the tech companies view your content as nothing more than a loss leader for selling phones and tablets, thereby attracting a demographic ripe to spend money on anything other than music.

How is an artist supposed to make their next record, if they can't get paid for people listening to their last one?

Even Apple's music sales are crumbling at a remarkable pace, given the advent and popularity of Spotify and Pandora. According to a January 2014 article in *Billboard*, "digital track sales fell 5.7% from 1.34 billion units to 1.26 billion units while digital album sales fell 0.1% to 117.6 million units from the previous year's total of 117.7 million." This would explain why Apple is scrambling to get into the streaming business. This downward trend is likely to continue.

As a consumer, I love Spotify and Pandora. As one who creates material for those two streaming sites, it's a disaster. Why would anyone pay for music if they can get it for free? In the case of Spotify, I do pay a subscription for the sound quality. It costs me $120 a year for all the ad free music I want, anytime I want, anywhere I am. This is a good thing, so long as the artists are getting paid. According to Spotify, they do pay fairly. According to reality, they aren't paying a rate sufficient to sustain the music business.

Mark my words, the labels will do what they must to survive in the short term, and will make deals that all but cut out the artist if that's what it takes. Only an act of Congress can set a fair statutory rate per stream. Suffice it to say, we could be waiting a long time for that to happen. Currently, the only battle in Congress is the one for ideological power. Meanwhile, we're all left in the lurch. Pardon my U.S.-centric rant for a moment, but without some U.S. government intervention that establishes statutory payment for music, the needs of a technology industry, interested only in free content, shall prevail.

If you think that's an ideological statement in its own right, think again. The copyright act of 1909 is what built this business in the first place, and the copyright act of 1976 sent the business into overdrive for the next 30 years. Statutory levels of payment to creators forced distributors to operate in a manner that all but guaranteed profit-sharing by the creator. Until the technology companies are forced by law to pay fair statutory rates for content, they will continue to use the fruits of our labor as nothing more than a means to sell their products.

The big problem is the sheer level of competition. There are so many people desperate to be heard, they'll give away their product in the hopes that they may one day charge for it. This has bled into the recording services side of the business, made even more apparent given the relatively low price of entry into recording. That's a mirage, of course.

The price of entry is indeed low. The price of continuing is where the problem lies. I mean, you'll need a microphone collection; a mic pre collection (or an analog desk); a room buildout; quality converters; a compressor collection; multiple monitor varieties; instruments such as a piano, acoustic guitars, electric guitars, basses, amplifiers, a variety of percussion; soft synths; plugins; etc. etc. *ad infinitum* and *ad nauseam*. Surely you can run a commercial facility with less, but you might want to take a look at what you're competing against.

Then there are the crowdfunding sites like Kickstarter, which have brought the age-old patronage system back into vogue (albeit with a twist). There's a reason why that system was abandoned. It's not capitalism. In fact, I would argue we are currently operating within the technological version of feudalism, in which land (or in this case server space) is offered in exchange for our labor.

You'd think this would be distressing to the politicians who claim they are the champions of all that is capitalistic. Meanwhile, as music distributors and publishers have pivoted to the television business, and labels to the management business, music has become nothing more than the tech industry's bitch.

If you aren't dissuaded after all of that, your future in this business bodes well.

Opportunity Knocks

The sheer volume of music created every year has had the effect of devaluing music. If we took just the hits from the 60s until present, the number of recognizable songs would be staggering. As the pool of great songs increases, the disbursement of total revenues is diluted.

The good news is that as devalued as music has become, consumers still have a thirst for *relevant* music. It's been over 50 years since The Beatles first came to America, and their influence on modern music is still apparent today. At some point in the future, another artist or band will come along and change everything. You could be a part of that if you can manage to put yourself in a position of opportunity. Much like the business itself, opportunity is fickle and could require some manifestation on your part.

By the time I moved to Los Angeles, I had a number of years under my belt recording in a 24-track studio in Boston. My first gig in Los Angeles was a six month stint at Capitol setting up the sessions for large orchestral dates. That was followed by a gig as one of several house engineers at Hollywood Sound.

Mike Ross, the president of Delicious Vinyl, was mixing the first Pharcyde EP at Hollywood Sound and had already made the decision to record an entire album, which he was going to cut at a competing studio. I had assisted on a number of other sessions for Mike, and on multiple occasions I would listen to him complain about the quality of the recordings.

Jesse Hodges, the owner of Hollywood Sound at the time, had recently installed a small recording and production suite on the scond floor of the complex. He just happened to be charging the same price for that room as Mike was paying to track at the other studio. I'm sure you can see where I'm going with this. When the moment seemed right, I invited Mike upstairs to the new recording suite.

"Mike, you know you're always coming in here annoyed with your experience recording at that other studio, and I just wanted to show you this room, because Jesse is offering it for the same price."

His eyes lit up. Not wanting to leave anything to chance, I continued my pitch.

"I realize I have no track record here in Los Angeles, but I spent several years recording in Boston before coming out here, and can deliver you professional results."

I was recording the Pharcyde the very next day, and spent eight months recording what would soon become my first gold album and the start of my music career in Los Angeles. Better yet, *Bizarre Ride II the Pharcyde* is widely considered one of the quintessential hip-hop albums in the history of the genre, and I still get work because of that album today. Bonus!

Had I not approached Mike and sold him on the concept, I would likely never have recorded that album. The opportunity was not one that presented itself purely as a lucky break, but rather in the form of an unhappy client, one ripe for the taking. I had no allegiance to the other studio, nor did I know the people who were working on the project at the time, so I certainly had no moral obstacles. Further, I didn't have to bag on the competing studio— Mike was already doing that. All I did was provide him a better option—one that I was already prepared to deliver on.

The funny thing is, given the nature of a production in which the underlying track was composed purely of samples programmed in an Akai MPC60 drum machine, my only real job was to record the vocals. Any schmo could have done that competently, and with very little experience. Of course, that didn't stop the last guy from losing the gig.

I had very little, if anything, to do with the success of that album. I had nothing to do with the opportunity presenting itself. That was pure happenstance. I had everything to do with taking that moment to sell myself. The point is that you have some influence on generating work, but this requires a willingness to speak up.

There's another lesson in that story. I was the only house engineer at Hollywood Sound interested in recording hip-hop. All of the other recordists were rockers at heart, and couldn't imagine parlaying a hip-hop gig into a career in rock music. Yet that Pharcyde album led me directly to mixing Ben Harper's iconic *Fight for Your Mind*.

After hiring and firing three well-known rock mixers, I was given the call to mix Ben Harper's sophomore effort. Ben and his producer, J.P. Plunier, sought a roots-rock album with the kind of low end one could typically find in hip-hop, and who better than a mixer who knows how to mix with a ton of low end to accomplish the goal? Now, you have to understand, no one was putting that kind of low end on rock records at the time. Yes, I'm staking claim to being the first.

I completely lucked into that Ben Harper album in 1995. That said, I was called based on my past works. Success begets more success. That's how this business works. In fact, after several years of creating reels with my favorite mixes, I realized that the most recognizable songs on my discography were what garnered the most reaction from potential clients—not my best mixes.

Once I came to that revelation, I loaded my reel with recognizable songs, despite how I felt they stacked up to my other mixes, and regardless of the gig I was attempting to land. In fact, I went out of my way to avoid even remotely similar tracks to the job in question. That worked like a charm.

When you provide your most diverse selection of known records (even locally known), you change the evaluation process of the artist. No longer will she worry about the kind of sound you'll impart on her record. All she'll hear are familiar songs, which falls directly in line with her goals—success. Even mild success is an elixir that most artists can't pass up.

Which brings up the next logical question. If we're all competing against each other, how is one supposed to compete against engineers and mixers who have vast discographies chock-full of known artists and records?

For starters, you do have some advantage of proximity and price when it comes to the recording. Local artists are far more likely to work with local studios and talent. Albums have budgets, and if you can deliver a quality album within the proposed budget, then you're far more likely to win the gig than an outsider, who could very well be viewed with suspicion. Further, the perception still exists that producers, recordists, and mixers in my position are too expensive for local artists. In many cases that may be true; however, all free-lancers in this business will accept gigs for less than their usual price if they feel it's a project that could benefit them in the long run.

The problem is, of course, that you must have a certain level of competence to first win, and then keep, a gig. Competence translates directly into confidence, and from an artist's point of view, there is little more appealing than self-assurance. Confidence appears as success, so long as it's not delusional in nature.

Therefore, your first job is to put yourself in a position of competence and confidence. There is only one way to accomplish this. Practice.

Practice, Practice, Practice

It kind of boggles my mind that so many learning recordists, at least the ones who post on the Internet, don't understand why it's so difficult to get good results. Nothing worth accomplishing is easy to do. You're not going to become an NBA player without years of practice. You're not going to become a good lawyer without years of practice. You're not going to become a great surgeon without years of practice. Why would anyone believe they're going to become a great recordist, mixer, or producer without *years* of practice?

At any time, you can be accidentally thrust into a position of success by factors outside of your control, and well before you're ready for it. That doesn't mean you'll sustain that success—not without practice. When you find yourself asking why your records don't sound big—like the "pros"—the answer can't be provided in the form of step-by-step instructions. I can guarantee, anyone who tries to answer this sort of inquiry with suggestions like, "it's all about the compression, man" aren't in a position to answer in the first place. So how do the pros do it? Practice!

I realize that's not a particularly satisfying answer. Given the limited mentoring opportunities of today, many of you turn to the Internet for answers and encouragement. Hey, I like positive reinforcement as much as the next guy, but who are you seeking reassurance from? People in your same position who likely know less than you?

The good news is, you're reading this book. And books can certainly help, so long as they're not laden with misplaced encouragement. That's the last thing you'll get out of my books. In fact, I'm often criticized for being too opinionated. I can assure you, my strong opinions are far more useful than the usual milquetoast advice. At least you have somewhere to start. And besides, I encourage too!

Unplanned Moment of Encouragement

You will get better each and every time you record. It's a frustrating process, in a competitive field. Only those who refuse to be denied will turn recording music into a career. And there's a good reason for this. It's a tough dog-eat-dog world full of subjectivity, self-loathing, and doubt, and generally requires operating as a business. If you don't have the stomach for running a business, and you view constant stability as a necessity, you won't last beyond your first reinvention.

Oops. So much for encouragement.

I've reinvented myself multiple times over the course of my career thus far, and expect more to come. Times change, discographies age, and on those occasions when you find yourself out of favor within the business, you must rebuild. The good news is that once you're in the position to reinvent yourself, you've already been through the process of building your business in the first place.

Personal Relationships

To be perfectly honest, it's far easier to make it in this business when you have a life partner able to bring in a steady income. You should choose your partner based on love and compatibility, not a W2, and I wouldn't suggest otherwise. But if you're purposely putting off marrying that great gal or guy because you first want to be in a financial position to do so, you're ignoring the fact that you'll likely find yourself in similarly hard times in the future.

That said, partnership with someone who is unable to deal with the difficult times in this business will result in one of two possibilities. Either you'll be out of the business completely, working a job you hate in order to keep your marriage together, or you'll be divorced. Possibly both. Life balance issues will put a constant strain on your relationship, even with the most understanding of mates.

This is not the kind of job that allows for balance when it comes to your personal life. Statistically speaking, it's a business that's fraught with waves of feast or famine, and you will often have more work than you can handle one month, followed by an empty studio the next—the very definition of feast or famine. There very well could be times in your life when work is steady and dependable. I have experienced those times. Unfortunately, periods of feast can be just as detrimental to the well-being of a relationship as spans of famine.

When you're working, your absence will breed resentment. When you're not working, your lack of income will breed resentment.

Life balance in this business is not achieved in the short run, but rather over the long haul, and I'm not sure we can reasonably call that balance, since you will somehow manage to foment resentment regardless of whether you're working or not.

Further problematic is the stress of operating a business with a robust overhead. Disagreements over money can be traumatic to a relationship. Your mate could very well want to save money in order to soften the blow of the tough times. Good advice if there ever was any. Unfortunately, in order to build a business you must invest in it. Your mate will not likely understand a decision to sink a large chunk of money on a microphone when you're suddenly flush again, after a month of mac and cheese dinners.

Mates who have never built a business often can't truly comprehend what's needed to keep it growing, and your expenditures could be viewed as nothing more than personal whims, rather than necessary investments that will allow you to compete. That said, cash flow problems are certainly not unique to this business. It's your dedication and discipline that could prove the real downfall to your relationship.

Here's the painful reality. If you're the kind of person who is so passionate about making music that you refuse to do anything else, your career becomes your first loyalty, which by definition would place your mate as second. A close second, but second nonetheless. This is often problematic to a good relationship.

When you're driven to create, you're coming from a different mindset from most, and conventional relationships don't typically survive the rather unconventional lifestyle of a recording professional. Even a mate who admires your drive and creations will feel the resentment of playing second fiddle, and money doesn't tend to solve this problem. On those occasions when money comes to you in great abundance, you could find yourself pressured by your mate to take some personal time off. This can be counter to your business needs.

Time off is the kiss of death in this industry. I know—I took an entire year off in the 90s to spend time with my newborn son, and I virtually killed my career in the process. Not that I'd do anything differently in that regard, but it did take some time to rebuild.

Far be it for me to give anyone relationship advice. Believe me, as someone who views my purpose in life as a creator of art, I've failed with marked predictability in my relationships. But then that's the point. I'm not suggesting you can't have a loving and fruitful relationship that lasts a lifetime. That depends completely on the personalities of both you and your partner. What I'm saying is that you must have a mate that is fully supportive and understanding of what's at stake, and I'm not sure that explaining it is sufficient.

Let me put it this way: If you can figure out how to maintain a healthy personal and love life as you operate in this business, you should write a book about it, as I have yet to figure it out myself.

Whether self-inflicted, or out of pure happenstance, the difficult times in this business will come. If you rest on your laurels, as if your run of success will never end, you could be in a world of hurt, both financially and personally. It's tough to enjoy your time off when you're dealing with a mate pissed off that you're broke, as you personally deal with feelings of failure and inadequacy. Negative thoughts are destructive in nature, and often include concerns of permanence. I have wondered countless times in my career whether I've made my last record. I don't care who you are, when you're not working, your confidence will suffer. Therefore, vigilance is a necessity, and you must at all times adjust your position as it relates to the business.

Positioning

From *Zen and the Art of Producing*:

"Positioning" is a well-established marketing term. It refers to your position in the market (go figure). For instance, a Volvo is positioned as a "safe car." A Lexus is positioned as a "luxury car." All successful products have a position in the market, and that position offers appeal in niche markets.

Despite their specific positions, the Volvo and Lexus are both cars, and perform the same overall function. Yet, the makers of these cars focus on one specific selling point in order to attract a particular customer. Generally, the position of a product is purposeful. Lexus loads its cars with features that make them luxurious, and advertises them as such. Volvo makes sure its cars get high safety ratings, and markets that safety record to stay-at-home soccer moms seeking to protect their children. As service providers, we also have a position. We just have limited control over it.

How much you charge is one way to determine your position. You will attract a wholly different client at a rate of $100 per day than 10 times that. There will be reasonable expectations of competence from anyone who charges $1000 per day. Conversely, there will be unreasonable expectations at the $100 day rate. That said, the higher-end daily rates plummeted after the crash of 2008, and it's a rare recordist indeed who can command that kind of money as a freelancer today. Many fully stocked commercial studios are having trouble bringing in that kind of rate.

Frankly, you're way better off working for free than for $100 a day. At least then you can negotiate a stake in the product. Of course, negotiating for points on sales probably isn't worth the price of admission at this stage of the game, at least until the artist and songwriter pay structure is fixed. I'm not going to go through how points work in this book, because recordists don't get points. Once you start negotiating a stake in the product, you should be doing so as a producer or as a production company. I go through all of this in *Zen and the Art of Producing.*

Charging money for an incompetent job due to inexperience is generally a bad idea, especially in this business. I realize you have to make money, but you also have to record everything that you can before you can reasonably charge for your services. I'm sure some of you are thinking, "Fuck that!" And if that's your reaction, I get it. But I'm not sure that charging $10 per hour as the owner of a recording business is worth the demands that come along with it.

When you're first starting out, you don't set your price, the market sets it for you. Without a discography of some kind, there is no market force that will bring price to bear. Even a disc laden with local talent will work in your favor. Unfortunately, if you charge the local talent before you're ready, your position will suffer, as you will have managed to sully your reputation. While it's true that you can overcome this perception with just a single record, you might put yourself out of the running before that record even comes to you. Therefore, I advise you to learn how to record well, either in a relatively pressure-free environment, or one in which you can be mentored.

Mentoring has been a long tradition in this business, and it's all but dead. Between name engineers holding multiple master classes all over the world, audio schools, forums, blogs, instructional videos, and of course, books, one might start to wonder if it's more profitable to teach recording than to actually record.

It's not, really. Many of us, myself included want to give back to our profession. This is a tough business to learn without mentoring.

Every mistake that can be made, will be made without some sort of guidance. But hey, you learn from mistakes.

Once you're in a position to charge money, you'll know it. At that point, you can begin to build your discography, and every record you're a part of will have elevated importance. It's your discography that keeps you working.

The principle of parlaying work into more work is true whether you're a performer, songwriter, producer, mixer, recordist, or all of the above. You win your next record off the perception of your last. You can accomplish this by networking, and keeping everyone in your sphere aware of your latest projects. That may seem obnoxious, and to some extent it is, but you can't wait for your phone to ring. You have to generate work for yourself.

You don't need an aggressive personality to sell yourself, although it doesn't hurt. Really, there is no personality trait that lends itself better to sales than pure honesty. You need to figure out how to sell yourself in a way that's honest to who you are. Get to know every local band and let them know about you. Invite local musicians to your place if you have one. Play them your work. You should also network extensively on the Internet. Get to know other musicians and engineers everywhere.

This business is far too competitive not to hustle. The work won't come to you until you've put in the effort to find it in the first place. Selling yourself is a worthwhile skill to develop. This way, when you're sitting in an empty studio wondering if you've just finished your last record, you'll have the tools necessary to fill your schedule again. Use them.

As much as you're competing against everyone in the business right now, you have the power to build your perceived brand and position. My good friend Slipperman and I will likely never compete for the same record. Our tastes in projects don't align, nor do our positions in general, and we therefore attract wholly different clientele. As much as you're competing with every professional in the business for your services, your position serves to narrow the field.

It's Not About the Money, It's About the Money

There are a few ways to get paid in this business, which break down to three possibilities: your time, your skill, or your name. Producers and bona fide mixers get paid by the track. Super-producers and -mixers get paid for their name. Recordists and studio owners are paid by the hour, the day, the project, or the track. There are advantages and disadvantages to each.

In the long run, I advise against charging based on time. This removes skill from the equation. Anyone can rent space and time, and the perception will be that you are being hired to facilitate your client's every whim. Such is the nature of a time metric.

Corporate gigs, which could include voice-over work, commercials, and jingles, are best charged by the hour. Your role on a corporate session is indeed to meet your client's every whim, and you should bill accordingly. Of course, corporations don't want to go to your house. The corporate mooks prefer large vibeless commercial studios.

I personally prefer to quote a price by the project or track. This puts the onus on my skill, and not my time. Inexperienced clients will view your efforts to spend time on tones with suspicion—as if you're milking them. Charging by the track is a good way to give your client a budget she can depend upon.

While it's somewhat unusual for a Recordist to charge by the track in the upper echelons of this business, it's a totally reasonable method when your reputation is more important than the short-term money. Charging by the track is also subject to abuse by the client, and requires some protection.

I wouldn't advise charging by the track without including a limit on the total time. You have to protect yourself against a client who might take advantage, and you never want to remove your time completely from the equation. There must be some expectation of a time budget, otherwise, your client might not view the completion of the record with any kind of urgency. Even as a mixer I will begin to charge for time on those occasions when a client relentlessly wanks with my mix.

When charging by the track, you should set both the price and the time limit based on your best estimate of the number of days it should take. If you believe it should take three days to record, then offer four or five as the limit. You set these boundaries based on your comfort level. This allows you to retain the thrust of time constraints on the session, while simultaneously keeping your client relaxed.

When you're paid as a producer, and you have a stake in the product, it becomes considerably more problematic to charge for overages. You're a part of the team, and it's your job to deliver a final product within budget—famous last words from someone that will rarely put time above quality. Overages technically come out of a producer's advance, although in my experience, that's not all that common.

Most professional freelance recordists and commercial studios charge a flat rate for the day. Whether you charge $600 per day or $50 an hour for a full 12 hours, the results will be the same. It's the perception that changes. A client who is paying you by the hour will not understand why you're paid to take breaks. Invoicing by the day all but eradicates this view.

How you work, and the tools you invest in, will also dictate your position. If you've invested heavily in guitars and amplifiers, it makes sense that you're going to attract clients in need of these tools. Which means a significant portion of your work will come from rock bands. As a consequence, you might get pretty good at recording rock music, which will only further solidify your brand.

Your collection of recording gear will affect your position, as well. If you have a small room with nothing more than a couple of mics and preamps, then you're really not in a position to record anything other than overdubs. And if you fill your studio with prosumer gear, not only will you have a difficult time getting results, you'll have a tough time charging a reasonable rate due to the inherent perception issues.

Imagine if you hired a guitar player, referred to you by a friend, who came in to your session with just one poorly intonated guitar and a small practice amp. What would your impression be of that guitar player before he even played a note? Would you be comfortable knowing that your guitar player for hire hasn't invested in the gear that allows him to do the job at a high level? He could be the greatest guitar player ever, but his gear limitations have now relegated you to simulated amplifiers, and Melodyne.

If you're honest with yourself, your perception of our imaginary guitar player can be characterized in one word. Unprofessional. When you send him on his way, will that decision have anything to do with his skills? His main axe is essentially broken, and will cost you hours of time. What do you think the likelihood is that you're going to be blown away by his skills?

So why is anyone going to pay you even $500 a day to record in a shitty little space, with subpar converters, on your fucked-up mic pres? I mean, 90 percent of your potential clients will already have that level of gear available to them. Do you really think you'll be perceived as professional? If you can't even put together a semi-decent rig, then how could anyone possibly trust that you know what you're doing?

This is about the time when someone insists that results aren't about the gear. It's all about the skill, man. Right, so let's see if I've got this straight. You have mad skills, yet you can't seem to work enough to invest in professional quality gear? You think anyone is going to believe that?

If success in this business is purely predicated on skill, then why do we all covet a nice collection of microphones when we record? And if it's all about the skill, why is analog gear still valuable? If it's all about the skill, then shouldn't the stock plug-ins suffice? If you're going to be a professional recordist, then you have no choice but to invest in your tools, if for no other reason than for purposes of perception.

Anytime someone pays you to help them make music for the first time, they are taking a tremendous leap of faith. There are certain indicators that a potential client will use to make a determination of value, and like it or not, your gear collection is one of them. Frankly, your personality and general bedside manner will have far more to do with your success than any other factor. But if a potential client walks out the door because you're using a Sound Blaster for conversion, they'll never get the opportunity to truly experience your shining personality.

So you can scream from the rooftops that your success has everything to do with your skills. You can insist that talent will prevail over any and all recording gear. And while that's a comforting thought, and there may be a grain of truth to that, it completely ignores the realities of perception and basic common sense. Listen, I'm not suggesting that your skill is of no consequence. I'm saying that running a business requires considering your position, and it's difficult to convince potential clients that you're the man (or woman), when you have only the bare minimum gear to accomplish the job. It doesn't instill confidence.

Home Recording Facilities

Recently a poster argued that home studios would make professional facilities obsolete. By the term "professional studios," of course, the poster meant commercial facilities. Not only is this a ridiculous notion, it can't possibly happen that way.

The first big wave of home studios came in the 80s, and resulted in an epic freakout from the industry, which then resulted in the enforcement of zoning laws at the behest of the legitimate commercial facilities. A home studio used for professional recording in an area zoned for residential is not subjected to the requirements of a commercial facility. An underground home studio doesn't have to build wheelchair access, designate bathrooms by gender, or pay city business taxes, workers comp, unemployment, payroll, etc. That is, until the city figures out what's going on.

It's true that many studios have closed because there's more competition for less work and money overall. It's true that many mixers like myself rarely hire professional studios for mix work these days, and choose to operate from a personal mix suite. Both of these trends will certainly affect the total number of commercial facilities over time. That doesn't make home studios a replacement for commercial facilities. Home studios are merely a launching pad, just like they've always been. I mean, if you're successful out of your home studio, your business will outgrow your home. And if you're not able to make a viable business out of your home studio, you too will close.

The home studio will never replace the commercial facility. Home studios are the upstarts of our business, and frankly, most will fail miserably, just like all other businesses. I can guarantee you that more home studios close in any given week than commercial facilities do.

The commercial studio's success in the long run often includes real estate in the equation. When you build a studio in your home you devalue it. Not so with a commercial facility. Commercial real estate makes the business model more viable, as the property becomes your means of retirement. You can certainly lease commercial space, but in the long run, if you're going to operate as a studio business, it's almost a requirement to involve commercial real estate into the plan.

If you're running a home studio as a musician or songwriter, you're probably not going to have any issues. Even as a mixer you can likely get away with it, especially if your sessions are generally unattended. As a recording facility, clients will come in and out of your doors throughout the day, they will smoke cigarettes and weed and engage in loud arguments on your patio. That's what musicians do. You can only get away with operating in a residential area for so long before the city comes snooping around.

There's a reason why we insist as a society that certain businesses are zoned as commercial and industrial. It protects the consumer from fraud and the neighborhood from nuisance.

I'm not here to police home studios, nor pass moral judgment. I have no problems with the home studio, as it's often the only feasible way to build into a legit operation. But you'll only get away with it for so long, and you should be careful just how much you invest in a home studio, particularly where the buildout is concerned.

The idea that home recording facilities are the wave of the future falls in line with another rather perplexing concept. One that I must take a moment to rant about, as frankly, it irks me. Every few weeks some dumb ass posts on the Internet claiming in frustration that the youth—who have been recording for all of two minutes—are taking over this industry, as if youthful exuberance is somehow going to win over high-level experience. This sort of absurd rant typically comes after a poster has been smacked down repeatedly for doing something inadvisable—like using headphones while mixing.

"What kind of headphones should I use for mixing?"

We may as well set aside the stunning lack of both insightfulness and expansiveness in the question. It's the premise that's fatally flawed. More often than not, this sort of question will have garnered 18 responses in a short time period, all of which list the best headphones for mixing. These sorts of answers bring on feelings of goodwill. Posters often congratulate each other for being part of such an encouraging group. Then someone who knows what they're doing pipes in, suggesting one should never mix in headphones, as if it's a rule.

Of course, it *is* a rule. One that a great many seasoned recordists have concluded as such. Yet somehow, this suggestion often gets a hostile reaction from the Internet Chatter Class, interested in one thing. Validation.

I understand it's difficult to live under rules when you just want to explore and be creative and be you. To blaze new trails. To make a name for yourself. All good. Break all the rules you want. Then you'll understand why there are certain things that are generally long-settled rules.

The fact that there are so many new recordists has only resulted in a veritable feeding frenzy for information. Unfortunately, this has also manifested into an enormous volume of misinformation and mythology being passed about. And while this was true even in 1999, it's reached new levels of madness in recent years. It's gotten to the point that the guys who actually know how to record don't want to bother explaining it, because it's mostly falling on deaf ears.

Nowhere is this more evident than on the Internet, where I found literally hundreds of posts asking how to set the attack and release settings when compressing. That kind of depends on what compressor you're using, for what application, and you know, *the music* itself. Of course, the Internet Chatter Class pipes in with a whole slew of useless answers offering specific compressor settings, and advice that completely ignores the fundamental principle of what we do—listen.

There are a number of things that I find disturbing about the whole Internet Chatter Class, but none more than this seeming inability to do basic research. I mean, when I enter the words "compressor attack release" in my search engine, I come across dozens of good articles from *reputable sources* that explain how attack and release settings work. Why then, would anyone ever ask this sort of question on an audio forum? How is it that I, a Gen Xer, am somehow considerably more adept at using a search engine than a seemingly large percentage of millennials? If you're that interested in learning recording, then why do you not seek the answer from a verifiable source? You're going to just trust some shmo on the Internet who is in the same position as you are?

Would you ask a first-year lawyer your best defense? He's never seen a courtroom. Why are you asking him?

Frankly, the Internet Chatter Class is more a social club for purposes of validation and camaraderie. Telling someone that they shouldn't use headphones to mix is seemingly tantamount to changing an artist's lyric. That's my art, man.

I just don't get the fascination with going online and putting your ignorance on full display. And when you answer someone's question about a good preset with your idea of a good preset, then you are just as ignorant as the person asking the question. When you finally realize five years from now that you were an idiot, do you really want to be on eternal public record in this regard?

If you're the kind of person that goes online to get validation for every fucked-up idea you have, let me save you some time.

There is nothing you can do that is unique. There is no trick or idea that you can come up with that someone else isn't already doing. So there's your validation. You can do anything, anyway you like. It's an art, and so long as your clients are happy, and you're happy, and you can make a living doing it, then I'm happy. But please don't for a moment think that validation from strangers in a similar position is worthwhile information. It's rather easy to get affirmation from people who likely know less than you, and are every bit as shameless in putting their ignorance on grotesque display. Given the right audience, you can validate every fucked-up thought you ever had. So why bother?

If you're in your early 20s or younger, you are no doubt going to take over the music industry from anyone and everyone my age or older. You have time on your side, I don't, and I really don't see myself recording for a living when I'm in my 60s. I'll be too tired, and I'd just as soon sit down and write books by the peaceful ocean roar of a tropical paradise. But that's a while from now. I'm not that old!

Anyway, to you kids that insist your youthful exuberance some-how trumps experience, please don't be a knucklehead. You don't last twenty years in this fucking business because you're not able to adapt to changing times. Besides, I recorded my first gold album on a DAW in 1993. You think any of this shit is new to me? You think your youthful enthusiasm gives you an advantage? Admit-tedly, in some ways it does. It makes me want to hire you to work for *me*, because I can use your enthusiasm to my advantage.

But let's be super-real here for a moment. Should I get a whiff of a record that I find interesting, and you happen to be vying for the same gig (perhaps it's local to you), I can assure you, many more times than not, I will win that gig. I'm being conservative with that estimate.

And you can set aside my skills in the studio. Between my dis-cography, and my ability to talk to a potential client—a skill that

I've honed and fine-tuned over my career—you will have no way of defending against my advances. Your client won't look at my discography and think that I'm old. More often than not a potential client will look at my discography and recognize successful songs, at which point you're at a formidable disadvantage.

When your potential client realizes I have a deep understanding of music, due to decades of studying an instrument, years of studying music theory at the college level, and a verifiable discography that can be reviewed on Spotify, you're more than likely out of the running.

Okay?

So fucking stop it. Yes, yes. There are no rules. Except for the fucking rules, which we all ignore, and regret later only to return back to the rules again. Believe me, there is plenty of room to experiment without deciding that *faux* stereo of a mono source is the way of the future. Every neophyte engineer thinks that's a good idea, until it's clearly not. At which point it's a rule again.

When you decide to place condenser mics on toms, and you're in absolute misery because now you have to strip silence and essentially choke those gorgeous tom tones, and your mic over the rack tom that got whacked by a spastic drummer still isn't back from the shop, you'll likely stick with dynamic mics on toms. When you decide to record your vocals in a closet that instills a "boxy" sound that you simply can't remove, you might decide that your room is indeed a critical part of the sound, just as I've told you seemingly *ad nauseam* throughout this book. You might even make a "new" rule: Don't bother recording in a shitty room.

That's a really good rule.

To the morons that make these kind of absurd and obviously trolling statements: Go ahead and keep telling your delusional self that your drive, motivation, and fearless experimentation makes you more valuable than someone who's already gone through that phase. Convince yourself all you like that you are destined to forge new ground in recording, as if there's anything you can do that's new when everything you use in your bedroom computer is designed to mimic exactly what the old shit did, just not as good (yet).

But if you think you're reinventing music and recording, you're sadly mistaken. While there are a seemingly infinite possibilities, there are also patterns of similarity that are necessary for creating art for commerce. If you work in a manner that is so far outside the mainstream that it's not understandable by the general population, your genius will be viewed as nothing more than cluelessness until many years after you're dead. You want to eat now? Or do you want your mook great-grandchildren living off of your supposed "genius?"

If you take my advice, if you try the techniques that I'm offering you here, if you open up your mind to what those with experience are telling you, you will reduce the learning curve significantly.

You can also reject all of my advice, and forge ahead trying to succeed in areas in which we've all failed. This won't prevent you from success. But make no mistake, you will come to many of the same conclusions that the rest of us did—it's just that now you've got to learn them the hard way.

 Conclusion

This is now the third book I've written on the subjects of recording, mixing, and producing music. I encourage you to read all three. I realize that may sound a bit self-serving, but this is an industry now in which it's not sufficient to specialize. Today, you're almost forced to operate as a jack-of-all-trades, which is the opposite of how things were when I started in this business. You were far better off specializing in the 90s and 00s.

Learning to mix raised my abilities as a recordist by several levels. Understanding the end game by dealing with the mistakes of others allowed me to record towards the mix, and much of that has to do with how I think about the music. Everything that I consider when I'm mixing is contained in my first book of the series, *Zen and the Art of Mixing*.

Zen and the Art of Producing goes into detail on all the responsibilities of a producer, including running a session, inspiring performances, making a budget, dealing with politics, and most importantly, establishing a vision. Given that we all must perform producer's duties at times, it's important and useful information that will only make you more dangerous as a recordist.

All of the concepts that I've weaved into these books require time to fully grasp. There are ideas in this series that can't be understood until you reach certain plateaus of growth. As simple as I try to make things for you, many concepts require years of practice before you'll make a connection, even if I spell it out in the plainest terms I can muster. Which I have.

All three books are designed to work together, and this book is, without a doubt, the most technical of the three. You can find countless articles on the technical aspects of all of our tools, and it's quite easy to find reputable sources for this kind of information online. It's the strategies that you implement based on the music itself that require time to learn, regardless of how well you understand the technical aspects of how everything works.

I'm a prime example of someone with limited technical expertise who has managed a long career making records in a variety of creative capacities. You don't have to know how the attack and release settings work on a compressor; you can hear it for yourself. Of course, that requires learning how to listen, and that is the part of this job that, frankly, most people never get.

Just because you don't hear something, doesn't mean that no one else does—nor does it mean you won't hear it in the future. I've watched a ton of basketball in my life, and I've played it too, but I will never see basketball the way someone like Phil Jackson does. He sees countless more levels of what's unfolding in an instant than I ever will as a fan. He has court vision.

When it comes to the recording arts, you need to develop your court vision. There's really only one way to foster this, and that's through constant practice and evaluation.

Not only do you have to understand how to listen musically, you need to be able to accept input from your creative team. I can make a record without anyone else's input, but that's not what I'm being hired to do. I'm hired to make the most effective record for the artist or band, and that *requires* their participation.

You are at the mercy of the quality of song and performers. Therefore, all you can really do is limit the weaknesses by accentuating the strengths. Of course, sometimes that means presenting a weakness as a strength. An embarrassing solo is often better placed loud and proud, as no one will ever doubt the intent. These are the sorts of things I discuss in *Zen Producing* and *Mixing*.

Some of you could very well be frustrated reading this book, given the millions of dollars in equipment I've discussed throughout. Don't let a minimal collection of gear get you down. It can take years to put together an adequate rig. If you're currently relegated to plug-ins in order to process your audio, this shouldn't be an impediment to good results. You can learn how to use your limitations to your advantage.

Your monitoring will be your biggest Achilles' heel, and this includes conversion. You can't take advantage of the gear that you do have available if you can't accurately evaluate what's happening. You can't adequately compensate for shit you can't hear, no matter how good you've developed your ability to listen. The good news is, quality converters really aren't a prohibitive expense any longer.

The biggest mistake that I see is the almost knee-jerk reaction to reach for gear. EQs and compressors are often implemented before a determination of necessity is made. This is all part of learning to listen. Rather than deciding in advance that your kik drum needs a compressor, make that determination based on what you're hearing. Not from your past experiences with other drummers. Every Source Player, Instrument, and Room offer their own challenges.

EQs are often engaged in lieu of mic adjustment, and everyone is guilty of this, myself included. Time is a reasonable factor in this kind of decision. I mean, if all I need to do is add a little top end in order to move forward, then that very well could be the best decision. It's still a decision that's made based on the realities of my session. It's not made as a matter of course.

Plug-ins can perform the basic functions necessary for recording and mixing music. Over time you will learn how to use those tools to your advantage. There may be a day when a computer can adequately replace analog gear; that time has not come. That said, plug-ins have improved tremendously in the past five years alone, and we can expect that trend to continue. Analog gear can make your recording life easier. It will not preclude you from making and recording great music.

Still, we can't get around the fact that as a business you will be virtually forced to make purchases in order to compete. Believe me, if you're paying attention, if you're listening, at some point your recordings will result in more gigs, at which point you'll be able to supplement your gear collection. For now, focus on the musical decisions. Your gear deficiencies will begin to reveal themselves as you get a basis of comparison.

For now, all you need to do is operate within your position. That might require working for free or very little money. It's more important at the early stages that you record as often as possible, and your only real leverage is price. And while this will certainly bring in some rather atrocious gigs that someone in my position wouldn't touch for any amount of money, that's only because we've been through that learning process already.

I worked for free on many occasions early on. I wasn't good enough to charge money. So I'm not suggesting that you do something that I wouldn't. I'll still take the right gig for no money up front if I think it makes sense for my longer-term goals. This career requires you constantly look ahead and adjust your position within the current realities. Your discography is your best weapon in improving your position over time.

For now, offer services that you can deliver successfully. If your room and equipment list are only useful for the overdub process, then try to position yourself for that kind of work. This way, you can build up your clientele to keep you financially afloat as you gain experience.

Don't misrepresent your abilities. Admit to your shortcomings, admit that this is all a learning process for you, and that you would like to learn on some music that you enjoy. There are always artists and bands in the early stages of their careers that need someone in a similar position. Form a partnership and deliver the best record you can. Everyone benefits from that experience, even if the resulting product is unusable.

Throughout this book, I've suggested you simplify the process as much as you can. This advice is given largely because it keeps you out of trouble. Most of us are distracted by other, more important duties, and it's paramount that you're not sacrificing your music and performances because you're complicating the process with technique.

There's nothing wrong with putting two mics on an amplifier, but there's no point in complicating the process until it proves necessary. Rather than automatically putting two mics on an amplifier, start with one and add a second only when one mic reveals itself as insufficient. Approaching technique in this manner will allow you to keep the focus on what's important: the music itself.

If you have a knack for music, you'll have a knack for recording too. If you know nothing about music, take my advice—pick up an instrument and learn to play it. Take lessons. I can't tell you how many sessions I've been on as a recordist in which I was given no respect until the clients realized I understood music. It's an advantage, and you need every advantage you can get.

While it's true that we don't have control over how any individual reacts to our music or sound, we do have certain tried and true techniques available that will cause a similar reaction from listeners. A soaring reverb on a Celine Dion vocal is designed to enhance a feeling of grandiosity and drama. A filtered "radio" vocal makes the listener feel as though they're listening to a character. This technique allows the artist to distance herself from a disturbing or off-kilter lyric. A record devoid of ambient information is designed to cause a feeling of intimacy. An automated tap delay on a single word offers a haunting feeling.

Many of these techniques you may already know innately. Your job is to convert that innate understanding into concrete and usable knowledge. This way, your decisions are made with intent.

One way to do that is to listen to a ton of music, from all genres and eras, across the board. As you listen to music, you will notice things that you can apply to your recordings. And after you've been recording a while, it can be difficult to listen to a track without dissecting it down to its working parts. Welcome to the negative side of this business.

Instead of dissecting everything that you hear down to parts and sound, try to evaluate your favorite records based on how they make you feel. Now listen to the production and recording decisions through that prism. Think about the lyric and then listen to how the producer and recordist used sound to enhance the feelings brought on by the song. The music and the song are always the main drivers of emotional impact. But the sonic decisions can be used to enhance the feelings brought on by the music itself. There's really no way around it. Sound evokes feelings.

Music is merely the organization of sound in a manner designed to manipulate the emotions of the listener. The music starts out as nothing more than an abstract thought in the mind of a songwriter.

It isn't until the thought is converted into sound that it can be shared. Therefore, music does not exist without sound, and how that sound is presented will influence the listener.

If I were to deliver an R&B production with drums that sound like they were straight off of a Metallica record, you would question my sanity, and rightly so. The sound of the drums would be nothing short of distracting. If I were to deliver a hard rock production with clean guitars, you would likely recoil.

Those may be extreme examples, but they illustrate my point. Your sound must be contiguous with the music. They go together.

Many of your sonic decisions will have to do with precedence. Clicky kik drums are commonly heard on hard rock records; not so much in R&B. Now, you certainly don't have to adhere to what's usual and trite. Just what works. In general, rock drums on an R&B track don't work, mostly because rock drums are performed too aggressively for the genre in general.

Rock drums must be big to counter the crunch guitars, and as a consequence, they are played with aggression and often with many cymbal crashes. R&B drums are more about groove. Here's the thing, though. Although I can't actually imagine it, you could very well successfully record rock drums on an R&B track. Someone could come to you with a song in which that treatment would be appropriate. So long as it's a decision of intent, no matter how far-fetched, that's a good decision. There's nothing wrong with going for a concept and failing. And you need to trust in your sensibilities to judge what works and what doesn't.

I'm suggesting you simplify matters, I'm not asking you to play it safe. The fact that I suggest you should record so aggressively is the opposite of safe.

If you're thinking musically, you are thinking sonically. If you are thinking sonically, you are not necessarily thinking musically.

Therefore, you should think musically at all times, and leave the sonic evaluations purely to how they relate to the music itself.

This is why every old-timer will give you the same broad advice when it comes to recording. Follow the music.

As opinionated as I am, I can assure you, I'm far less dogmatic than I used to be. Much of that has to do with experience. Over time, you start to recognize where and when to prioritize. There isn't a single piece of advice that I can give you that you couldn't or shouldn't ignore under the right circumstances. You could even flip one side of the track 180 degrees out of phase, and if that's done with intent, knowing full well the ramifications of such a decision, then it's a reasonable treatment. Of course, now you have to convince your clients. Good luck with that.

All of my advice is meant to increase your odds at success. This is why I use clarifying words like "often" and "typically" throughout my books. My intent is not to present you with rules in which you must abide, but rather guidelines on how to think as you record. I've provided countless strategies that you can use based on the music that you're recording. Once you understand all the concepts in this series, there is absolutely no situation that you won't be able to handle appropriately. As you progress, you will recognize patterns and solve problems more quickly.

As complicated as music is, there are really only five basic functions in any given composition: melody, rhythm, harmony, counter-melody, and often a lyric. You could bring me a band of aliens with instruments I've never seen nor heard before, and it won't make a difference. Musically speaking, every instrument, no matter how foreign, will fill at least one of those five functions, and the sound of the instrument will dictate how it's used within the context of the music.

Sound travels based on the laws of physics, and an instrument has to emit a sound in a room. There is no musical instrument, no matter how foreign, that I couldn't record well. It would cause me no consternation whatsoever to be presented with an alien instrument so complex in nature that I would have to literally surround it with microphones in order to capture it in balance. I've already learned how to record an instrument like this. It's called drums.

There is nothing stopping you from being successful in this business, regardless of how much competition there might be. Should you find yourself frustrated over a lack of results, then you are not in a unique position. There is not a single seasoned recordist or mixer who has not experienced this. There are literally tens of thousands of hours behind every success story, regardless of outward appearances. If you work hard, if you invest in yourself and this craft, and if you refuse to give up, you can become a great recordist. For this, I'm grateful.

Now, go forth and record.